Too Much Te...

AN AUTOBIOGRAPHY
OF CHILDHOOD AND YOUTH

CHRISTOPHER ELLIOTT-BINNS

Routledge & Kegan Paul
London, Boston, Melbourne and Henley

First published in 1983
by Routledge & Kegan Paul plc
39 Store Street, London WC1E 7DD,
9 Park Street, Boston, Mass. 02108, USA,
296 Beaconsfield Parade, Middle Park,
Melbourne, 3206, Australia, and
Broadway House, Newtown Road,
Henley-on-Thames, Oxon RG9 1EN
Typset in 11/12 Garamond by
Inforum Ltd, Portsmouth
and printed in Great Britain by
St. Edmundsbury Press
Bury St. Edmunds, Suffolk

Library of Congress Cataloging in Publication Data

Elliott-Binns, Christopher, 1924—

Too much tenderness
1. *Elliott-Binns, Christopher, 1924—*
2. *England—Biography.*   I. *Title.*
CT788.E57A37   1982   942.082'092'4[B]   82–16582

ISBN 0–7100–9418–3

Love has no desire but to fulfil itself
But if you love and must needs have desires let these be your desires
. . . To know the pain of too much tenderness
To be wounded by your own understanding of love

Khalil Gibran

Contents

Author's Note

This is a true autobiography because it is how I remember things. However, recalling the past is a complicated and fickle affair, a 'mixing of memory and desire', and I expect I have portrayed some people not quite as they would have seen themselves from their particular standpoint. I hope I have not offended anyone.

The people and incidents are real but, to avoid overcrowding of the stage, I have taken the liberty of introducing two composite characters. Tom represents three people, all friends whom I knew in sequence and who played similar parts in my life. Janet too is a mixture of three people.

I dedicate this book to all those who appear in its pages but especially to the girl who became my wife, and to our three children, Jane, Caroline and David.

I also express my gratitude to Laurie Fallows, Mary Nicholls and members of my family who helped me with the writing and to Dorothy Barrington who typed and retyped the manuscript.

Finally I thank the executors of the estate of C. Day Lewis, Jonathan Cape Ltd and the Hogarth Press, for permission to use the quotation from 'The Image' (*Collected Poems*, 1954) on page 120, Messrs Faber & Faber for the extracts from 'Little Gidding' by T.S. Eliot (*Four Quartets*, 1944) on pages 172 and 214, and the editor of *Medical News* for permission to use the case history in Chapter XI.

PART I

I

Pamela

1931

I first fell in love at the age of six with a small, plump girl called Pamela. The affair was almost entirely make-believe. It happened like this. My family lived, at that time, in a house called Springwell which stood alone in the Essex countryside surrounded by gently sloping grassland with here and there small woods and copses. The market town, Saffron Walden, was about four miles away and every Wednesday my brother Michael and I were taken to a dancing class in the dark and dusty hall off the main square. Here we were herded together with some forty or fifty other boys and girls under the instruction of Miss Davenport. It was stuffy and boring and we hated it from the moment we got there to the moment we left and continued to think of it with horror long after we got home.

Mother thought it was good for us and, because father thought so too, we could not argue the point. What we could do, and did, was to make a habit of appearing at the last moment in such a state of filth that mother and Eidy, our old nanny, had to do a thorough cleaning-up job to make it possible for us to go at all. We hoped this behaviour would eventually wear everyone down and, indeed, I once heard mother say to Eidy, 'I don't think the boys enjoy dancing. I wonder if it really does them much good.'

Unfortunately this perceptive and completely accurate remark did not override the theory that boys of our age and class should learn the art of dancing because, as mother put it, 'You'll come to regret it if you don't at least try. What will happen when you are older and go to a dance? You'll be miserable. And think of your poor partners. Their toes will be black and blue.' As it turned out mother was absolutely right.

The class started with the boys standing in a long line facing the girls. At a signal from Miss Davenport the boys bowed and the girls curtseyed and, this preliminary completed, the cry would be, 'Take

3

your partners for the dance.' I hated this moment because I did not like girls as a breed and it made me feel uncomfortable having to put my arm round any one of them. Fortunately I was very small for my age so I did not have to look them in the face, the focus of my eyes being somewhere between their chin and upper chest, and that was about all I saw of them.

Miss Davenport was tall and always dressed in black. She rarely smiled and when she did it had the effect of freezing the blood rather than making anyone feel happy. Her voice was monotonous. 'A-one, A-two,' she would call out and the piano would tinkle in the odd way pianos do at dancing classes.

It was not all dancing in pairs; we had some marching and one jolly dance called the Sir Roger de Coverley, while all the time Miss Davenport kept up her chanting and the piano its tinkling. There was no personal instruction and the only time I can remember Miss Davenport speaking to me was when she unexpectedly put a boney hand on my shoulder and whispered, 'Don't shuffle, young man.' It gave me quite a start but I was to remember her remark years later when my dancing partner at that time referred to what she called my 'all-purpose shuffle'. 'It's completely predictable,' she said, 'except in the waltz when you give a little hop now and then.' This is what Miss Davenport's class did for me.

After an hour or so of this torment the proud parents were allowed in to watch the final stages until, at long last, we were permitted to scamper away to the changing room to take off our dancing pumps and escape into the open air. In the car going home mother would say sadly, 'I wish you would look as if you were enjoying yourselves. It makes me quite embarrassed seeing your glum faces.' Once, she told us, a lady sitting next to her had asked which her little ones were and she had pointed out two entirely different children who happened to be dancing extremely well. If this was an attempt to sow seeds of guilt it fell on stony ground.

Then one day things were different. It was Michael's doing. He suddenly decided we ought to fall in love. Being eighteen months younger than him I did not really understand what it was all about, so he had to explain. It meant a boy choosing a girl to 'like very specially much'.

'But I don't like girls one little bit,' I pointed out reasonably.

'That's because you're a baby.'

'I'm not.'

'Well then you'll have to be in love.'

4

The logic of this seemed difficult to refute.

'Are you?' I asked.

'Of course.'

I thought hard for a bit.

'Who with?'

'Peggy.'

I tried to think of anyone we knew by the name of Peggy, then the penny dropped. At the dancing class there were two sisters called Peggy and Pamela. I can't remember how we knew their names because communication between pupils was virtually non-existent. However, I did know Peggy and Pamela. Peggy was a rather tall long-legged girl, an agile dancer, far above the general moronic level of Miss Davenport's class. She was, as even I realised, very good-looking. She wore a green frilly dress.

'Oh, yes. Peggy,' I said.

'Well,' continued Michael, after a pause, 'if I'm in love with Peggy, you ought to be in love with Pamela.'

'Why?'

'Because it's fair.'

I thought hard. Once again the logic was irrefutable. It was like tidying up the nursery floor. As Eidy frequently pointed out, if one of us put his toys away in the cupboard, so should the other. 'What's good for the butcher is good for the baker,' was her rather odd way of explaining this idea. So what was good for Michael was good for me, and it was only fair for me to be in love with Pamela if he was in love with Peggy.

Pamela was much shorter than her sister and a little on the dumpy side. She, too, wore a frilly dress, but hers was yellow. Her hair was fair and shiny and she had a pleasant but plain face. For a moment I felt I was getting the worst of the bargain but I put these thoughts to one side.

'All right,' I said.

'Good.'

'When shall we start being in love?'

'Next Wednesday.'

I was not quite certain what one did about falling in love and on this point Michael was strangely unhelpful, although I suspected he had read about it in a book which was why the idea had come to him in the first place.

As far as Pamela was concerned I supposed that, at the next dancing class, I should somehow contrive to dance with her while Michael danced with Peggy. Being extremely shy as well as very small this worried me a lot and I dreaded Wednesday coming round again. But come round it did and we were both clean and ready half an hour before we were due to set out.

Mother was surprised and vaguely pleased but Eidy was highly suspicious.

'Those boys are up to no good,' she kept muttering to herself and for some extraordinary reason she started a complete and thorough search of the nursery. She looked under the cushions on the settee, foraged into the toy cupboard and even climbed on a chair to peer at the top of the wardrobe. It was like the police searching a building for a suspected bomb.

Mother was obviously puzzled by Eidy's behaviour but said nothing. Finally Eidy decided everything was all right, gave our hair a final brushing and watched us suspiciously from the nursery window as we crossed the drive with mother and got into the car.

When it came to the point, dancing with Pamela presented no great problem. The technique was similar to a rugby line-out, with which I was to become familiar years later, but was obviously less exuberant. One just pushed into the line of boys at the right point and when Miss Davenport exclaimed, 'Take your partners for the dance,' I stepped forward and, with eyes averted, put an arm tentatively round Pamela's waist.

Unfortunately Pamela was not very tall so I could not avoid catching her eye. She shook herself slightly to escape from my grip and gave me a half smile but did not seem to realise what a momentous occasion it was. From then on the dancing class was just as boring as ever and I came rapidly to the conclusion that it was not much fun being in love.

In the car coming home we were both silent and I had a feeling that Michael hadn't enjoyed herself any more than I had. So I did not mention Peggy to him, expecting that he would raise the subject that evening when we did our talking.

The expression 'did our talking' needs some explanation and, because one explanation always leads to another, it might be a good idea to forget about Peggy and Pamela for the time being and describe the strange life we led as children, in that secluded house in the Essex countryside.

The focus of our existence was the nursery which was more an institution than a place. It was presided over by Eidy, whom we loved dearly. She was old and round and her throne was a wicker chair by the coal fire from which she kept an eye on the goings on around her. Her nanny's uniform was old-fashioned even for those days, a blue-striped dress going down to her ankles with the white apron littered with numerous safety pins. On her feet were black lace-up boots but in the evening she wore loose-fitting slippers. A lot of her time was spent looking after our clothes and I remember her hanging up the washing on the line in the garden with clothes pegs stuck in her mouth and a black hat on her head. Winter or summer she never went out of doors without her hat. In the evening she would sometimes do the ironing and there would be one iron heating on the grate while the other one was in use. She was an exponent of the damp cloth technique and used to stand with clouds of steam encircling her. The hiss of steam and smell of the freshly ironed clothes are one of the most vivid memories of my childhood.

In her way she was shrewd — witness her suspicion over the Peggy-Pamela affair — and was a very experienced Nanny. She had been with the family over fifty years, having started as a 'tweenie' in my grandfather's house, and had nursed my mother when she was a baby. She lived long enough to hold a third generation of our family in her arms.

We loved her and teased her unmercifully, pulling out her hairpins when she was dozing in her chair or undoing her apron strings when she was bending over the fire. We would then run to the corner of the nursery where we were seized with paroxysms of laughter. Dear Eidy! She enjoyed being 'played up' as she called it, but if we went too far she became 'tucked up' and would sit in her wicker chair breathing heavily. Once we made her cry by calling her a silly old woman and I have not forgiven myself for that, even today.

The nursery belonged to Eidy and us children. My sister Joan, who was three years older than me, was by now at boarding school so was away much of the time. My other brother Edward was seven years older and his life was half-way between the nursery and 'downstairs'. He was more a grown-up than a child.

Mother used to come to the nursery frequently. In those days we had family games every evening after tea because there were no ready-made amusements like television. Our favourite was a vicious form of patience called racing-demon but we used to play all sorts of word and picture games such as Consequences and an educational game called Lists in which you were given a letter of the alphabet and a subject such as birds, colours or towns of England. In five minutes you had to write as many as you could think of beginning with that letter. Penguin, pelican, pippit and so on, ending with ptarmigan if you were clever enough. Being the youngest I usually came last but if any form of handicapping system was suggested I would go into a sulk even worse than the sulks when I lost. These games were considered too pagan for Sundays, when we were given biblical texts in large capital letters to colour with crayons or water colours. The one exception was an extraordinary game called Missionary Lotto and for years I retained information from this which never proved of great practical value. The questions and answers went something like this:

Q. Who were the first bishops to visit the province of Hang-Chow?

A. Billings, Burkinshaw and Harvey Jackson.

We used to have these off pat, but gradually their memory has faded and now I cannot even remember who is 'the monkey god of India' — one of the easier questions.

Father rarely came to the nursery and when he did it was usually as a duty visit to 'get to know the children' and we did not enjoy it because we had to stop whatever games we were playing and do what he had planned. He probably hated it as much as we did. Poor father!

Looking back I think he would have been much happier if he had been compelled to help with the feeding, washing and nappy-changing from our baby days as men do now, but for a middle-class father of those days it was unthinkable. So he came to the nursery as a visitor and, partly because of this, remained a stranger to us all his life. He was a shy person and the system was against him for by nature he probably preferred to be alone in his study with his books and writing. He was a clergyman by profession, a writer of books on theology and history by choice.

The other important feature of nursery life was our toys. All children have loved, love and always will love their toys but because there was so little else to amuse us toys became a very personal matter. Some of them were, for practical purposes, living creatures. Joan naturally went for dolls, in particular a rather scruffy golliwog and I have a photograph of her clutching this ghastly object to her chest. We boys went for lead soldiers. We had hundreds of these. They came in red cardboard boxes, usually eight infantrymen or five cavalrymen to a box, superbly made by modern standards. The officers we knew personally by name, while the other ranks we recognised by various features such as a broken sword or head missing. Usually missing heads were reattached with a match stick but tended to swivel round the wrong way. My favourite was a cavalry officer in the Dragoon Guards called Sherbrooke. He was a gallant figure on a rearing horse and his existence was one of perpetual suspense – was he going to fall off or was he not? Michael's favourite was a Highlander called Picton who was in a permanent squatting position which must have led to severe cramp. These names were taken from characters in the Peninsular War – shades of G. A. Henty – and Edward's favourite was called Crauford, another of Wellington's generals, in spite of being clad in khaki and ready for action on the western front.

My other special favourites were a group of light cavalry, four on black horses with lances couched, the fifth a bugler on a white horse, everlastingly at full gallop with legs outstretched like the horses in old racing prints. I loved these beings as much as my family and I distinctly remember on one occasion making a list of people in the order in which I liked them best which read as follows:

> Mother } equal first
> Eidy
> Sherbrooke
> Joan
> Edward
> The Bugler
> Father
> Jemima (a china egg-cup in the shape of a duck)
> Michael

Jemima was an Easter present and had arrived bearing a chocolate egg.

Michael was at the bottom of the list that day because he had trodden on one of my farmyard animals and broken off its hind legs.

At the beginning of the holidays Edward organised a complicated battle game in which we all took part. The conflict extended from the nursery down the corridor to the spare bedroom and everyone, even father, had to tread delicately to avoid causing casualties amongst the soldiers. Sherbrooke, Picton and the lancers were requisitioned for this along with Roman legionaries, angry Zulus with clubs, and khaki-clad infantry from the First World War in gas masks. Unless or until they got killed, we could not play with them on our own and as the battle usually lasted two or three weeks before Edward won, we felt deprived.

This situation set me one of the first ethical problems of my life.

Should I make Sherbrooke charge the Zulus single-handed and get killed on purpose so that I would be able to play with him? It will be remembered that King David had a rather similar problem over Uriah the Hittite.

The battle game was a highly organised affair based on the use of dice and rulers. Each soldier, cavalry or infantry, had a measured distance which he could move, fire his rifle or attack the enemy with a sword. Similarly each gun had a known range and explosive spread. The dice decided exactly where the shell or bullet went and also who won a personal combat. It was a fair system and gave everyone a chance. For example a Red Indian with a tomahawk could dispose of an elite squadron of dragoons if he was lucky enough with the dice or, at a pinch, he could have a go at an enemy tank of First World War vintage. Joan was not in command of an army but she had a couple of dozen Red Cross nurses who did devoted service. If ever a soldier was really destroyed, that is to say trodden on by mistake, we would bury him in a match box in the flower bed by the privet hedge.

Apart from this battle game Edward treated us very fairly, although we must have tried his patience sorely. He was fated always to be one age group ahead of us and, as everyone knows, no one is more irritating than the person who a few years previously was similar to what you yourself are now.

At the time of the Peggy-Pamela episode my favourite toy was an aeroplane. It was a silver high-winged monoplane and I used to carry it wherever I went rather like a medieval squire with a hawk on his wrist. I was at my happiest running around the garden, or through the waist-high grass of the paddock, holding my aeroplane at arm's length against the wind. Once I flew it from the car window but this practice was forbidden because mother thought it might confuse the driver of the car behind into thinking we were about to make a left turn. This aeroplane was a present from an aunt, and it is interesting to ponder the effect of toys given to children by their relatives. I am sure that a child's future is, to some extent, influenced by the presents he receives at Christmas or on his birthday. This particular aeroplane eventually led me to join the RAF.

The point of this description of our childhood way of life is to show that we were intensely creative. Our toys and everything else were fitted into a pattern, part reality and part dream, and if Peggy and Pamela were to have any meaning at all they would have to be drawn into this pattern which was devised, for the most part, after we had gone to bed and 'did our talking'.

Bedtime was ritual. It started with Eidy warming night-shirts on the fender in front of the nursery fire and helping us to get undressed. We would then light our candles – there being no gas or electricity in the isolated Springwell – and be taken along to the drawing-room to kiss father and mother goodnight. The next stopping place was the pantry where we collected brass jugs filled with hot water and were then allowed to go up to the bedroom by ourselves. It was a time of mystery with the candlelight making strange patterns on walls and staircase and, once we had left Eidy, there was a feeling of suspense.

> The door opens
> In the tiger leaps

Although bedtime was a nightly routine something *might* happen, just as every time you open a door a tiger might be waiting on the other side. I knew what that something would be. Once upstairs in the bedroom we would pour the hot water from our jugs into china washbasins and give our faces and hands a perfunctory going over with a flannel. Then to bed where we read books by the light of our candles, until Eidy came up to say goodnight. My candlestick was of chipped orange enamel and I would watch the candle wick as it curled over until the flame flared up and drops of liquid wax ran down the sides of the candle. The used matches were blackened and distorted because as a point of honour we never dropped a match until it was burnt through, which meant holding the hot end as soon as it was cool enough to be bearable. A collection of these lay heaped in the candle-stick, like the grisly relics of a holocaust, and many years later I was to remember this. We then said our prayers, each ending with the word Amen, which I took to be 'Our Men', that is to say the gardener and chauffeur who seemed to have more than their fair share of spiritual support. Eidy always said A-men, presumably referring to the AA men in their yellow mackintoshes who saluted us from their motor-bikes with side-car as we drove by. Eidy's last act was to kiss us goodnight and recite a ritual jargon rhyme which we found very funny although we had heard it many times before. Our favourites were

> Good night, sleep tight
> And mind the fleas don't bite.

and

> I saw some lambs and lots of sheep.
> And naughty boys go off to sleep.

Then the sound of her footsteps would disappear down the passage and when we could no longer hear them and the last flickering of her candle had vanished we would be alone, not however in complete darkness because we had a small night-light with the wick turned low. It was now that we 'did our talking', partly to keep at bay the terrors of the night and partly to create our fantasy world.

I can remember little of this strange world because it was so long ago. It contained what we called our dream people, characters who came and went, were invented and discarded in a never-ending story which carried on night after night. It was not unlike the prolonged serials of today's television and radio except that we had to make up the story as we went along. At times I had the distinct impression of the characters taking over and doing what *they* wanted.

Who were these dream people? Some, of course, were real: ourselves, Eidy and so on, but in the shape which we desired rather than what they were. Others were fantastical. Perhaps the most famous of all was a creation of Joan's called Sky-blue Pink, who did many exciting things over a period of months or even years. As a younger child I had followed the adventures of three teddy bears called Binkie, Winkie and Christmas Pudding but by now I had outgrown this fascinating trio. Christmas Pudding was the youngest and naughtiest but he always came out on top – in other words myself as I would like to have been. Michael had his own special dream people too and each of us jealously protected our individual collection. I had no control over Sky-blue Pink while Michael was not permitted to put words into the mouths of Binkie, Winkie and Christmas Pudding. This unwritten law made story telling a very complicated business and, now that Joan was mostly away at boarding school, Michael and I kept the tales going by a strange dialogue, rather like the antiphon of a church choir, a series of responses which were not answers but maintained a theme of their own.

At the time of the Peggy-Pamela episode the story had developed along the lines, literally, of a train journey. This was because the family had recently returned from a holiday in Norfolk and due to an engine breaking down had arrived home after dark. The incident had impressed us enormously and anything which impressed us automatically became incorporated into the story. Our dream train must have been amphibious as well as high-speed because it took a bewildering course between such unlikely places as Bury St Edmunds (where our aunts lived), Zanzibar, London, Hang-Chow, Llandudno and Sydney. Many of these names originated from Missionary Lotto.

As soon as we were certain we were safe from Eidy we would part the curtains of the bedroom window and look out across the lawn. Sometimes it was pitch black, sometimes moonlit so that the shrubs and greenhouse stood out with clarity and we could see the shape of the hills and woods beyond. Occasionally, in summer, we could see the dim phosphorescence of glow-worms in the flower-bed beneath the window (what has happened to glow-worms today?). But whatever kind of night it was we would see the railway station on the lawn outside with the engine puffing and groaning to a halt. There would be the slamming of carriage doors, the rumbling of porters' trolleys and the chatter of passengers. Some we would recognise, others were blurred figures against a background of smoke and sparks from the engine. The question on this particular night was, 'Will Peggy and Pamela be on the train?'

This was one of the few episodes of the story I remember and our conversation went something like this:

Michael	It's Saffron Walden station. I can tell because I can see the fat porter with a beard.
Me	Eidy's got some flowers in her hand. Pink and red and gold. Can you see them?
Michael	He has a beard because he doesn't like drinking his cocoa at night so he dips his beard in the cup to soak it up then goes and wrings it out on the lawn.
Me	Eidy's talking to some Zulus. They seem terribly cross. One of them's waving his club over his head. He's got white teeth.
Michael	Butterflies love cocoa so in the daytime there are swarms of Red Admirals and Peacocks on the lawn all drinking the cocoa where he's wrung out his beard. People come from miles round to see it, even from Calcutta.
Me	They are banging their shields and jumping up and down. Eidy's telling them they'll be sent off to bed if they don't behave. There's someone else talking to them. It's a girl in a yellow dress.
Michael	I can see a girl in a *green* dress. It's as green as grass and very long, right down to her feet. She's got golden shoes on and a golden crown on her head. I think she must be a princess. (pause) It's Peggy.

Me	(crossly because Michael had pinched my idea) Mine is Pamela. The Zulus have pushed Eidy out of the way and are getting cross with Pamela. They are holding their spears up and making funny noises through their teeth.
Michael	The porters are bringing something on a trolley. It's large and shiny. Yes, I can see it now. It's a throne all covered with jewels. They've put it on the platform and Peggy's sitting on it. All the porters are bowing and all the women are curtseying just like at Miss Davenport's.
Me	Someone's jumped off the train. He has a great big silver sword in his hand. The Zulus are all running away. Their eyes are sort of bulging and they're terrified. Pamela is standing all alone in her yellow dress. The someone with the sword is going up to her and kneeling down. He's offering her his sword and she's smiling. Who is it? I think it's me. Yes, it is.

The two stories had, by now, become so exciting that our voices must have gradually got louder until they reached the danger point of grown-ups hearing us. Eidy, who could move with cat-like stealth, had crept down the passage and suddenly pounced on us.

'You're talking,' she said accusingly.

Talking at night was one of the deadly sins. If Eidy caught us at it she was disproportionately angry and as a punishment would, sometimes, turn out the night-light. Father, on the other hand, would listen to the rumbling of our voices with increasing irritation until it became unbearable when he would come rushing up the stairs from the drawing room. Before we knew what was happening he would be in and out of the bedroom and we would both have had our bottoms smacked. These visitations were infrequent but devastating and stopped us talking for several nights but we had to start again because the story must go on.

Eidy repeated her accusation.

'You were talking,' she said, 'and what's more you've pulled the curtains back.'

She went to the window and peered out. Of course she was unable to see Saffron Walden station with Peggy and Pamela, the Zulus and her own self. All she could see was the empty lawn.

'H'mm,' she said, 'No light for you tonight.'

'Please, Eidy,' I said, 'please don't put it out.'

'That's what happens to boys who talk.'

'But we were only talking a little.'

'Talking a little is talking too much.'

She took a box of matches from her apron pocket and lit Michael's candle. Then she went over to the washbasin where she turned down the wick of the oil lamp until the glow vanished.

'Please,' I said desperately.

Eidy did not reply. This time when the flickering of the candlelight disappeared we were left in total darkness.

All children, I suspect, have night terrors and my particular fear was a patch of damp wallpaper above the wardrobe. About three months previously I had happened to glance at it and discovered it was in the shape of a witch. Because the candle was flickering it appeared to move, which seemed to bring it to life and I was at once convinced it was a witch. Naturally I was terrified. I dared not look at the wall above the wardrobe but my eyes inevitably kept moving in that direction. My fear was that one evening I would find the patch had disappeared and that would mean the witch had escaped and was loose in the room. It was dressed in black, rather like Miss Davenport, but its body was humped up so that the long, pointed chin almost touched the black slippers. It wore a shovel hat on its head but I never saw the face because it was concealed by long, ragged skeins of hair. It is strange that I thought of the witch as 'it' rather than 'she' but this, perhaps, was a measure of my fear and loathing. It may also seem strange that I was perfectly aware it was a discoloured piece of wallpaper, but that is the way children think – and adults, too, for that matter. Religion and myth are full of this double-thinking.

Now, lying in the dark, I could not tell if the witch was in its wallpaper form above the wardrobe, or roaming at large about the room. I lay in bed terrified, listening to the creaks and whispers of the old house and expecting, at any moment, to hear the shuffling of slippered feet across the floor and feel bony fingers round my throat. Eventually I went to sleep but the witch rode hag-like through my dreams and even now sometimes appears to me in nightmares. Little did Eidy know what she was doing when she turned down the wick of the nightlight.

Next morning, with the sun shining through the windows, the witch seemed unreal and I pushed it into a corner of my mind from which it would emerge only when darkness came. Michael felt let down because the story had been interrupted at a crucial point so we decided to make an exception and continue it during the day. While Eidy was washing clothes in the back kitchen, we leant over the brass fender of the nursery fireplace and tried to recommence the story at the exciting point where it had been abruptly terminated.

We tried hard but the dream people seemed colourless in full daylight with sunbeams making patterns on the nursery floor and the sound of laughter coming from the kitchen. So we gave up and Michael decided to play with his soldiers while I went into the garden and wandered down to the yard to see how the chickens were getting on. They were clucking about happily and I sat and watched them for some time. The cock crowed and clapped its wings then, for no obvious reason, attacked one of the hens, pinning it to the ground and pecking its neck. I chased it away and the hen stalked off indignantly. I was a little puzzled as to what the hen had done wrong for the cock to attack it like that and, because I had seen the same thing happen before, I mentioned it to mother later that day. She could not think of a reason either.

'I suppose he was just in a bad temper,' she said.

'Well couldn't we get rid of him?'

'I don't think that would be a good idea. The hens need him.'

I had a feeling mother was going to tell me something more but she decided not to and for years I was puzzled why the hens needed the cock because it seemed to me he gave them a pretty rotten time.

I thought a lot about Pamela that day and wondered if I really was in love. In the afternoon I went by myself up what we called the Long Walk. This was a continuation of the paddock in the form of a grass track between pine trees which extended to the top of the hill and was the limit of our safe territory. I had never been to the top by myself before and it gave me a thrill of apprehension. I leant over the gate looking out across the fields. In the distance was a scarecrow with its black sleeves flapping in the wind. It reminded me of the witch and I turned and ran back to the safety of the house.

I continued to think about Pamela and wondered how things would turn out for her in the story that evening. When last seen she had been saved by my opportune arrival, which had sent the Zulus scampering away, but they might come back again.

They did. We kept our voices low so as not to disturb the grown-ups and by the time we stopped talking I had, with my sword, beaten off a counter-attack of Zulus aided by a detachment of the Household Cavalry and a naval mountain gunnery team. Pamela was very grateful and without realising it, I had forgotten to be frightened of the witch.

Wednesday and the dancing class came round once more. I had no difficulty in taking Pamela as my partner, and this time she smiled at me in a friendly fashion but we did not speak to each other. I wondered if she knew about the Zulus. For me her appearance in the story was just as real as her appearance at the dancing class. It was puzzling and that evening I asked Eidy, in a roundabout way, 'If you dream about someone do they dream about you too?'

Eidy put down her knitting. 'Lawks, what a funny question to ask.'

'But I want to know.'

'You get on with your game and don't worry your head about such things.'

So that was not much help. I noticed Eidy was watching me furtively and I suspected that if I asked her again she would send me off to bed with a dose of medicine from the cupboard above the washbasin in the bathroom, black treacly stuff which made me feel sick. This was Eidy's stand-by for all troubles.

Michael was going great guns with Peggy. Mother had recently read us the story of Perseus and Michael, seizing upon this, had rescued Peggy from the jaws of a seamonster as she lay chained to a rock. It was such a good idea that I performed a similar feat but Pamela was chained to a smaller rock in a cove down the coast and the sea monster was not a very large one. Neither girl was in the nude as they were in the picture of the incident which mother had shown us and which had a decidedly erotic flavour.

Sadly the next dancing class was the last time I met Pamela because, soon after, I went down with scarlet fever. In those days 'the fever' was taken seriously and I was quite ill. The doctor came to see me several times, a big man in a brown suit, who grunted but never actually spoke, at least not to me. I think he was afraid of catching the infection because he would not come close to me but touched my chest with his stethoscope which seemed to have yards of black rubber tubing attached so that he could hold it at arm's length. I genuinely believed it had magic qualities.

When I was a little better, I lay in bed tearing strips of skin off my legs like peeling wall paper. Michael did not catch the fever so I spent a fortnight in isolation and when it was all over the season of dancing classes had come to an end and we never went again.

Two things did, however, happen. Being alone I was unable to carry on the story with Michael so had to make do with daydreaming on my own. The distinction between imagining things while awake and imagining when asleep – true dreams – was blurred and one night, when I was running a high temperature, I was aware of Pamela sitting on the end of my bed. Actually she was sitting on my feet so I asked her to move.

'You don't look very happy,' she said peering at me in the dim glow of the night-light.

'Nor would you be,' I replied, 'if you were cooped up all night with a witch over the wardrobe.'

'Nonsense.'

'See for yourself.'

Pamela climbed off the bed and walked across the room to the wardrobe where she stood gazing at the wallpaper.

'You're quite right,' she said at last.

She came back to the bed and noticed a walking stick, which I was meant to use for thumping on the floor if I needed anyone and which was leaning against the bedside table.

'Here, give me that,' she said.

She took it and turned it over gently in her hands, then pointed it at the wardrobe and started calling 'witch, witch, come along witch,' rather like a farmer's wife calling the chickens.

There was a rustling of wallpaper and the witch slid down on to the floor.

'Come here, you silly old witch,' said Pamela imperiously. It sidled cautiously across the floor between the wardrobe and the bed. I did not feel at all frightened. When it was quite close Pamela unexpectedly lifted up the stick and brought it down with a crash on the shovel hat. The witch seemed to disintegrate and when I leant over the side of the bed and looked down to the floor all I could see was a crumpled heap of wallpaper.

It would be untrue to say the witch never came back again but, because of Pamela, it never held the same terror for me. I was grateful to her but I suppose it was a fair deal because I had saved her from the Zulus, not to mention the Household Cavalry and naval gunners.

The other incident had occurred at the last dancing class. We were just finishing and Miss Davenport had clapped her hands and said, 'All right, children. See you next week.' I was about to turn round and go to find mother when Pamela gave a little cough. She put her head close to mine and whispered in my ear, 'I like you.' Then she was off to the changing room leaving nothing behind but a faint fragrance, a fragrance I cannot describe except that it was somewhere between the smell of soap and Seville oranges. It's a strange thing that I cannot now remember what Pamela looked like but I still recognise that fragrance.

Twice recently it has come back to me – once in a supermarket and once at a party –and with the fragrance came a picture of Pamela in her frilly yellow dress at Miss Davenport's dancing class. It was a love affair after all.

II

Miss Brownlees
1932

Nowadays children have to go to school at the age of five or there-abouts. In the early 1930s tutors and governesses of the Jane Eyre type were not quite extinct, a few still lurking in the homes of the wealthy. We were not among the wealthy but mother was allowed, under a system run by an organisation called the PNEU to teach us at home because she felt this was the best way to start us on the right educational path. Probably she also wanted to have us around as long as possible.

Teaching was formal by modern standards but none the worse for that. We were all able to read, write and do our sums at a very early age. My first reading book, which I remember well, was dark green in colour. It was of the traditional type and on the first page was the word CAT with a picture of that animal so there could be no possible confusion. The story, I thought, unfolded rather slowly but by the middle of the book it was noted that 'the rat sat on the mat.' A few pages later 'the cat ate the rat on the mat.' This was a tragedy but I was confused when the rat appeared later in the story this time described as the 'fat rat'. How could being eaten by a cat allow him to survive at all, let alone grow bigger? It was a real puzzle to me but mother was unable to understand my problem and I thought I was being either stupid or naughty to mention it.

Lessons were held in the dining room and were associated with the smell of vinegar because the maid used to polish the surface of the table with vinegar after clearing away the breakfast things. They were also associated with green baize which was used to protect the table.

Mother was a good teacher and I enjoyed learning from her. The three of us, later two when Joan went to school, had personal attention of a kind that no school could provide and even mundane tasks like learning the four times table were fun. The teaching was imaginative and mother told us stories from the bible, mythology and fairy tales in such a way as to make them seem real. I have already described how Michael and myself, in the guise of Perseus, rescued our respective Andromedas, Peggy and Pamela, from the jaws of the sea monster. Many other stories were equally vivid and became incorporated into our being, which is what children's stories are for, because, after all, they originate from the depth of being.

Another special lesson we had was called Picture Study. We were shown a picture, usually an old master, and had to describe in detail what we saw. This was a wonderful training in observation and we noticed things like a dog gnawing a bone under the table, a bird perched on a tree in the background and the shape of the clouds, all of which had been included by the artist for a special reason of his own and were therefore important. Is Picture Study done today?

If the weather was nice we would sometimes be taken for nature walks instead of doing lessons indoors, usually up the Long Walk, through the gate and across the fields. Mother was especially keen on flowers and there were crowds of cowslips in the short grass of the chalky soil and bluebells and purple orchises near the edge of the woods. These we were taught to treat with respect and we were not allowed to pick them.

Mother was not so good on animal life and because all animals, birds and insects fascinated me I outstripped her in knowledge at an early age, mostly from what I learnt by looking at picture books. My search for knowledge was insatiable and I used to embarrass comparative strangers by asking them impossible questions such as, 'If a lion fought a tiger which would win?' or, 'Which flies the fastest, a swallow or a martin?' I really wanted to know and became quite annoyed by the ability of grown-ups to turn questions aside without admitting they did not know the answer. 'It depends,' they would say but would never explain what it depended on.

I was by now seven and that summer the sun seemed to shine all day and every day. We played with our toys in the garden and the Hornby engines pulled their trucks, laden with twigs and pebbles, along the track laid down the paths between flower beds, the farmyard animals cropped the grass on the lawn and the soldiers fought their battles in the rockery amongst the blue lobelia, with behind them giant hollyhocks which attracted the bees more than any other flower. Swarms of tortoiseshell butterflies fluttered round the buddleia by the back door. Those were golden days at Springwell.

The world was still wonderful – the house, the garden, the fields and woods, our private dream world and the fascination of our lessons in the dining room. But autumn was coming and black clouds loomed on the horizon. Soon we would lose 'the clouds of glory' as Wordsworth described them and once lost they can never be regained except in rare moments. Even to remember them, as I am now doing, is to dull their clarity with the haze of nostalgia.

The particular black cloud was school. Father and mother decided that Michael and I should both go to boarding school at the same time to keep each other company, although I would be only seven at the time. They chose for us a preparatory school on the Sussex coast, a part of the country where preparatory schools congregate, and the rivalry between the various schools was, in those days, as intense as between animals guarding their territorial rights. I was not especially worried about going to school because I could not imagine the possibility of being away from home and the security of the nursery. What is beyond comprehension is usually beyond fear.

Mother took us up to Gorringes, the big store in London, to be fitted with school uniforms and she and Eidy spent days poring over lists of clothes, which they put in piles, ready to be labelled and packed in our trunks. Once I found Eidy with tears running down her cheeks and I tried to comfort her. I did not know why she was crying but I suppose that, for her, it was the end of an era. She was to sit alone in her wicker chair in a silent nursery.

Two nights before we left for school there was an eclipse of the moon. It seemed that the powers of the universe had arranged this specially for us and it was, perhaps, the most vivid memory of my childhood. We were allowed to stay up late and watch from the paddock. Edward was in a scoffing mood, having seen an eclipse before, but Joan, Michael and I were filled with primitive awe. We watched the moon over the beech trees. It seemed to race through the sky amongst wisps of cloud and I could not understand it was the moon that was still and the clouds that were moving.

Father called out, 'It's starting now.' There was a tiny black dot or blemish on one side of the moon and gradually it spread inwards, gnawing its way across the surface. I thought of the witch and clung to mother's arm.

'It's only an eclipse,' she murmured.

But for me the moon was being destroyed by an evil power and the scientific explanation mother had given us meant nothing. What we could see going on before our eyes was the reality. Slowly, but inevitably, the moon's face was eroded and the darkness around us deepened so that I could no longer see the outline of the house or the hedge at the top of the paddock. For a moment the moon was a black disc, then on the far side a silver rim appeared and gradually it came out from behind the shadow. I had a feeling of enormous relief. What if it had got stuck and remained a black disc for ever and ever?

Edward remarked that it was not at all a bad eclipse and we wandered back to the house in the light of the restored moon. As a treat we were allowed to drink mugs of cocoa in the drawing room which was lit with oil lamps whose flames sometimes flared up and blackened the glass with soot. Then we collected our candles and hot water jugs and went up to bed.

This was the last memory of my true childhood. The next picture is Victoria Station in London. At the age of seven and nine, never having been away from home except with the family, and having had no experience of being with other children apart from Miss Davenport's dancing class, Michael and I were put one September evening on the Brighton train which took us to a world remote from anything we had known before.

The platform was crowded with boys all dressed like ourselves, most of them apparently excited and pleased to meet each other again, with porters pushing trunks and tuck boxes on their trolleys and parents standing round smiling brightly. I was confused and had no feeling except that I wondered if I was there at all.

Father had gone off to find out what they were meant to do with us and came back to say that Michael, who was old enough to be in the senior school, would travel in a compartment with Mr Culbertson while I, being in the junior school, would go with Miss Brownlees. At that moment Miss Brownlees came and introduced herself.

'The train will be starting in a moment, Binns,' she said to me. 'You had better say goodbye to your parents.'

I shook father and mother by the hand and followed Miss Brownlees into the train. I was in a daze. Why, having been Christopher for seven years, should I become Binns? Why did mother and father not kiss me goodbye? As I climbed on to the train I turned and I looked back. Michael had by now been led off and I saw, for a moment, the despair on mother's face while father grimly looked down at the platform. Mother saw me and raised her hand a fraction, then a porter came between us and I did not see them again.

In the carriage I sat on one side with four other new boys, with opposite us another four and Miss Brownlees. One of the boys was crying, little gurgles and sobs coming from his round face, but my desolation was too much for tears and besides, a sixth sense told me that I must not cry. The train gave a jolt and moved slowly from the platform amidst a hail of goodbyes and waving hands and when I at last came to my senses I was aware of the dingy houses and backyards of London rushing past the window.

Miss Brownlees was my only hope. She had not spoken to us before the train started, being too busy jumping up and down to check who was there and who was not but once we were on the move she closed the door to the corridor and shut out the noise and laughter of the other boys and surveyed her new charges thoughtfully. Her eyes dwelt on me for a moment then passed to the fat boy by the window who was still crying.

'You'll run out of handkerchiefs, you know,' she said in a matter of fact voice, 'so you had better stop crying.' The tears stopped immediately.

'If you want to start again I have got a spare one,' she added and, opening her handbag, pulled out an enormous handkerchief almost the size of a hand towel. On one corner were embroidered the letters TW.

'Can anyone tell me what that says?'

I looked at the letters but from the depth of my despair I could not say what they were. A boy on my left whispered 'TW.'

'My, what a high educational standard we have,' said Miss Brownlees and she laughed to herself but in such a way that we were included in the laughter if we wanted to be. I did not want to be.

'TW,' she repeated, 'now try to think what it stands for. As a start I will tell you it isn't my initials. I'm RB. B for Brownlees and R is such a ghastly name that it remains a deadly secret for all time.' She laughed again and my numbed brain stirred and began to try to work out what TW stood for.

'I'll tell you later,' said Miss Brownlees, 'and now lets introduce ourselves.'

It is strange that, after so many years, I can remember the names of the boys in that carriage and the order in which they sat. Saunderson, Joyce, Williams, Binns II, Baxter, Hazeldene, Smith II, Watson and Talbot-Jones. I, of course, was Binns II, Michael being Binns I, and the fat boy who had been crying in the corner was Hazeldene.

Miss Brownlees continued a sporadic conversation with us throughout the journey. She had little response and did not expect it, nor did she ask us about our homes or families because she knew this would start the tears flowing. Her silences were as comforting as her moments of speech but, for me, her efforts did not lessen the dumb horror I felt but gave a faint hope that, in time, the nightmare would end. She was like the silver rim on the black disc of the eclipsed moon and I will never think of her with anything but gratitude.

Our journey took us through fields and later the humped Downs but I scarcely noticed these. As we neared the end of the journey and the train slowed on its approach to Brighton Miss Brownlees said, 'You had better start getting your suitcases off the rack now and try not to knock yourselves out. We don't want you to arrive unconscious. By the way TW stands for Tear Wiper. Thank heavens I didn't have to use it although it could do with a wash.'

Of course this was a professional ploy but Miss Brownlees was a very professional teacher.

We were bundled out on to the platform at Brighton and Miss Brownlees sorted out our tickets for us and led us into the station yard.

'You had better stay close to me,' she said, 'you might as well make a good start by getting on the right bus.'

I looked round for Michael and saw him standing with a group of larger boys, a hopeless look on his face. Our eyes met for a moment but there was hardly recognition in them. And it remained like that. At school we were strangers and if we did meet it was a painful reminder of home and things that had ceased to be. We had nothing to say and avoided each other. For Michael the hurt was greater than it was for me. He had no Miss Brownlees to cling to, no babyhood to retire to because there was always a brother younger than himself who had first claim.

Two coaches arrived. Miss Brownlees pushed the juniors on to the first one waving the older boys aside.

'Let the new boys on first. Where are your manners?' There was a muttering about filthy new bugs and Miss Brownlees rounded on them.

'Well, you were new bugs yourself not so long ago and a lousy lot too from what I remember. What's more I haven't seen much improvement.'

In the coach Miss Brownlees left us to ourselves and went to sit at the back with one of the masters. We sat in silence as the coach took us out of Brighton and along the main road. It was not a long journey and after about twenty minutes in the gathering dusk we turned in through tall, wrought-iron gates and went up a long drive with tall trees on the right and what seemed to me an enormous expanse of playing fields on the left. The coach swung round on the gravel surface and came to a halt outside a large country house. On the steps of the front door stood Mr and Mrs James, the headmaster and his wife. This was my new home.

The memory of my first day at school fills me with horror. In fact I still use it as a yardstick against which to measure any deprivation or sadness I suffer in life. I was lost. I did not understand what was meant of me.

It started on the first evening. It was quite late when we arrived and we were taken over by a teacher called Miss Morris, who took us up to our dormitory and stood watching us silently while we unpacked our suitcases and put our belongings in the bedside lockers. I had brought with me my aeroplane, from which I was still inseparable, and Miss Morris took exception to this.

'That thing should have been in your tuckbox,' she said brusquely. 'Dormitories are for sleeping in.' I don't think she meant to be unkind but I found it difficult not to burst into tears and I did not know what to do with the aeroplane, so I just stood holding it.

'I suppose you had better put it in your locker for the time being,' she said.

She took us downstairs where we queued for cocoa and biscuits. I realised I was hungry but when my turn came I found the cocoa didn't taste like cocoa nor the biscuits like biscuits, or at least not like any I had eaten before. At home I had been used to a family dinner in the evening so I went to bed miserable and hungry. I was pleased it was Miss Brownlees who came to put our lights out. I had never before gone to sleep without being kissed goodnight by Eidy and although I realised Miss Brownlees would not do this it was some comfort to hear her cheerful voice saying, 'Well, goodnight. Life's not too bad really and if I hear anyone talking I will come and skin you alive.'

There were six boys in the dormitory, four new boys and two older boys called Peterson and MacDermott who unfortunately turned out to be the bullying types. As soon as Miss Brownlees had gone they started on us. I forget what they said. I was determined not to cry but later in the night I was woken up by the sound of someone sobbing and discovered it was myself.

Peterson had been woken up too. 'Someone's blubbing,' he said, 'is it you, Binns, or whatever your name is?'

'No, it's not me.'

'Well, it had better not be. We don't want blubbers in our dormitory.'

Next morning I woke to a day of despair. It is difficult to describe why I felt despair. It wasn't so much that anything very dreadful happened but I was in an unreal world from which, unlike the dream world of my childhood, I could not escape. I suppose it was comparable to an older person's grief for loss of someone they love dearly, an emptiness and lack of feeling rather than pain.

After breakfast we new boys were taken to the headmaster's study where he talked to us kindly but I did not listen to what he was saying. The only remark I remembered was, 'If ever you feel unhappy come and talk to me. It doesn't matter what time of day or night.' In the afternoon we were taken for a walk up the Mile Oak Road, which I learnt in time to hate, walking two by two in the charge of Miss Morris. I was with another boy called Joyce who was older than me and cheerfully grumbled about the food. 'That stuff we had for breakfast wasn't bread. It was *grey*. I've never seen grey bread before.'

It was then that an extraordinary thing happened. One of the pair immediately in front of us was Peterson. He turned round and said casually to Joyce, 'You don't like the food then?'

'Not very much.'

'Well, how do you like this?'

He hit him hard on the mouth then turned back and continued talking with his companion. A trickle of blood ran down Joyce's chin. It was so unexpected and so far removed from anything I had experienced before that I went numb. Joyce wiped the blood from his face with a handkerchief. Neither of us spoke for the rest of the walk. I am sure if Miss Morris had seen the incident she would have done something about it but she was at the back of the column.

I did not see Miss Brownlees all day and another teacher put the lights out in our dormitory. Immediately she had gone the ragging started. I remembered what the headmaster had said and I quietly got out of bed, put on my dressing gown and slippers and went out into the corridor. I had no idea where the study was so I wandered round for some time until finally I met a maid who seemed surprised to see me and asked what I was doing. I told her I wanted to see Mr James and, obviously puzzled, she took me to the study then went to find him. I am sure Mr James was puzzled too. For years he had been making the same remarks in his talk to the new boys but he had never expected any of them to take him up on it. Now he found himself called away from the dinner table to a diminutive figure in a dressing gown sitting in his study. He was a kindly man but he did not know what to say, so he puffed at his pipe and looked thoughtful while I sat staring at him.

The furrows on his brow deepened and finally he decided to send for Miss Brownlees.

Miss Brownlees knew just what to do. The headmaster backed out of the room still puffing his pipe and making inarticulate noises while Miss Brownlees sat on the arm of the chair opposite and looked at me with her head on one side.

'What's up?' she said.

'I want to go home.'

I was expecting Miss Brownlees to put her arm round me and let me sob out all my unhappiness on her shoulder. I had pictured this scene while we had waited for her to come and, even in my unhappiness, it was by no means an unpleasant prospect.

'Well, you can't,' she said, 'not in what you are wearing at the moment. You would look ridiculous.'

'I want to go home tomorrow.'

'You can't.'

'But I don't like it here.'

'Nor do I particularly. At least not all the time.' She looked at me intently and said, 'You may be a nitwit but at least you've got courage, haven't you?'

'I don't know.'

'Getting up and coming to the study at this time. How did you find your way?'

'I asked one of the maids.'

'Was it the one with a face like a pancake?'

'I don't know.'

'Well, if you don't know, it wasn't. Can you find your way back to the dormitory?'

'I don't know.'

'In that case I will take you back myself. We can't have you wandering about the corridor at night. You'll frighten people out of their wits. Come on, you can hold my hand, but don't tell Mr James otherwise you'll get expelled and I'll be given the sack.'

She led me back to the dormitory. Outside the door she whispered, 'And I don't want to hear any more nonsense from you,' gave me a pat on the shoulder and went off, presumably to finish her dinner. This incident gained me some renown because I refused to tell Peterson and MacDermott where I had been and it remained a mystery to them and made me a figure of interest.

After that first day things improved. In the morning Miss Brownlees did an assessment on the new boys. I had to go up to the desk and read out loud, which I did badly because I was nervous, then we all had some dictation to do, also a few simple sums. We were then called up to the desk one by one and Miss Brownlees said to me, 'Even if you are a nitwit your mother taught you quite well,' and she smiled at me most fondly.

In the afternoon we played football. Although I had often kicked a ball about with Michael and Edward, I had never played football in the sense of being on a pitch with twenty-one other boys and real goal posts. I loved it. Although I was small I was quick and I pursued the ball tenaciously all over the field and once nearly scored a goal. There was no question of team work and when we stopped for half time Miss Brownlees said to me, 'If you want to charge all over the place like a maddened bull, Binns, that's your affair. It might be better if you limited your activities to one side of the field.' Miss Morris, who was in charge the next time we played, quite rightly insisted on positional placing and although at first I was on tenterhooks in case the ball never came my way I finally accepted the idea as reasonable.

For a short time I had forgotten Springwell and mother and Eidy, and as the days went by I became more and more interested in what I was doing and in the boys around me. Joyce became my best friend. But there were still problems.

One of my biggest worries in the early days was that I did not know how to tie my tie. No one had taught me. I used to loop it round my neck and let it hang down loosely but someone would notice this and say, 'Go off and put your tie on properly.' I used to walk round with my chin almost on my chest to hide it. I never thought of asking anyone to show me how to do it and I cannot remember who finally taught me.

Another problem was the food. It was remarkable that in a fairly expensive and well-known school we were underfed. On paper the menu would have appeared reasonable with meat, vegetables and pudding, but the meat was always the same, a form of stringy beef, except that sometimes it was hot with gravy on it and sometimes cold and served with a bright yellow pickle. The vegetables were nearly always potato and cabbage. Cabbage can be delicious but not the way it was served at that school. The standard puddings were prunes and custard or tapioca. For tea we had the peculiar grey bread and a substance called jam which, rumour had it, was a form of jelly with wooden pips put in it. On three evenings a week, Mondays, Wednesdays and Fridays, as a special treat we had food which we had brought with us from home at the beginning of the term, tinned fruit, cakes and so on. This was shared out amongst everyone at each table. Mondays, Wednesdays and Fridays stood out as the best days of the week and even now have for me a particular flavour of their own. I think of Friday as tinned fruit day. On these days we boys would spend a lot of time wondering what we would find on our table and as teatime approached we would go to the dining room and peer through the glass door to anticipate the pleasure. A jar of potted meat was treasure from heaven. I spent nearly all the term looking forward to my tin of sliced peaches, which did not appear until early December.

The staff fared better. They had white bread and at breakfast toast and marmalade. A master or mistress sat at the head of each table and we would long for them not to want their second piece of toast and prayed that we would be the one to receive the precious gift. I dreamt of food, especially making toast in front of the nursery fire and eating strawberry jam with strawberries in it. Starvation and inhumanity were our spectres and I suppose the school I went to was no different from all the other schools lining the Sussex coast in this respect.

The worst problem was the dormitory at night. Peterson and MacDermott made life very unpleasant for us younger ones. Fortunately one of the other new boys, Saunderson, sometimes wet his bed so he became the target of scorn and I am ashamed to say I, with the others, held my nose and called him Stinky Saunderson in the knowledge that when he was being baited I would be safe. There was a horrid old lady called Madge who looked after the bed linen. She was meant to be 'quite a character' but, in fact, was a sort of perverted form of Eidy. She treated us unkindly and when Saunderson had made one of his mistakes she would storm into the dormitory and call him a filthy, dirty swine. Poor Saunderson! I hope he was not ruined for life.

Bullying by day was bad too. In theory there was always a member of staff present but Peterson and MacDermott ganged up against other boys in turn. Once they had a go at my friend Joyce but he fought back and although he lost they left him alone after that. I was too small and shy and did not have a chance. I can remember spending one Sunday afternoon hiding in the toilet so they would not find me.

In spite of this I was tolerably happy and in my letters home gave no hint of my troubles. I know this because when mother died we found, in the bottom drawer of her desk, stacks of letter from us children. They were mostly highly uninformative, usually requests for things to be sent or results of school matches which would have been of little interest to mother or father.

'We plade St Rolands. We lost 3–1. Please send green crocodile.'

Only the first letters I wrote showed my deep-seated misery but I was pleased to find this was never openly expressed. Maybe Miss Brownlees was right and I did have courage but when I read them I could have wept for the person I then was. What I wrote was genuine feeling, even if it was highly unoriginal and the spelling could have been improved.

'When I look up at the stairs I no you can see them to.' This was one of the first letters I sent home and I can remember I had lain awake one night in a state of despair and through the window watched a single star shining down on me. Years later I read a passage in a book where one of the characters with all hope gone, waiting for the end, looked up and, through a break in the clouds, saw a single star like the one I had looked at and 'the thought pierced him that in the end the Shadow was only a small and passing thing.' When I read these words I was cut to the heart.

My great stand-by and love was Miss Brownlees, and the time has come for me to describe her. She was dark-haired and very pretty with a touch of colour in her cheeks, a smile that glowed, almost palpably warming the air around her. I remember her best sitting at her high desk in the classroom. She liked to have flowers on her desk in front of her but a little to one side so as not to obstruct her view and, in my memory, these are a part of her presence. Daffodils in spring, Michaelmas Daisies in autumn but during winter a mass of everlasting flowers, sometimes called immortelles. She grew these herself and was proud of them. From a distance they looked lovely but, close to, were dry and dusty.

As she sat there her gaze would wander from boy to boy, pausing at each one and, I am sure, knowing exactly how he felt. If she was puzzled her head would tilt to one side and she would look long and thoughtfully. She was a highly professional teacher, showed no favouritism and rarely permitted close intimacy but when she did it was like a benediction. Looking back I realise she was already too 'school-ma'amish' to be attractive to the opposite sex in spite of her good looks but we boys worshipped her. I am sure she was destined to become a headmistress rather than a wife.

She taught history and for her sake I learnt the dates of all the kings and queens of England. Throughout my school career I always came top in history and have loved it ever since. The stern Miss Morris taught us arithmetic. I sometimes wonder what would have happened had their roles been reversed. Maybe I would have developed a love for higher mathematics and abhorred anything to do with history. As with our childhood Christmas presents, which I have mentioned before, chance takes a big part in the sort of life we choose.

Miss Brownlees had a great sense of humour and would laugh loudly at some of the things we said, but never maliciously. She liked reading to us in her deep voice and would sometimes get completely carried away by what she was reading. She would go on and on and we would sit spellbound because she spun magic in the words that came from her mouth. Finally she would come to, shake her head and laugh. 'A prize for anyone who's still awake,' she would say, 'what will it be? Extra cabbage for lunch?' We would groan and laugh too.

Once I remember she read us Hiawatha out loud and the words have stayed with me ever since.

By the shores of Gitche Gumee
By the shining Big Sea Water
Stood the wigwam of Nokomis,
Daughter of the Moon, Nokomis.
Dark behind it rose the forest,
Rose the black and gloomy pine-trees,
Rose the firs with cones upon them . . .

On and on she went, because it is a long poem, and when she closed the book the room was almost dark. This time she shrugged her shoulders and said nothing but I noticed the glint of tears in her eyes.

She kept everyone at arm's length perhaps because she was aware of the attractiveness of her own personality and the dangers that could arise from it. Two occasions I especially remember because each time the curtain opened for a moment and I saw her as she really was.

The first took place the following Lent term. Peterson and Mac-Dermott still terrorised the junior school. Their usual prey was Saunderson or Hazeldene, but on one particular day they turned on me. They had raided my desk and tuck box and had me cornered in the classroom where they were pouring scorn on my belongings which, as I have explained before, were very personal things. Peterson was flying my aeroplane upside down and, on purpose or by accident, he dropped it and broke the wing. I was standing clutching the back of the desk at the time and the wooden piece came away in my hand and I found myself hitting Peterson again and again with it. I remember his frightened face with saliva and blood dripping down his cheek.

Of course I was in deep trouble, but the headmaster was fair and the final punishment was a 'spatting' for both Peterson and myself. When a boy had a 'spatting' he went to the study where he held out his hand and Mr James, after saying untruthfully it was going to hurt him more than it hurt you, took a thick leather belt from a hook on the wall and slashed it across the outstretched hand four times. It was exquisitely painful because the strap would hit the palm and then swing round and catch the back of the hand. If the boy withdrew his hand he got an extra two spattings.

After this ordeal my final punishment was to go and see Miss Brownlees. She was sitting in the office and when I came in she swung round in her chair and looked at me. She gestured to me to raise my hand, which was swollen and red. Then she looked at me solemnly and nodded her head four times. Not a single word passed between us but I knew that she *understood* and approval or disapproval did not matter. She turned back to her desk and I went back to the classroom.

Later that term I was ill and had to go to the San for a week, a pleasant building, separate from the main school and reached by an iron bridge over the road which climbed up a hill with high perpendicular banks on either side. The bridge is still there although the school and its grounds have long since been demolished and are now part of a housing estate. It gives me a strange feeling to think that what is so clear in every detail as I write no longer exists.

At any rate my illness was not very severe. The diagnosis, as I learnt years later from the letter I wrote home at the time, being, 'I am in the San with dire rear.' I remember Miss Brownlees coming in, smiling and sitting comfortably in an easy chair on the far side of the room. Usually visits of this sort were a bore because, once the visitor had asked how you were, there was not much else to talk about, but Miss Brownlees stretched out her legs and started talking about herself. I wish I could remember what she said but it is a long time ago. The one thing I recall is that she told me her great ambition was to go to Africa.

'You mean to see the elephants?' I asked.

'No, to teach black children.'

'Zulus?'

'Perhaps. Who knows?'

'Aren't they dangerous?'

'No, but I think they want to learn. Anyway,' she added, 'I don't suppose it will ever happen. Dreams seldom do.'

Another vivid memory of Miss Brownlees is an incident that took place about a year later on the last night of term. The bullying of Peterson and MacDermott was by now a thing of the past and I got on well with the other boys. It was the custom to celebrate the last night in some way, usually with a midnight feast, which was splendid in theory but in practice was not much fun because everyone was too exhausted to enjoy the food and anyway we would be going home next day to the joys of a civilised diet.

On this particular night we did what came to be called the Jerry Trick and I am proud to claim that it was I who invented it. This later became something of a school tradition but I suppose disappeared with the demise of the jerry as a standard utensil.

The jerry was of course the china pot which every boy had under his bed for use during the night. The trick was to tie a length of dressing gown cord to the handle and at the critical moment give the cord a jerk. We selected Hazeldene as victim because he was rather deaf and was an invariable user of the jerry soon after lights out. On this occasion he let us down and appeared to be dropping to sleep. We must have been good amateur psychologists because we decided the best thing to do was to get out of bed in turn and by a process of suggestion stir him into activity. It worked. I pulled the cord and the jerry shot along the floor away from poor Hazeldene, leaving him stranded.

Unfortunately he was a very nervous boy and to our surprise jumped on the bed and started screaming. We could not stop him. It was Miss Brownlees who came to see what was going on and after she had calmed Hazeldene she noticed the jerry in the middle of the floor with the dressing-gown cords leading to my bed. It took her only a moment to work out what had happened and she was very angry. I was prepared for the lash of her tongue when the expression on her face suddenly changed. A smile appeared at the corner of her mouth and she was soon sitting on the edge of the bed laughing as uncontrollably as, a moment before, Hazeldene had been screaming. I loved her for that.

This was one of my last and happiest memories of Miss Brownlees. Her dream came true after all and she left the school to teach in South Africa.

I met her once more and that was several years later when I was one of the senior boys in the school. We were going for a school run on a damp autumn day and I was taking a short cut with Talbot-Jones through a beech wood. As we emerged on to the grass of the Downs, I saw two figures approaching. One seemed familiar and I paused while Talbot-Jones ran on. It was Miss Brownlees. She tilted her head to one side and looked at me.

'It's Binns II,' she said, 'you haven't grown much, have you?' I was embarrassed and muttered some unintelligible words. She smiled. 'I can see you're still a nitwit,' she said, 'but never mind. You always were one of my favourites.' She turned and walked on with her companion. I caught up Talbot-Jones and together we ran down the slope towards the school.

III

A Sprig of Heather
1935–6

About three years after I started school we left Springwell, another nail in the coffin of my childhood. The reason was some financial disaster which befell us although I never discovered what exactly happened, nor do I even know why father was fairly well-off in the first place because as a clergyman his income must have been tiny. I suppose he inherited money from his own father who was in the brewery business and the 'disaster' was due to an unfortunate investment.

The whole affair made a great impression on me at the time. It was the custom, when we came back from school at the end of each term, for father to 'show us round the house'. This was a strange ritual and very frustrating because all we really wanted to do was go to the nursery to give Eidy a hug and get our toys out of the nursery cupboard. Instead we were conducted from room to room by father who would say, 'Now, what changes are there here?' We were expected to notice any alteration in the furniture and so on and he became quite put out if we failed to do so. Mother realised our predicament and when his back was turned she used to point silently at, say, a table which was normally in the study but had been moved to the drawing room. On this particular occasion the ritual did not take place so we knew something pretty serious had happened.

There was an air of gloom about the house and father was nowhere to be seen. Eventually he emerged from the study with a grave expression on his face. 'Has your mother told you we are going to move?' he asked. We shook our heads and he went on to talk in words we did not understand and finished by muttering, 'We are on the brink of ruin.' I could see mother was trying desperately to shut him up, and although she explained afterwards that things were not as bad as they appeared, the damage had been done. I was haunted by pictures of the family living in poverty with us children going about shoeless and in rags, like the pictures I had seen in various children's books which were a relic of the Victorian era, especially one of a family begging by the roadside while a lady seated comfortably in a carriage, drawn by two horses, was condescendingly tossing a coin in their direction. The picture was entitled 'Charity'. The coin looked suspiciously like a penny and I do not know to this day whether the moral was that it was a good thing to be generous to the poor or whether the artist was a secret Marxist portraying the inequalities of the social system. Be that as it may the prospect of being on the receiving end of such charity was frightening and I don't suppose father had any idea of the effect of his words. I even started packing up my toys on the assumption they would have to be sold.

The disaster could not have been all that serious and if we were on the brink of ruin we came nowhere near falling over the edge. In fact, we moved three times with bewildering rapidity but each house seemed as large as the one before and it was only years later that I partly understood what was going on. We finally settled in a house called Dalberg on the outskirts of Cambridge. It was about this time that our name suddenly changed from Binns to Elliott-Binns. There was some dark mystery about this but I never did discover the reason. I expect it was due to some financial or legal complication in our family affairs.

Dalberg was quite pleasant from the front but when viewed from the back was one of the most hideous houses ever built and it was the back that most people saw because this aspect faced across what we called the fens, a stretch of flat grassland leading towards the town. The house was one storey higher than its neighbours which made it stand out like a sore thumb. It was exactly symmetrical apart from an extraordinary rectangular structure stuck on the wall, high up to the left, rather like an unsightly mole on someone's back in the shoulder-blade region. Strangers were puzzled by this excrescence, a possible conclusion being that the house was short on lavatories and this had been added for the benefit of some incontinent old gentleman. It was, in fact, a wardrobe attached to the main bedroom which was not very large, so it was decided to put the wardrobe outside the house because there wasn't room to have it inside. I have never heard of this sort of thing being done in any other house, and the story behind it was even more amazing. The house had been owned by a merchant from the Far East who was very fat. He was also very aggressive and used to treat his wife badly, often knocking her about. She was thin and when, at her suggestion, the wardrobe was grafted on the outside of the house, she arranged for the entrance to be narrow so that her husband could not squeeze through it. In fact it was an escape hole for her when the going got tough.

One can conjure up a delightful picture of the thin wife cowering behind the dresses and coats on their hangers while the fat husband stormed and raved outside, occasionally making fruitless attempts to force his way through the door. I was grateful to this merchant because, whatever deficiencies there may have been in his personal life, he had the good taste to create a genuine Japanese garden in the grounds. This consisted of a U-shaped pond surrounded by a rockery. There was a real pagoda and also a tiny hump-backed wooden bridge. Both were in a state of decay with the woodwork rotting but the impression was that of a faded willow-pattern plate, turning brown with age. One could not perhaps quite imagine beautiful Japanese ladies with fans tripping lightly over the bridge, but the tiny garden had a haunting beauty about it. I loved it and I think it is the only place I still dream of exactly as it was. Sadly the bridge and pagoda have long since been pulled down and the pond alone remains.

Although we all loved the Japanese garden it became my special territory because of my fondness for natural history. I stocked the pond with goldfish and also hunted for sticklebacks, crayfish, newts and many other strange creatures in the stream which ran along the back of the houses and in the river Cam itself. Anything I caught went into the pond and it was soon vastly overpopulated but nature has a habit of sorting these things out. The newts, as is their wont, took to the land and moved elsewhere while the sticklebacks, who are notoriously quarrelsome, could not tolerate the overcrowding and there must have been many fights to the death which benefited the crayfish who fed on the remains. I finally bought an eel from the fishmonger, two and a half feet long, at threepence a foot. This, having devoured all the crayfish and anything else it could catch, succumbed either from starvation or from despair because it had no chance of finding its way to a river and hence to the ocean where all eels have to go to fulfil themselves. My ignorance of ecology caused a lot of suffering to the creatures I loved.

I was thus left with the larger goldfish and also a pair of pond tortoises. These were delightful creatures with flat, dark shells and yellow speckles on their long necks. They used to climb on to a sloping stone at the edge of the pond and slide off, falling into the water with a sound like someone clapping hands. Their favourite posture was lying just beneath the surface with their heads above water like the periscopes of two submarines. I fed them on raw meat and the cook always cut a bit off the joint for 'Master Christopher's tortoises'. Another visitor we had was a grass snake, a beautiful blue green creature which slid gracefully through the water. The gardener killed it with a spade and when he told me this with pride I burst into tears and could have killed *him* with a spade. There were also lizards which basked on the rocks and disappeared in a flash if your shadow came between them and the sun. For me it was a paradise.

Occasionally the Japanese garden changed from a place of peace and meditation to a scene of unutterable chaos. This was because Edward had invented a game of golf which included the Japanese garden as part of the course. It was, I imagine, the most difficult golf course that has ever been devised. Since the first four holes consisted entirely of rockery and water it was by definition impossible for the ball to lie anywhere you could hit it in orthodox style and we had to adopt a kind of scooping motion with the club which we learnt to do rather well. The course extended over the rest of the garden and I think mother and father were very tolerant to put up with it because the flower beds suffered dreadfully and the gardener more or less gave up and retired to the vegetable garden.

The real family game was tennis and everyone, sometimes even father, took part. I wish cine cameras had been in use in those days because it must have been extremely amusing to watch and was worth recording. Edward found our tennis rather a bore, being old enough to be a competent player, and took part only out of duty. Joan was pretty hopeless but she had been given tuition at school. This meant that when she served she threw the ball very high and sometimes lost touch with it altogether. On one occasion it landed on her head. Michael used to ward the ball off as if it was a dangerous missile while I had the habit of falling over whenever I got excited. The family used to say I tripped over the white lines.

Mother and father were, perhaps, the oddest of all. Mother played with careless abandon which had little relevance to the actual court, while father took it all very seriously. He used to prefer playing at the net where he would crouch in a highly professional manner but if the ball came his way he would slash at it and nearly always hit it out of court or into the net. He was rather unpredictable and sometimes would remain immobile and shout 'partner' which put his startled partner in an impossible position because he had no chance of getting anywhere near the ball. The result of all our oddities was chaos.

Sometimes we had proper tennis parties which we children were allowed only to watch, the players often being athletic young men from the university. I looked upon them as heroes and this was borne out by a particular incident when one of these undergraduates had the misfortune to have a wasp crawling up his trouser leg. It turned out he had been stung five times but with casual courage he mentioned he had not wanted to interrupt the game, so had done nothing about it. The only thing he could have done was to take off his trousers which was unthinkable with ladies present.

There was another game in connection with the tennis court which involved Bingo, our bull-terrier, whose name was not worthy of such a fine animal. Father chose it because it was the name of a character in one of P.G. Wodehouse's novels, which were one of his chief relaxations – and this leads me to diverge from the subject of tennis to that of dogs. We were more devoted to them than to people, our immediate family circle excepted, and in one sense they were our first loves. Bingo was the second dog we had, the first being an Airedale called Jock who, I think, joined the family at about the time I was born. Jock was a trained police dog and if he saw anyone who might be a burglar he would circle round his victim getting ever closer until the poor man was paralysed with fear. To Jock anyone carrying something such as a bag or sack was a potential burglar and this led to problems and quite a lot of apologies to harmless tradesmen. In spite of his police training Jock used to kill hens and for a time had to wear a muzzle whenever we took him for a walk. He also had a habit, which was only talked of in a whisper, of 'doing nasty things on the beds'. On these occasions he had a thrashing and was confined to his basket under the stairs all day. I did not know what nasty things he did on the bed but I used to feel very sorry for him and when no one was looking I would creep under the stairs and sit with my arms round him to console him.

Jock died when we were away at school and because we all missed him so much we got Bingo, who was my companion and the companion of all of us for many years. He arrived as a tiny puppy with a lovely puppy smell and strapping round his tummy because he had a small rupture. It was the size of a marble and we had to put a collar stud over it to push it in and then strap it tight. This gave Bingo frightful indigestion after meals and I can remember nursing him in my arms while he whimpered in pain.

Bingo grew up quickly and became a handsome dog, mainly brown but with white socks and a white face, an unusual mixture for a bull-terrier. There was a brown patch on the side of his forehead which made him look like Hitler. He was not, like Jock, obsessive about burglars but as with all dogs of his breed once he got his teeth into something he would not let go. One of our ways of giving him exercise was to get him to bite on a stick and then lift the stick with Bingo attached and support it between the two uprights of a gate. He would hang on growling and wriggling for minutes on end enjoying it immensely. Once he took a dislike to the blue pin-stripe trousers of a visiting theologian from Austria and having fastened on would not let go. Fortunately there was only cloth, not flesh, between his teeth but the theologian justifiably took umbrage and, after swearing in German, left the house abruptly.

Bingo had a sense of humour. For a time we had a rather fussy aunt staying with us. She obviously did not like him and used to withdraw from him saying 'good dog' in an offhand way. One afternoon he stole a Stilton cheese from the dining room, carried it up to her bedroom and proceeded to dismantle it and at the same time a feather pillow. When she went up to bed the floor was covered with feathers and cheese. It was Bingo's turn to do a stint in the basket under the stairs and I did not console him because I knew he had done wrong.

Apart from these two incidents I cannot remember Bingo being hostile to anyone and the only enemy he had was the wheelbarrow. He hated the wheelbarrow and would bark at it hysterically or lie on the ground watching it in case it moved. It was our fault because one of us, I forget who, had invented a wheelbarrow game. This consisted of Bingo being held by the collar, while someone rushed round the wire surround of the tennis court pushing the wheelbarrow in front of him. Bingo was let loose when the wheelbarrow pusher had done one length of the court and the object of the game was to get back to the starting-point before being caught. Edward was rather fat at this time and I remember Bingo once catching him on the final corner, leaping up and nipping his grey flannels which, being under stress, split all the way down. I found this game rather frightening because I hated being pursued, even by Bingo, who I knew would do me no intentional harm.

Family life was good in those days at Dalberg, and I was lucky to have so much tenderness, which excluded the need for any other form of love. My home and family were all I needed and I remember waking up one night at the beginning of the holidays and longing for daytime to come. The nursery was still our refuge although Joan, Michael and, to a lesser extent, I were outgrowing it and we were secretly ashamed at having a nursery. It was not something one would mention at school and one of several reasons why we never thought of asking our schoolfriends back home.

There is no doubt that at this time mother was the pivot of our existence. She was a remarkable woman and almost everyone who met her was attracted to her. Looking back over the years I think her secret was that she was a deeply religious person and, although she seldom talked about it, it pervaded her life. I wish she had spoken more of it but for her generation it was not a subject one discussed openly except in its most superficial aspects, such as what hymns one liked or whether the sermon was too long. As young children we had almost too much instruction but when we had reached the thinking stage religion became just as taboo as sex and we, as children, missed out on both. Church was something we went to on Sunday and sex had not yet reared its ugly head, or beautiful head, depending on how one looked at it. Mother was such a good mother, and the nursery was such a secure stronghold, that we did not need anything else at home and it was at school we fought our battles.

She was not intellectual like father, but had deep insight. She was full of the prejudices of her generation but compassionate when it came to individual cases. For example she disliked on principle Germans, the Labour Party and, to a lesser extent, the Roman Catholic Church and made her feelings clear but she would have been kind to any German she happened to meet and she visited and was adored by the most labourite of parishioners at the times when father was a practising vicar of a parish. Later in her life she was surprised to find that Roman Catholics were ordinary people like Anglicans but she still had her reservations and was very upset many years later when I attended a Roman Catholic service.

She had a great sense of humour although not an especially subtle one. Once when we were visiting a house one of the bones in her stays became loose and made a twanging noise when she bent down – she must have been about the last woman in the country to wear bone stays. It was something of a crisis because it happened outside the front door after she had rung the bell. She just had time to pull the bone out and stick it in the ivy in the wall. During the visit she kept on having attacks of the giggles which she managed to control with difficulty. When we left she remembered to reclaim the bone from its place in the ivy.

She was prone to errors of speech which sometimes took the form of outrageous statements which puzzled people. Once, when giving a talk to the Mothers Union, she opened with the remark, 'I can remember many years ago when I was standing on top of Mount Everest . . .' She actually meant Ben Nevis but no one thought of correcting her and such was her appeal that some of the older people actually believed her. 'The vicar's wife would never tell us an untruth,' one of the old ladies said.

Mother was terribly forgetful and she is the only person I have known who would come back from a shopping expedition on the wrong bicycle. Once she thought she had lost her false teeth while on a walk and organised the Brownies to search for them in the field next to the rectory where we lived at that time. She later found them in her tooth mug in the bathroom but instead of keeping quiet about it, as most people would, she told everyone. The Brownies thought it very funny.

She also did odd things like leaving a dish cloth in the silver teapot which was used only on special occasions. I can remember her pulling out the sodden rag covered in tea leaves after one particular tea party which she gave for the local clergy and their wives. When we all laughed she exclaimed, 'Sh! You should always show respect to the cloth.' Such witticisms, however, were more typical of father than mother.

Her chief fault was that she was over-protective. She never realised that many people prefer to fight their own battles even if they lose them. I suppose this was a kind of inverted selfishness on her part and as far as we children were concerned she, like most parents, unconsciously preferred to see us emotionally backward and intellectually advanced. In other words she wanted us to stay children, and who can blame her? To what extent she succeeded and whether it was a good or bad thing I cannot judge.

In spite of my contentment at Dalberg it was here that I first raised the standard against parental authority, although in the mildest way imaginable. One of my crazes, apart from natural history, was roller-skating. It happened that the road in the front of our house was a cul-de-sac and, because there was very little traffic and the surface was fairly smooth, mother thought it safe for us to skate there. Joan and Michael were not nearly as keen as I was so I usually skated alone to the top of the road and back at least once a day. I managed to get up quite a good speed but always fell over if I tried any clever tricks. One morning I was doing my usual trip when I saw Joan skating at the bottom end near the main road. This rather surprised me but I waved to her and she waved back. When I got closer I discovered it was not Joan at all but a *strange* girl. It was most embarrassing. I was twelve or perhaps thirteen, and at that age I simply did not speak to girls apart from Joan who, being my sister, did not count. I had no idea what to say because I had never met a girl on my own before.

She was about my own age, fair-haired and slight of build and seemed as embarrassed as I was. There was great likelihood that neither of us would say anything but I summoned up courage and asked her, 'Are you roller-skating?'

'Yes, are you?'

'Yes, I am too.'

This was not a very intelligent bit of conversation but, when one analyses it, just about as sensible as one adult telling another it's a nice day when both are aware the sun is shining.

'Have you been to the top of the road?' I asked.

'No, have you?'

'Yes, I've just been there (pause). Would you like to come?'

So we set off up the road skating side by side. The conversation did not sparkle but I discovered her name was Heather and she discovered mine was Christopher. We skated to the end of the road and back and agreed to meet at the same time next day.

I did not tell mother and father about this incident. It so happened that Edward was going out with the girl next door and, although it was all above board and legitimate, and she was a nice girl and even survived playing tennis with us, none the less the matter was never actually mentioned. I therefore took it into my head that it was wrong to talk about such things.

I met Heather next day and this time we were both a bit more forthcoming. I discovered her parents had recently moved to a house near the main road. Once again we skated to the top of the road and back and once again we agreed to meet the following day. This was the beginning of a tentative friendship that lasted for several weeks. We devised a peculiar game of roller-skate hockey using a toy wooden brick as a puck and I found her company pleasant. She was very much a tomboy and did not mind falling over, so when we were playing our game of hockey we used to bump into each other and push each other over on purpose. She was also very pretty. This slowly dawned on me. I became aware of an undercurrent of deep feeling which remained an undercurrent. If this was sex rearing its ugly head it decided to keep its head down for the time being and I had no particular wish to hold her hand or kiss her. It was just that *I liked her being pretty*. It was as simple as that.

I was perplexed that mother and father never commented on the fact that we skated together most days and it was very sad that they did not. If only they had made a joke of it by making such remarks as,

'How's your girl friend today?' it would have put the whole matter in perspective. But that was not their way and I came to think that skating with Heather was rather naughty. Once, when her parents were out for the day, we went into her garden and sat talking behind the privet hedge. This seemed more than naughty.

We found that at the very top of the road there was an alley which led between two houses. It was not suitable for roller-skating so sometimes we would take our skates off and wander down towards the field. It was innocent and harmless but at the same time wicked. I have a feeling that Heather's mother and father had the same kind of attitude as my parents and she, too, felt she was being naughty. It was a shame we didn't go and play in each other's gardens, as we should have done, because we were still children.

This affair, if it was an affair, came to an unfortunate end. One day we were roller-skating at the top of the road and probably being a bit more noisy than we should have been when an old gentleman came storming out of his house and started shouting at us.

'How dare you make all this rumpus,' he yelled, 'there's not a bit of peace and quiet with all your clattering and banging.'

I was struck dumb. I could not have argued or apologised to save my life.

'If you want to roller-skate do it in your own gardens and leave other people in peace. What's more,' he continued, wagging his finger at us, 'I've seen you slipping off down the field. Do your parents know about that? Well, do they?'

I shook my head.

'It's not the last you'll hear of this, my son. Nor you miss.' And the old gentleman stormed back into his house. By now Heather and I were white-faced with alarm. We took off our roller-skates and walked dejectedly down the road, like criminals on the way to execution. I don't think we said a word to each other and when I reached the gate of Dalberg I was just able to say goodbye and she said goodbye in reply.

I went to bed terrified and that night I dreamt I was chained up in the dog basket under the stairs. Next morning father told me, without rancour, that there had been complaints about the noise I made roller-skating and in future I must only do it in the drive. The name of Heather was not mentioned.

It was all so stupid and at the time made little impression on me because girls were unimportant compared with such things as dogs, tortoises and goldfish. It is only on looking back that I feel angry.

IV

Frankenstein's Daughter
1937–8

We were still at Dalberg when I left the preparatory school in Sussex. My final memory of that school was a visit to the headmaster's study for a talk about sex. At first I did not know what Mr James was on about. He mentioned tulips bursting into bloom and then started telling me about the sacrifices women have to make when they have babies. For this reason they should always be treated with respect. 'They may even have to give up playing hockey,' he added with great seriousness and this was the one thing I learnt from the talk. The tulip bit I found merely confusing.

Thus prepared I moved on to Harrow, the famous public school on the outskirts of London. Michael had gone to Winchester, it being thought wise to separate us because at home we quarrelled quite a lot, as brothers near to each other in age nearly always do. I still had the advantage of being 'the baby of the family' and capitalised on this in a most unscrupulous fashion because, as I have already mentioned, mother and Eidy wanted us to remain children forever. This used to irritate Michael, and quite justifiably.

Going to the new school was nothing like as damaging as the Victoria Station incident but it was bad enough. Edward drove me there in the car. He had left that same school the term before, and it was felt better that he should introduce me to my new surroundings rather than me having the usual tearful farewell with mother and father. It did not work out very well because Edward was welcomed joyfully by his friends while I was left standing shyly in the back-ground. It must have been the custom for his particular group to have 'friendly fights' because I remember he and another boy – actually the head of the house – had a real set-to, rolling about on the floor in a wrestling match. It was all good fun but I found it alarming and wondered what I had been let in for. Edward finally drove off in the car and I was left standing miserably by my trunk.

Public schools have changed enormously in the last decades and I suppose the life I led was half way between the schools of today and the wicked era of *Tom Brown's Schooldays*. It might be worth recording the extraordinary daily routine I had to get used to and soon did.

I shared a room with another boy called Cavendish and on my first morning, following his instructions, we got up at ten to six and slipped silently downstairs in our dressing-gowns and slippers and concealed ourselves in a corridor on the first floor, where we waited, shivering with cold. I was aware of other boys peering through partly open doors and it all seemed very peculiar.

At six o'clock the bell rang, doors flew open and there was a mad stampede to the bathroom which was on the ground floor. We were the first to arrive, having been strategically stationed in the corridor, and Cavendish showed evident satisfaction. The system was that the younger boys had their baths first to make way for the older ones and because there was not enough time allotted for this it was important not to be at the end of the queue. There were three baths, two hot and one cold and not to finish with a cold bath was a serious crime. Cavendish and I had a room on the top floor and this is why we had to creep downstairs before the bell went. The other boys soon got wise to this and there was a tendency for everyone to get up earlier and earlier and station themselves closer and closer to the bathroom. The system was completely mad.

After the bath we would get dressed, collect together the schoolbooks we needed, then go downstairs where we had tin mugs of tea and special early morning biscuits. If it was winter we would stand round shivering with cold and still half asleep until it was time to set out, in the dark, for the classrooms. The idea was that we had one forty-five-minute lesson before breakfast during which no one learnt anything and the hardship was as great for the staff as it was for the boys. I suppose it was part of the toughening up process.

We returned to our houses for breakfast and this is when we came to life. On my first morning we were offered a second helping of bacon and eggs and this impressed me enormously because such a thing would never have happened at my preparatory school. After breakfast the whole school attended chapel, then we had lessons until one o'clock. Instead of us having our own classroom and the masters coming to us, it was the masters who had the classroom and we had to go to them. Since only five minutes were allowed between lessons, and the school covered a wide area we had to travel pretty fast from one classroom to the next. It was quite a good idea because to sit in the same room all morning becomes monotonous.

The afternoon was dedicated to exercise and no one was allowed in the house between two and four. This was all very well if one was down to play rugger or cricket but otherwise the time passed slowly and it could be thoroughly unpleasant if it was raining. Sometimes we would cheat and cower in the squash courts reading books, or we would go for runs and break bounds just for the devil of it. The rules were strict and there were both masters and school monitors on the prowl to catch boys who were neglecting to take proper exercise. To be found in the house during the afternoon was a serious crime, one of the few which might merit a beating.

After exercise we changed and the entire school attended Bill, not a person but an elaborate roll-call which took place in the yard outside the old part of the school. This was an age-old custom and presumably dated back to the time when boys tried to escape from the hardship of school life or did wicked things like going to London for the day. Each boy, starting with the most junior, trooped past the duty master in turn and said, 'Here, sir' when his name was called out.

We had further lessons before supper and prep afterwards, the younger boys doing this in the dining room under the supervision of a monitor who was also expected to help them with their work. Cavendish made a speciality of thinking up impossible questions and, with a puzzled look on his face, would take his book up to the monitor who, if he was wise, would admit he just didn't know.

It may appear from this account that we had no time to ourselves. In fact, although life was at first rather confusing. I soon got the hang of it and found I had plenty of freedom to do what I wanted, even though there were many other rules, some sensible, some petty and a few, in my opinion, sadistic.

An example of a petty rule was the system of doing up the buttons of the school blazer. In your first year all the buttons had to be done up, in the second year one button could be left undone, the third year two, while in the fourth year the blazer could be worn open. This was really rather ridiculous because if it was hot the first year boy suffered, while if it was cold pride would not permit the fourth year boy to do the sensible thing and fasten up his blazer. Incidentally, we called them 'bluers', not blazers, but throughout this account of school life I have avoided using the peculiar vocabulary which would only be understood by someone who had been to Harrow.

The fagging system I accepted at the time but, on looking back, I find it obnoxious. If a monitor wanted anything doing he would open his study door and call 'Boy' and the fag on duty would have to arrive at the double. If the monitor wanted several things doing, or if the duty fag was not available, he would call 'Boy, boy, boy'. All the fags within earshot had to come and the last one to arrive was given the job. It was one of the most heinous offences not to answer the call of 'Boy'. In addition the fag had to polish the monitor's shoes and also light his study fire in winter so that good firelighters were an essential part of a fag's equipment.

Like all systems it was reasonable if not abused. I was lucky in my monitors who treated me well and I formed a sort of friendship with them. Others were less fortunate and would be sent on unnecessary errands to the other side of the school or given unfair tasks to do. One power-mad monitor, I remember, called for his fag to pick up a book he had dropped on the floor. On another occasion the same monitor did a 'three boy call'. I was the last to arrive so had to do the task. The monitor said to me, 'Fetch me a piece of string.' I happened to have some string in my pocket and I at once produced this. Unfortunately the other fags thought this funny and laughed.

'No,' shouted the monitor, 'I said *fetch* me a piece of string,' so I had to go and find another piece of string in my room. I also got punished for 'lip'. One could tell endless tales of the misuse of the fagging system which would give a false impression but I must admit that when, years later, I was a monitor I rarely called 'Boy'.

The other possible abuse was that of homosexuality because the fags were very much in the power of the monitors and had little redress. I only heard of this happening once but it was, I think, one of the reasons why the fagging system was modified not long after I left the school so I feel I belong to a bygone era.

Although I tolerated fagging I objected strongly to some of the punishments which were inflicted on the junior boys. One was to report to the monitor before early morning school in 'corps kit'. This was military uniform of First World War type with puttees which took a long time to put on and were almost impossible to put on correctly because there had to be an exact distance – I think it was one and a half inches – between each band when the puttees were wound round the leg. I remember my punishment for not *fetching* the string was to report to the monitor on five successive mornings and on each occasion I had got the puttees wrong and had to come back a second time. This, together with having a bath and doing my regular fagging, put an impossible strain on me and I became very tired over those days. I suppose I might have gone to the housemaster or the head boy, who was kind and tolerant, but the whole system was a replica of the army life of that era when 'a private could only bypass his immediate superior in exceptional circumstances.'

The worst punishment was the beatings. This was reserved for serious offences, such as hiding in the house during the exercise period, repeated insolence or failure to answer a fag call on more than one occasion. It was carried out by the monitors but there was some restriction because the housemaster had to give his permission first.

The victim was summoned to the monitors' room in the evening when he was in his pyjamas and dressing-gown and was made to stand on a chair while the head of the house berated him. He then had to kneel over the chair with his trousers down and was restrained by the third and fourth monitors. The second monitor held the door open so that the head of the house had a good run in to deliver his stroke. I was fortunate in never having to suffer this indignity and, indeed, in my day it was rarely done but the ritualism of it nauseated me, and when I was a monitor myself I found the courage to object. There was quite a fuss about this and I had to go and see the housemaster who told me in confidence that he agreed with me entirely and ritual beatings of this sort were stopped not long after. It was one of the few occasions when I felt I had struck a blow for the oppressed which is better than striking a blow *at* the oppressed.

Harrow is famous for its songs and once or twice a term we had an event called House Singing. It was the custom for each new boy to stand up and sing, as a solo, the first verse of 'The Men of Harlech'. This was not meant to be a sadistic practice but in my case no one could have devised a more effective form of torture. I worried about it for days in advance and when the moment arrived I gave a terrific hiccup at the end of each line. This earned me the name of 'hiccups' but the matter was finally forgotten and other nicknames were found for me. At that time I had the distinction of being the smallest boy in the school and I was quite cross when an even smaller boy, called Ashe, came to another house the following term.

From what I have said it may appear that I did not enjoy public school life but this is because I have dwelt on the peculiarities of the system rather than its merits. On the whole I was happy there, largely because I was good at games in spite of my small size. It was an all-male society in which sport was the quickest path to renown and I used to idolise the older boys who played for the school at rugger, cricket or our own peculiar brand of football designed to be played on waterlogged pitches, which they often were.

This idolisation did not overstep the mark to the point of homosexuality which is popularly believed to be rampant in public schools. Some boys did get into difficulties with this problem because it was impressed on us that it was a 'bad thing' yet we were completely bereft of female company, apart from distant views of the younger masters' wives, or the older masters' daughters, who would have been embarrassed (or pleased) if they had realised the amount of sexual fantasy woven around them. I expect we all played this delightful game but did not talk about it. Our 'dream people' were kept secret.

I had a few advances made to me, if one can use this delicate expression. One older boy put a note on my desk on which was written, 'May I hold your hand?' I wrote 'No' on the reverse side and gave it back to him and that seemed to be the end of the matter. On another occasion a boy came into my study with 'evil intent'. I did not at first understand what was going on but when I did I hit him hard on the face and gave him a black eye. It was the second time I can remember hitting anyone in anger and I was quite proud of myself. The boy in question was a very likeable person and he was so upset that I later felt a bit ashamed. Of course I had every right to resist a homosexual advance but I had an inkling that I was a little bit of a prig and did not really fit into the pattern of a clean-limbed English youth giving a cad the punishment he deserved with an English straight left.

I rather laid myself open to these advances because I took the female lead in the house play, reluctantly I may say, because acting so scared me that I forgot to come to rehearsals on purpose. The producer was a serious-minded boy called Wilson, who later was to become famous as the writer of *The Boyfriend*. If ever he reads this I am sure he will agree I was the worst leading lady he ever had and it is surprising he wasn't put off showbusiness for life. I had no talent at all.

The part I played was Frankenstein's daughter, whose name I think was Elizabeth, and I didn't have to do much except look frightened. The play was a complete disaster. My big moment came when I was sitting alone on the stage and through the curtains suddenly appeared the monster, all teeth and clawlike hands, making grunting noises. At the last moment I was to become aware of his presence, give a piercing scream and proceed to be strangled. An English straight left might have been a more sensible response but this was not written into the script.

One night the monster had a cough and I mistook this for the grunting noise – I was shortsighted without my glasses – and, half turning in my chair, began to scream while he was still waiting to come on stage. The audience were completely mystified as to why I was screaming and even more surprised when they saw a bulge in the curtain at the back of the stage moving rapidly from left to right. Unfortunately the monster in his hurry tripped up and fell so the bulge temporarily disappeared only to appear again and continue with its progress. It was, of course, quite impossible for me to scream that long so, like a rather poor singer in an oratorio, I had to keep taking breaths and start again. When the monster finally emerged through the curtains he was in such a hurry that he knocked me flying so I missed my dramatic moment of being strangled gracefully like any Victorian maiden worth her salt and instead had to pretend I had died from concussion.

I would have thought this disaster should have put anyone off me, even with a stuffed bra and my spots covered with make-up, but one or two manly hearts did beat a little faster and I was conscious of this for a week or two.

My only love at school was for Miss Wilmott, the house matron, but this belongs to a later era of my life.

V

Barbara Allen
1938–9

Father was, I think, a disappointed man because he had not received the advancement he expected and probably deserved. This was one reason why he lost faith in himself and found it easier to be a scholar than a parish priest. As it was he seldom seemed able to survive more than two years in a parish before moving on, either to an ordinary house where he could get on with his writing, or to another parish which for some reason or other had caught his imagination. This must have caused agonies to mother. When father first showed signs of restlessness, usually by pacing up and down the drawing room or round the garden with his hands behind his back, she knew another move was on the way. Once again mother and Eidy and the maids would start preparing to pack and in due course the familiar furniture vans would appear in the drive. Our worst batch of moves was at the time we were 'on the brink of ruin' but I eventually concluded this was more in father's mind than in reality. He was escaping imaginary ruin by fleeing from house to house.

Father was impressive in church and preached good sermons, scholarly and compassionate. Outside church he felt at a loss and, in his later years, I cannot remember parishioners coming to our house for advice or comfort, or him being called out to someone dying or in distress. In this I am probably doing him an injustice because we children did not really know what went on but it seemed to us that mother did most of the work. When we moved to a new parish she would drag father round 'visiting' and when this obligation was fulfilled it was she who would run the various parish organisations, arrange bazaars and jumble sales, but more important, talk to people. She was immensely loved and as she went round the village, either on foot or riding her tall bicycle with a wicker shopping basket on the handlebars, people would wave and smile. She seemed to know everyone, and probably knew a lot about their personal lives.

53

I think father felt this keenly and was, in his way, jealous of mother. She had so many friends and he so few that he felt he must move somewhere else where, perhaps, things would be different. Jokingly he would say he was moving because he couldn't stand the Mothers Union another moment and there was some truth in this because the Mothers Union epitomised *people* – people who wanted to talk about their own mundane lives while he was primarily interested in theology. He never seemed able to wed the two. I can remember him once preaching a moving sermon on the importance of love and the curse of possessions and, after coming out of church, going black with rage because he found some of the village lads had come inside the garden gate to pick up conkers from under the chestnut tree.

Our frequent moves upset mother, although she used to say that at least it saved her from spring cleaning. She was left with a string of friends and admirers scattered across the south of England from East Anglia to Cornwall, to whom she wrote regularly but seldom saw. She had, incidentally, probably the finest collection of prayer books in the country because, being absent-minded, she invariably forgot to leave them in the pews of the churches she visited and, although she always meant to return them, she never got round to it.

The constant moving affected our lives. What with this and being away at boarding school much of the time, we seldom had a chance to make friends with people of our own age and if we did make friends as I had done with Heather in the roller-skating days, they seemed to be snatched from us. Our contact consisted mainly of tea parties, which we hated, or tennis parties, which were quite fun, but it was always under the watchful eyes of parents. Like dogs kept on a lead we treated other children with hostility, although we never got quite as far as growling at them.

From Cambridge we moved to Newton St Cyres, a delightful village near Exeter. This proved a remarkable journey because Joan had a craze on goats at the time and the only way we could transport the nanny goat of the moment was to have her standing in the back of the car. It was a terrible squash because we also had to fit in Bingo the bull-terrier. I was sitting at the rear end of the goat who was so nervous she lost control of her bowels, but fortunately the consequences were in pellet form and it was like being fired at with grape-shot from time to time. At the other side Bingo was being sick over Michael and Michael was being sick over Bingo so I really did not do too badly.

Fate decreed we should stay in Devon for nearly five years because the war soon descended on us. Of the eight different houses we occupied before I finally left home it was this vicarage near Exeter and Springwell in Essex which I remember best and I think of these two as our true homes.

I was fifteen when we moved to Devon and had been at public school for over a year. I had only just got out of the habit of crying profusely when I went back to school. It was more of a reflex than anything else because, by now, I knew how to cope with boarding school life and, although still desperately shy, was generally popular. Even so, whenever I said goodbye to mother and father at the end of the holidays, the spectre of Victoria Station would loom up and, indeed, even today when I leave home for any reason that terrible feeling of desolation is not far beneath the surface.

Eidy was still with us, so was the nursery. Of course we had our meals downstairs with mother and father, and after dinner we were expected to sit in the drawing room but the nursery was still our refuge, even though Michael was now sixteen and Joan eighteen. There was never real freedom in the drawing room because we always had to keep quiet. I had a regular game of bezique with mother every evening which I did not enjoy very much and I suspect she only suggested it to please me.

Eidy was a 'retainer' and did little work but we still loved her and teased her gently. Her chief function was to provide nursery tea. This was the great occasion of the day. There was a white cloth on the table, bread and butter cut to exactly the right thickness, raspberry jam, Dutch cheese, cakes and the black kettle on the grate. 'Come to the table,' Eidy would say and we would bring our books with us and munch away knowing we did not have to talk if we did not want to. Eidy seldom came downstairs and the nursery on the top floor was almost a self-contained unit to which grown-ups, apart from mother, were not welcome. Eidy still looked upon us as her children and the other day when I was talking to Joan she reminded me that whenever we left the house to go anywhere, Eidy would thrust her face out of the window high above us and call, 'Have you got clean hankies?' I can picture her now, the white hair, the small, oval-shaped spectacles and the slightly anxious expression.

We still followed many strange family customs, strange, that is, to modern readers. The day started with family prayers before breakfast, to which the maids came but not Eidy who was Baptist. We had a housemaid called Marjorie who had been with us almost as long as Eidy and was in a sense her rival, and a succession of cooks, usually young girls, whom mother used to train. As soon as they were proficient they left to get married bringing, I am sure, great culinary joy to their husbands. Marjorie was inclined to be snooty but I think she loved us almost as much as Eidy did and we were usually welcome in the kitchen and on friendly terms with most of the cooks. We did not think of them as servants and, although the idea of people being employed to do housework and cooking for others is now abhorrent, it was a happy relationship. I think Marjorie, with her duster, or the cook singing while she peeled the apples were in their way happier than the more highly paid workers of today.

Another family custom was reading out loud. This was a ritual performed after lunch and dinner. Mother would read for about half an hour and by the time I was fifteen I was familiar with all the books of Jane Austen and the Barchester novels of Trollope. In lighter moments she read P.G. Wodehouse or Agatha Christie, although when war came the P.G. Wodehouse books were discreetly removed because he had 'gone over to the enemy'. Sometimes it would be father who read and he usually chose the now forgotten books of W.W. Jacobs which were very amusing and at times he would chuckle so much he could not continue. This was the other side of father which we saw all too rarely. When I was younger I did not always enjoy the reading and would often have preferred to be out in the sunshine or playing with my toys, but I owe mother and father an eternal debt for giving me the priceless gift of liking books.

It was while we lived at Newton St Cyres that I fell in love with Barbara Allen. She was one of three sisters who lived with their parents in a hamlet about two miles from the village. Violet, the youngest, was generally thought to be the best-looking but Barbara and her elder sister Marilyn were both pretty girls. Mrs Allen was a middle-aged edition of her daughters and the four together made a striking picture. I can remember them standing in the churchyard talking to mother on the first Sunday after our arrival. They were all dressed in dark blue and I stood back shyly to avoid being included in the conversation. Mother must have tried to introduce me, although I was out of range, because they all turned and looked at me momentarily, but only one of the sisters smiled and I was immediately captivated. They soon moved off, going down the stone steps to the road where they had parked their car. Mother, too, moved off to talk to some other parishioners. I was standing by myself, when something strange happened to me. I noticed the sunlight had suddenly become very bright and I could see each leaf on the elm tree with crystalline clarity. The cooing of a wood pigeon from the other side of the church was soft and beautiful. I had fallen in love for the first time in my life.

Of course it was hopeless. Barbara Allen was a very attractive woman of nineteen or twenty while I was a boy of fifteen, small for my age and lacking all knowledge of the opposite sex. I wore small, round, steel-rimmed spectacles which made me look like an owl, except that owls are, I think, very beautiful birds. I also had rather bad acne.

But for that brief moment it did not matter. I was in a haze of glory because of the tender smile of a woman I had never met before and, for all I knew, might never meet again.

At lunch that Sunday I listened to mother and father, still half in a dream. Father was cheerful because his first service in the new parish had gone well and the church had been full. 'They even seemed to listen to what I was saying,' he remarked dryly.

'I thought your sermon was outstanding,' said mother, 'especially the bit about lifting up mine eyes unto the hills. After all it is hilly round here and I've been told that you can see Dartmoor from the garden on a clear day.'

Father obviously thought this remark irrelevant and mother continued, 'I was talking to a very nice lady called Mrs Allen after the service. She has three charming daughters and the middle one, Barbara, tells me she helps in the Sunday School. They seemed very friendly. In fact everyone I talked to was friendly.'

I knew, without being told, that it was Barbara who had smiled at me, and at once my mind leapt into activity. Somehow I must find a way of meeting her. I toyed with the idea of joining the Sunday School but obviously I was far too old for that and if I had asked to go along as a helper father and mother would have thought it most odd. The only way I could be sure of seeing Barbara Allen was to go to every church service possible.

That week Joan, Michael and I explored the countryside with Bingo at our heels. The best walk, we were told, was a lane on the other side of the village which led alongside a stream then up to the woods. On either side of this lane were masses of brambles and bushes over which climbed convolvulus with white, bell-like flowers and wild roses, which mother called musk roses because they filled the hot lane with their scent. Beyond was a field with bracken and more brambles, the home of hundreds of rabbits, their white tails bobbing up whichever way you looked. Beyond this again were the pine woods and if we followed the path we eventually came to the clearing at the summit of the hill, from where we could look down over the tops of the trees towards the Exe estuary and see the city and its cathedral in the far distance. Here we would rest, because it was a long climb, while Bingo rashly sniffed at the massive anthills of tiny twigs which abounded. The wood ants were large and vicious and his black nose seemed to bring out the worst in them, but he never learnt his lesson and I remember him frantically wiping them off his muzzle with his two front paws, then coming to sit down by us dejectedly.

Once, during that first week, we saw a herd of deer running through the trees, skipping this way and that, and on another occasion a fox ran across the path almost flattened to the ground. Its scent put Bingo into a paroxysm of excitement. Sitting at the top of the hill we decided we were going to like Devon. Below us to the left was the village and we could see clearly the vicarage and the church surrounded by elm and walnut trees. I wondered where Barbara Allen lived, and as I thought of her everything was pervaded with her smile. We sat in silence amongst the bracken. Michael and Joan had their own thoughts and Bingo was probably pondering on the subject of ants. My thoughts were secret. I could not share them because I might be laughed at or the image of Barbara Allen might in some way become tarnished.

I have often wondered since then whether most people falling in love for the first time find their lives suddenly changed, for that was how it was with me. Miss Brownlees I had worshipped and Heather I had liked but the nearest experience to love had been romantic feelings for girls I had known slightly or seen casually in shops, streets and so on. I also developed a habit of falling in love with people in books, which was convenient because they were easily accessible and my shyness was no disadvantage. Princess Flavia in *The Prisoner of Zenda* was one and another very odd choice was Margaret, the youngest of the three Dashwood sisters in Jane Austen's *Sense and Sensibility*. It was a remarkable choice because this Margaret is a very minor character, not mentioned more than a dozen times in the whole book and omitted altogether in radio and television scripts; but as mother read her way through the story I listened eagerly, waiting for the sound of the magic name. By an extraordinary coincidence the three Dashwood sisters and their mother had, according to the book, lived in Barton Cottage, 'within four miles northward of Exeter', and later I wondered if the Allen's house was, in fact, *the* Barton Cottage although with its slate roof there was not much of a cottage about it. The two families, fictional and real, became somewhat confused in my mind.

Next Sunday we all went to morning service. By tradition the vicar's family occupied the second pew on the left, the front pew being the privileged position of the squire from the manor house across the road. Captain Quicke was a true squire who owned most of the land round the village and treated everyone with natural courtesy. His family, too, were charming and we got to know them better than any of the hundreds of other families we met briefly on our peregrinations round the south of England.

But on this particular day the feudal system was against me. Being stuck up front I could not see who else was in church. I longed to know if Barbara Allen was there. She was. At the end of the service I caught a glimpse of her ushering some village children from the back of the church through the side door to the churchyard but it was only a glimpse and I had to wait until the following Sunday before I got a better view of her. I managed this by a simple ruse. I came to church without my handkerchief.

Of course I had to go back because the need for always having a clean 'hankie' had been ingrained into us by Eidy. I managed to delay my return until I heard the beginning of the first hymn. The door creaked as I went in and several people looked round but immediately opposite me was Barbara Allen with three or four children and I was able to slip into the pew behind her. Thus, for a whole hour I was almost in touching distance of her and, because I was sitting a little to one side, I could see her face in profile much of the time. Occasionally she would bend down to find a place in the hymn book for one of the children and her movements were gentle but purposeful. As I watched her I loved her more and more.

She had the sweetest face of anyone I had ever known, although over the years the image has become blurred and I don't suppose I would now recognise her even if it were possible for me to see her as she was then. She was dark-haired and had a rather round face with soft, deep red lips. I cannot remember the colour of her eyes. At rest her expression was gentle and it seemed to me she could never be angry with anyone although I am sure I was wrong in this. There was, however, nothing insipid about her and one gained the impression of great strength in a small body for she was small and neat and always well dressed.

I studied her closely throughout the service and did not feel guilty because I felt very much in love. I expect she was unaware of my presence but during the hymn after father's sermon when the offertory bag was passed round, she turned to hand it to me and smiled. It was this smile of hers that made her such a striking person and I used to think of it as 'Barbara Allen's all-embracing smile' because it expressed a kindness which included everyone within sight. Her tenderness was the complete antithesis of 'the cruel Barbara Allen' of the folk song although I could imagine people, especially myself, dying for love of her and this became one of my most satisfying dreams.

Sadly I was never again able to repeat my missing 'hankie' stunt. Mother was surprisingly cross with me after the service. She looked upon Matins as a sort of family church parade and to have one of us missing spoilt the effect. Father, too, was angry.

'It doesn't look very good having one of the vicar's children sitting all by himself at the back of the church. What will people think? We have to set a lead in the village and that sort of thing starts people talking.'

I suppose they were right although by present day attitudes it all seems absurd. It must be remembered that our family, like many others of that time, had strict rules. For example we had to be on time for meals, and if by mishap or forgetfulness we were a few minutes late there was an unpleasant atmosphere and sometimes open anger. The dinner gong ruled our lives.

During what was left of those summer holidays I was never able to get close to Barbara Allen again. Usually she was with her family and I was with mine, which formed an impenetrable barrier. On the few occasions I caught her eye she would smile but mostly I had to content myself with admiring her from afar.

From listening to scraps of conversation at the dinner table I soon found out where she lived and the only way I could show her my love was by going for a bicycle ride every day and passing by the house. It was about a four-mile ride and pleasant in itself as well as having the excitement of a secret mission. I pedalled between the high hedges of the Devon lanes, slowing as I passed the Allens' house, which was close to the road with steps leading up to the front garden. I never saw Barbara Allen although once her sister Violet came down the steps as I passed but she glanced at me without recognition. This bicycle ride was often very inconvenient but I had to do it every day. I was afraid I might meet her but was disappointed when I didn't. I would then pedal as fast as I could over the last part of the journey which ended with a steep descent to Newton St Cyres where the road at that time twisted sharply between the cottages. Twice I fell off as the tyres slithered on the wet surface after a shower of rain. It was worth it for the delicious unfulfilled expectation.

The long summer holidays came to an end and I was back at school, the other half of the strange dual existence we children lived. I might have forgotten Barbara Allen but I didn't. I thought of her more and more and the dreams became more real as time went by. Usually I dreamt of myself and Barbara Allen walking through the woods, or her coming to visit me at school where I showed her off to my admiring friends. This was a far cry from the fantasies of Pamela when I had to fight off the attacks of angry Zulus, supported by the household cavalry and naval gunners. It also protected me from other less pleasant fantasies which troubled some of my school friends.

It was strange that sex, in the present use of the word, entered very little into it. Like all boys of my age I had exotic and erotic dreams and I kept a secret envelope containing pictures of girls cut out of magazines of which the star was Tallulah Bankhead draped negligently across a settee. They were, however, reasonably well clothed because the present day type of 'girlie' magazines were not permitted to be sold openly, at least I never came across any. I was completely unfamiliar with the nude female figure. Barbara Allen was set apart from all this and it is probably a pity that she was.

When the Christmas holidays came round I was impatient to see her again. During the twelve weeks of term I had lived on the memory of her face and, during this time, the brightness had faded. It needed rekindling. I at once started my lonely bicycle ritual, although the weather was vile, but I was again disappointed. Michael and Joan thought I was mad and Eidy insisted on me wrapping myself in so many jerseys that I sweated profusely and was lucky not to catch pneumonia. It was on the following Sunday I saw her again. She smiled at me outside the church and said, 'Back from school?' I did not say anything in reply but I thought to myself, 'At least she's noticed I've been away.' After that I went to every church service possible. I realised by now that Barbara Allen attended different services in a rather unpredictable way and at evensong, which was not a family parade service, I could sit near to her.

Mother and father were impressed by my sudden interest in religion and I once overheard them talking about it. Mother, who had an archaic turn of phrase due to her reading out loud so much to the family, was saying, 'Do you think he's destined for the Church?'

'It may be,' father replied, 'but it's too early to say.'

They never guessed the true reason although in a sense my religion was genuine. Like many young people I confused the Love of religion with love for a particular person. The two often merge into each other and are not, I think, a bad mixture. When a girl goes to church because she finds the curate attractive it does not mean her attendance is a fraud. Many older people require a personal image such as a favourite preacher or a saint, the Virgin Mary in particular, to keep their belief alive. This was a part Barbara Allen unwittingly played for me and at least she saved me from the tedium of compulsory family attendance.

A few days before Christmas there was a carol service. Mother was in bed with flu and the others did not want to come so I went by myself. It was bitterly cold and there were sheets of ice on the path between the vicarage and the green side door that opened in the wall to the churchyard. The stars were tipped with steel that night.

Inside the church it was warm but the lights had been turned low to give advantage to the candles and Christmas tree by the pulpit. I found my way to the nearest pew where a woman moved up to make room for me. It was Barbara Allen.

One of my dreams had become real. I would never have dared to sit next to her on my own initiative but now we were close together and because there were not enough hymn books to go round she shared her book with me, holding it low so that I could read it easily. She sang as I knew she would, quietly but in a sweet and accurate voice. Her breath played almost imperceptibly against my cheek and its perfume was like the wild roses in the lane. Because the pew was crowded our arms touched. She did not draw away as most people would with a stranger but seemed not to notice it or to accept it as natural. I became submerged in her tenderness.

Particular incidents in my life are often associated with pieces of music and it was that evening that I heard, I think for the first time, the Christmas hymn, 'It came upon a midnight clear'. Most hymns I find drab and uninspiring but because of the time and place and, because Barbara Allen sang so sweetly, the words and tune burnt into my mind.

> Oh cease your strife ye men of wrath
> And hear the angels sing.

The angels were certainly singing for me that night and they have sung for me, one way or another, ever since.

At the end of the service the lights were turned on full. I knew I had to say something but the best I could manage was, 'Thank you for letting me share your hymn book.'

'I didn't hear you singing much.'

'I don't sing. I haven't got a good voice. I think you've got a beautiful voice.' She smiled and handed me the hymn book. 'As I fetched it it's only fair you take it back,' she said. I desperately wanted to say more but instead walked quickly away from her.

That was the longest conversation I ever had with Barbara Allen and the highlight of my love affair with her. Sadly, it was pure love, which cannot survive human contact and, as I came to realise later, is a phantasma, but something everyone should experience at least once in their lives.

During the remainder of the Christmas holiday I saw little of Barbara Allen. Always she seemed to be with her mother and sisters and I had not the courage to go and speak to them. When she caught my eye she smiled but only for a moment and would then turn away and carry on her conversation with someone else. Did she know how I felt? If she did I expect she was amused in a kindly way.

Once more I returned to school but I thought of her every night before going to sleep and at odd times, in the classroom or on the football field. In February I summoned up the courage to send her a Valentine card which I chose with great care – a picture of a girl walking through a wood, half hidden in the mist, and overleaf the familiar quotation,

> I did but see her passing by
> And yet I love her till I die.

As proof of my affection I put two penny-halfpenny stamps on the envelope, which was twice the usual rate. I cannot imagine what she made of the unfamiliar postmark, and I waited part in fear, part in expectation, for something to happen. I even imagined her father having sharp words with my father, which was a rather old-fashioned idea even for those days. Every girl likes to be flattered and I hope this mysterious Valentine gave her a little pleasure.

That was a strange year for me. Barbara Allen's image haunted me and, at the same time, the outside world was becoming topsy-turvy. The Munich crisis came and went and there was a feeling of expectation and doom which penetrated even my secluded life at home and at school. When we listened to the news on the wireless we would hear the strident voices of Hitler and Mussolini. The men of wrath were on the move.

My escape was the passion I had for natural history and I was happy in the woods with Bingo as my companion. I watched the squirrels running up the trees and peering at me between the leaves. These were the true Beatrix Potter squirrels with red bushy tails. Overhead there were usually at least two buzzards wheeling, sometimes so high that they were black specks, each the size of a fullstop. There were woodpeckers by day and owls calling at night and at dusk I sometimes saw a nightjar passing like a shadow or heard its churring from the edge of the woods. Where are the nightjars today? Like glow-worms they are little more than a memory.

Father and mother had given me a fishing rod for Christmas which I still have. There was a trout stream running through the fields of the manor house and Captain Quicke gave me permission to fish whenever I wanted. I never caught a trout but the roach and perch were less put off by the loud splash of my bait hitting the water and I caught quite a few of these. The stream was tiny but there were kingfishers to be seen and once I saw an otter. At first I thought it was a giant fish until it rolled over and rested for a moment with its head above water watching me. Then it was gone and I did not see it again.

My greatest interest was butterflies and moths. Painted Ladies, Red Admirals and Comma butterflies sunned themselves on the high wall of our garden amongst the peaches, and there were clouds of blue butterflies in the lanes and fields. In the oak woods were Purple Emperors but these flew high and I never caught one. However, I did form a good collection which I still have and the colours have scarcely faded. On looking back I do not know how I brought myself to kill these lovely creatures. I would juggle them from the net into a cyanide bottle, then watch the fluttering of their wings which became a trembling and, at last, stillness. I could not do that today.

I was busy and happy that last summer of peace but I did not forget Barbara Allen. My bicycle rides past her house became less regular but when I went into Exeter by bus I was careful to sit on the side facing the hamlet where she lived and I looked out with longing across the river which ran alongside the road. But I never saw her except at church where she was unapproachable and unattainable although she always smiled if she saw me looking at her. I accepted this was how it would be but I felt her presence as I walked through the woods with Bingo and dreamed of her at night or when I lay in the grass looking up at the sky where the buzzards circled.

War crept up on us. Then one Sunday it was there. Mother loyally went to church but we stayed behind in the vicarage to listen to Neville Chamberlain's broadcast. 'I have to tell you no such assurance has been received.' We were at war.

I can remember standing by the green gate in the churchyard wall waiting for mother to come back from the church. She came hurriedly but with hope in her eyes. When I shook my head silently I saw in her face that same look of despair I had seen years before at Victoria station. She had been through it before. Her favourite brother had died on the beaches of Gallipoli. This had been a special moment for her, perhaps the turning point of her life because, as she once told me – and I believe it to be true – she saw him standing in the room by her at the moment of his death.

For mother the word 'war' was a reality and tinged with memories but for me it was unreal. I had to pinch myself and say, 'We are at war.' What did it mean? That afternoon I went to the woods with Bingo and tried, once again, to catch a Purple Emperor. Things were not really any different and I felt a little guilty.

We had our gas masks of course, in square cardboard boxes. Mother made us canvas cases for these and we were meant to have them strung over our shoulders whenever we left the village, but after the first few days we didn't bother. The blackout took some getting used to but one soon learnt to walk straight across a darkened room to the window to pull the curtains across, then go back and switch on the light. But in the main, for those first few days and, indeed, few months, the war was something one listened to on the wireless. Except for the evacuees that was. I forget exactly when they came. It was soon after war was declared or may have been a day or two before.

That day our whole family spent the afternoon in the church hall filling large brown paper bags with food and necessities for them – an apple, an orange, a small pork pie, soap and other things which I forget. My chief concern was whether Barbara Allen would be there. I kept looking at the door but she didn't come. Her job was to go round the houses making final arrangements for the reception of the children. Her mother was there and I stood next to her for a time. As we filled the bags she seemed to make a point of talking to me and I wondered if she knew about the Valentine card and sympathised with my secret love. I asked her what she thought about the war and she replied, 'Last time I was your age and they said it would be over by Christmas.'

'And this war?'

'I don't know. I've got three daughters and your mother has four children.' I did not quite understand what she meant by this and I was surprised she was so solemn when everyone else seemed excited. I realised later it was only a forced cheerfulness the older ones put on, and it was Mrs Allen who was being honest.

The evacuees arrived long after dark, exhausted and frightened. I was by then in bed and asleep. The villagers were sorry for these children and, for the most part, took them to their hearts. Their ways seemed strange to us and, as father put it, 'All they are interested in is whether there's a fish and chip shop handy.' Even then I recognised this as an unfair judgment. The children were frightened at the sheer size of the country and, like cats in a new home, explored farther and farther afield by degrees. Within a few weeks most of them seemed happy although I expect many tears were shed in the upstairs bedrooms of the cottages at night and many children hid under the bedclothes when the unfamiliar owls called from the elm trees.

We were allotted a mother with a young baby. I forget her name. She had lank hair which hung straight down and a dark complexion which I did not recognise at the time as dirt. The baby cried a lot and its nose was always runny. They occupied half of the nursery suite and even I was horrified when I saw the mother chewing food in her mouth, spitting it out on a plate then feeding it to the baby. It was her way of doing things and I suppose her own mother had fed her in the same way.

Eidy became 'tucked up' about it and no one had the charity to understand the poor woman. I heard the maids talking in horrified whispers and even mother told us to keep away from her because she was 'different'. She did not stay long because she decided to go back to London which was her home and where other babies were fed with chewed-up food. I don't blame her.

In her place came two women who shared our spare room, one middle-aged and one young and rather attractive although her face rarely showed much expression. I found them a little strange when they were in the family circle but friendly enough if I happened to meet them alone when they were out for a walk. Neither mother nor father liked them much and many years later Edward told me they were lesbians. Fancy having lesbians in our Devon vicarage! I can't help smiling when I think about it. In those days it was, of course, a crime which was not mentioned in the Ten Commandments only because it was too dreadful to contemplate. Now I would wish them good luck. I wonder if mother and father knew.

They did not stay long and our next evacuees were an elderly couple called Brown. I liked them, too, and used to play cribbage with the old man in his room in the evenings. But once more a sense of strain appeared and, looking back, I think our family was too self-contained and father too fixed in his ways to tolerate guests for any length of time. I can remember once they were sitting in the drawing room with us and Mr Brown started talking during the news on the wireless. Father purposely turned the knob so that it was very loud and Mrs Brown, white with rage, led her husband from the room. Mother was angry but did not say anything in front of us children. I hated scenes like this and still do. The Browns did not stay with us long either.

It was time to go back to school again and near the end of term mother wrote in her weekly letter, 'A lot of the men round here seem to be leaving for the army. Do you remember Barbara Allen? She's in the Wrens now, training to be an officer.'

At first I could not believe that Barbara Allen had left the village, but I got used to the idea and learnt to picture her in naval uniform, her figure even smarter and her smile even sweeter than before. I hoped that when I came back for the Christmas holidays she would be on leave.

She did not come but she sent a Christmas card to mother. It may seem strange when I say I fell in love with her handwriting but it was true. She, of course, signed the card with a fountain pen using blue ink almost as dark as the blue dresses she was so fond of wearing. Fountain pens, unlike the modern ballpoint pens, could express personality because of the variety in depth of colour and width of stroke. Barbara Allen's writing was the most beautiful I have ever seen. It was not painstaking copy-book writing but had in it the curves and rhythm of the waves of the sea or, one might say, of a woman's body. I read an article the other day about fountain pen writing being seductive and this is exactly what hers was.

I took the card from the collection on the mantelpiece and for years kept it with my other treasures in my tin cash box. This could be locked but, since Michael and Joan had identical cash boxes with identical keys, security was not very good. Every evening I opened the box and looked at the writing,

> With love,
> Barbara Allen.

I never saw her again. But during those war years and right up to the time I met Alice she was my first love, 'Barbara of the all-embracing smile'. It is sad that I never really knew her.

VI

Miss Wilmott and Daphnia
1940–2

I was of an age when the war affected me only indirectly. I was too young to go into the services or, to be more accurate, I would have caught the tail end of the fighting had I not been deferred as a medical student. Edward was called up into the army and later worked in Intelligence. Michael, in due course, served in the artillery and was involved in the campaign in Italy. Joan spent most of the time away from home doing various jobs, finally settling down to be a children's nurse. And I . . . well, I made virtually no practical contribution and became very conscious of this later in the war and felt guilty about it. It was as if the finger of Lord Kitchener from the earlier war was pointing at me. 'Your country needs you,' and I was doing precious little for my country.

But this was all in the future. For the present our family had not split up, as all families must, and we continued our moderately idyllic life in the Devonshire countryside. Joan became a land-girl and worked as a dairymaid on the squire's farm which meant she could live at home but had to get up early to milk the cows. Much of the time she spent mucking out the cowsheds and I can picture her cheerfully pushing wheelbarrow loads of straw and dung across the yard. Sometimes I would call in to see her when I took Bingo for his daily walk but he still retained his ancient loathing for wheelbarrows and I had to hold him on a tight lead.

Michael and I also did farm work for Captain Quicke during the holidays. At first we were set to weed thistles in a potato field but, because the field was large and the thistles profuse, it was a hopeless task and became boring as the days went by. We used to quarrel quite a lot and took pleasure in pointing out each others' mistakes.

'How on earth could you miss that thistle? It's enormous. You must be blind,' was the sort of remark we would make.

Sometimes we were helped by one of the village girls, a stolid lass with a pleasant face. I soon realised that Michael 'had a thing about her' as the saying goes. I was an intruder and used either to pick the thistles very fast or very slow so as to leave them together as much as possible. I was quite pleased when we were moved to another job to work with the men.

I think the farm workers were suspicious of us at first and I noticed them having muttered conversations amongst themselves. I suppose they looked upon us as spies because we had direct access to the squire and could tell him if they were not doing their work properly. They finally came to tolerate us in their leisurely Devon way although we must have been far more trouble than we were worth. The only time I can remember them being positively angry was one day when we were carting hay. A dark brown shire horse pulled the wagon and I thought it would be useful if I led him forward when we had cleared a particular patch of the field. This I did, suddenly and enthusiastically, and the man on the pile of hay on the cart nearly fell off. It was then that I learnt that Devon people were not, in fact, always leisurely and had considerable mastery of the English language.

Michael got on better with the men than I did and I suspect he developed a deep love of country life, rather after the style of Thomas Hardy's books which he admired and I came to love later. For him, too, there was a feeling of the last of the summer because the prospect of going into the army was not far off while I could afford to be a child a little longer.

Those country days had a magical quality and it was the horses as much as anything which made this so. They were strong and patient and looked at us with intelligent, trusting eyes although they could have kicked us over the hedge with their great hooves. When the flies annoyed them they shook their heads and swished their tails so that their harness jangled. They knew just what was expected of them and the men rarely had to tell them what to do. In the evenings, when the day's work was done, they would stand under the chestnut trees, in groups of two or three, facing towards each other as if in conversation enjoying the cool of the evening. Once when I was very lonely and unhappy I went and stood with them and drew enormous comfort from their placid tolerance. We just stood there under the trees while the light faded and when I went back to the house the shadow of that particular trouble was but a small and passing thing.

Sometimes we would go up into the woods to help cut pit-props for the mines. We were not allowed to do the actual sawing but with bill hooks cleared the main stems of side branches and helped stack the pit-props in piles. The smell of freshly cut pinewood got into my nostrils and the coolness of the trees in midsummer delighted me. I came to love trees and still do – not only the beauty of their shape but the feel of their bark and the rustling and whispering of the leaves which is a language of its own. Trees have their moods like the sea. 'Dark behind it rose the forest, rose the black and gloomy pine trees', Miss Brownlees had read to me years before, and this is one of the moods. Another is of sunlight filtering through beech leaves and forming a moving pattern of light on the ground. Autumn is famous for its changing beauty and I love the winter trees too, 'bare ruin'd choirs where late the sweet birds sang.' Best of all I like trees half seen through mist.

When I was not working in the woods I often used to take Bingo for long rambling walks over the hills and it was during one of these walks that I decided to take up forestry as a career. This, by a weird chain of circumstances, led me to read science instead of Greek at school and put me on the path to becoming a medical student.

Perhaps the best time of all was in the cornfields in late summer. Harvesting was still a communal occasion, not just a technological routine with one or two men sitting on a combine harvester. When a particular field was near to being finished many of the villagers, including the evacuees, would turn up for the sport of chasing rabbits. As the square of uncut corn got smaller and smaller the rabbits were herded together and used to dart out and back again. Eventually they would have to make a run for it in ones or twos or sometimes as many as a dozen at a time, and we would pursue them with sticks hoping to knock them over or break their backs. I have a vivid memory of a particular rabbit leaping and swerving over the stubble ahead of me with its white tail bobbing. I finally got in a blow with a walking stick and held up its limp warm body in triumph. Nothing in the world would induce me to do that now.

Sometimes I took Bingo with me but he was hopeless. He was shortsighted and slow on the turn so if the rabbit changed direction sharply, he would carry on and chase nothing half way across the field before realising his mistake. He would then become patently embarrassed and pretend to lose interest unless I made a special fuss of him. Occasionally Captain Quicke came with his shotgun and, by tradition, one side of the field was left to him. Only the evacuees, in their excitement, would chase rabbits across this forbidden area and I am surprised some of them did not get shot by mistake.

Rabbits meant food and food was important. We were very lucky to be living in the country. The small square of butter in its tin and the half jars of sugar and jam, which were our weekly ration, amounted to very little. But we had fresh eggs from the hens in the backyard, masses of fruit and vegetables in the garden and even a small supply of milk from the goats, of which Joan now had two. They were never much good at producing milk and Joan, after working at the dairy, realised how pathetic was their yield. I can remember her once coming into the kitchen in floods of tears. 'Only four ounces today,' she sobbed.

So we got rid of the goats and I started breeding rabbits which was much more successful. One of the outhouses was fixed up with large wire cages and we purchased two does and a delightful buck rabbit called Horace. He was white with a black comma over his left eye and by committing incest, adultery and various other crimes, he kept us provided with young rabbits for two years. In the winter we managed to get a special ration of bran but the rest of the year we fed them with armfuls of dandelions and garden waste. It was all right when I was at home but in term time mother was hard put to keep Horace and his progeny happy. I am amazed that we did not mind eating the flesh of these rabbits which tasted like chicken. When poor Horace died we gave him an honourable burial and, to mother's relief, I lost interest in the project.

I cannot remember ever being really hungry. The spartan training of my preparatory school in Sussex had, perhaps, been a good thing after all but I was a little obsessive about saving food. I used to help mother by cutting hundreds of apple rings which we dried over the Aga cooker on bamboo canes to keep us supplied during the winter and spring. Even today I cannot resist chopping up apples and filling our freezer with them.

Natural food was also important. We used to collect beautifully flavoured mushrooms from the fields near the river and in autumn we had family blackberrying expeditions. These were a little spoilt because Joan, Michael and I had a childish rivalry about who collected most and used to get cross if we thought someone else had pinched a cluster which we had earmarked. We were happier picking from separate bushes. This was a pity because half the fun of blackberrying is doing nothing most of the time apart from looking idly round the countryside. Mother could not understand that there were people in this world who did not enjoy picking blackberries and I can remember her getting cross with Edward once when he came home on leave and showed unwillingness.

71

'I don't want to pick blackberries', he said.
'But we've saved up some special bushes for you.'
'I don't care if you have.'
'Well, I think you are being downright selfish.'

My sympathies were entirely with Edward who was exhausted after some night exercises and wanted either to go to bed or read one of the sophisticated novels he seemed to enjoy.

I am not sure when the bombing came but I think it was in the spring of 1942 when I was home from school after being ill with measles. These were the so-called Baedeker raids when the Germans bombed towns of historic interest but no special importance, or so we were told. Newton St Cyres was several miles from Exeter so we were not in great danger but stray bombs fell in the woods round us and for months I came across unexpected craters amongst the trees.

We huddled in the passage by the kitchen which was the safest place while most of the centre of Exeter was devastated in one terrifying night. Father, who put dignity above safety, stayed upstairs in the bedroom but the rest of us cowered against the stone floor and wall of the passage listening to the distant thud-thud-thud of the bombs and the occasional scream of one that fell near the village.

Eidy was terrified and moaned to herself when the bombs seemed to be coming closer and I nestled up to her hoping to give her strength. It is always a good thing to have someone more frightened than you are on these occasions. Marjorie, the housemaid, who had been her rival and enemy for years, also tried to comfort her and a fondness grew between them which they were at pains not to show once the raids were over. I felt a little superior about the bombing because I had previously been caught in the fringe of the London blitz but feeling superior did not stop me from being terrified. I looked up at the ceiling expecting it to split open and disintegrate. For a week or so after this first raid some of the Exeter people left the city at night. They streamed out in cars, on bicycles or on foot, pushing prams or carts. Some of them came as far as our village. They slept in the church hall and many camped in the open fields, believing that was the safest place of all. They returned to the city in the morning light.

I was forbidden to go near Exeter at this time but I can remember talking to one of the refugees, as we called them. I was taking Bingo for a walk and, at the side of the lane, I saw a woman sitting on the grass nursing a baby. I was usually too shy to talk to strangers but Bingo took an interest in her. She was a young woman and although she was unkempt and weary, having pushed her baby in his pram all the way from Exeter, she had something of the dark Devon beauty about her. This was in the late afternoon and, after exchanging a few words, I sat by the roadside with her. She seemed pleased to have someone to talk to and told me the houses on either side of hers had been destroyed and she was so terrified that instead of seeking refuge in one of the emergency shelters she had put her baby and a supply of milk in the pram and left the city at dawn. She had gone to sleep under some trees until the baby woke her with his crying and then she had carried on walking away from Exeter, but had gone by side roads and was not sure where she was. At that time all signposts had been taken down to hinder the enemy if an invasion took place. She seemed confused and I suppose was, to a small degree, 'shell-shocked'.

I longed to say, 'Come to us. Bring your baby with you and stay in our house as long as you want.' But I could not say this. I was too frightened that I might be doing the wrong thing. Father would be cross and mother would be puzzled. Looking back at the incident I now realise it showed the great failing of my upbringing and education. Compassion was harnessed to propriety and I could not step out of line. What if I had brought this poor woman and her child to the house? I hope she would have been welcomed and taken in but I am afraid she would have been escorted, kindly and firmly, to the village hall which was the 'proper place'.

After we had talked for some time Bingo started getting restless so I gave the poor woman directions to the village hall which was not far away and carried on with my walk. What an opportunity I had missed of following my natural inclination and growing up, but such chances do not come twice. I have told no one to this day about this strange meeting but I heard later that the woman and her baby had been taken to hospital 'for observation', so my dream of doing the right thing might have turned out to be the wrong thing after all.

When I was allowed to go to Exeter some days later I was horrified at what I saw. The cathedral had survived almost unscathed as cathedrals usually do, having been built to last forever, but there was a lot of damage in the precincts and someone told me that one of the houses which had been gutted was a nurses' home and there had been terrible loss of life. Part of the town centre was flat and lifeless, the only thing that moved being two men who idly prodded the rubble with spades. The thing that impressed me most was that our dentist's surgery had disappeared. I had been there a few weeks before to have a tooth stopped and found it impossible to imagine it no longer existing. Mankind is resilient and the centre of Exeter has been rebuilt but bears little resemblance to the city I once knew.

During the early part of the war our life at school was affected as little as our life in Devon except that many of the younger masters left and white-haired relics, with cracked voices, were dug up from somewhere to teach us French and Latin. There was little talk of the war. We were much more interested in the house rugger matches or getting our prep done on time, and my attitude to the fighting was much the same as it had previously been to the cricket season. I would sieze the evening paper to find out how the Finns were getting on against the Russians and was enthusiastic about the navy cruisers' 3–1 victory over the pocket battleship Graf Spee. Of course this came to an end with the fall of France and the Battle of Britain. Then, indeed, we did feel ourselves part of history and this was later enhanced by the annual visits of Winston Churchill. He loved the Harrow songs and came every year to listen to the school singing in the Speech Room. I thus heard the great man 'rumbling away' at first hand and some of these impromptu speeches became famous. 'Do not let us speak of darker days; let us rather speak of sterner days. These are not dark days; these are great days – the greatest days our country has ever lived.' This is how we all felt about the war, at least it was how we felt after hearing Winston Churchill in action.

On the whole I think the best adjective to describe the war at that time was 'grim', and when I went back to school in early October the blitz was at its height.

Although we were on the outskirts of London, and far from the docks, it was a frightening experience. In the evening we would hear the perverted music of aircraft flying overhead and the sound was not drowned by conversation or the radio. We pretended to be knowledgeable and would say, 'That one's a Jerry.' Sometimes we would switch out the lights, pull back the blackout curtains and look at the panorama of London ablaze. Then we would shake our heads and say wisely, 'They are getting it badly tonight', and these were the nights when there was an orange glow in the sky and the flickering lights of bombs and anti-aircraft fire ran along the horizon. The sound was like that of a distant giant striking an anvil with a hammer and, being of classical education, I would shut my eyes and think of Vulcan, the blacksmith of the gods, at work in Hades – which was not all that far from the truth. There was also the noise of anti-aircraft fire much closer and this used to keep me awake at night until I got used to it.

Then the bombing came our way. Some, I expect, were casual bombs but I think the reason was that our extensive playing fields were not far from a well camouflaged RAF airfield and the German planes sometimes attacked us in error but with considerable accuracy because they put strings of bombs across the playing fields without doing significant damage to the school. The town was not so lucky and many houses were obliterated.

On our first 'bad night' I was woken by an explosion some distance away and another one that rocked the house. The alarm bell went and this signified we had to carry our mattresses down to the cellar. A mattress is an almost impossible thing to carry downstairs and in the general confusion one of the younger boys, plus mattress, fell down an entire flight of stairs. Unfortunately he finished under the mattress and injured himself quite badly but this was the only damage done to the house or contents that night and I managed to sleep fitfully with my mattress on a heap of coal.

Outside, I heard later, things were more exciting. Showers of incendiary bombs rained on the school but these were put out quite easily by fire-fighting teams with buckets of sand because the incendiaries, in those days, were not the vicious exploding fire bombs of the later years of the war. All that was left of them in the morning were little piles of ashes and sand. One fell through the roof of the main hall on to the stage and this was the Germans' only great success as far as our school was concerned. The fire brigade, instead of letting it burn itself out harmlessly, sprayed it vigorously with a hose and ruined a very valuable organ.

After that we slept in the basement regularly. By next term the corridor in the depth of the house had been fitted with bunks and steel doors at either end. I learnt to sleep in these rather cramped conditions with eighty other boys in spite of the noises of the night. There were always one or two snorers and I used to be woken by the boy in the bunk above me whom we nicknamed Masturbatus Furiosus because his nocturnal activities rocked all the adjacent bunks. He probably could not help it, poor chap, but there were so many complaints that the authorities finally moved him to a separate room. It was considered a great joke at the time. Thus peace returned to the air raid shelter and the sound of distant bombs did not disturb us half as much as M. Furiosus had done. An interesting side light on life in a shelter!

The enemy persisted in aiming bombs at our playing fields and one landed in the middle of the 1st XV rugger pitch which caused our housemaster to comment, 'The war's beginning to bite.' I could scarcely believe he had made this remark and had to ask two of the other boys if it was true and they both confirmed it.

One evening I had a strange experience. I was sitting in my study doing prep, a piece of Latin translation. I was, in fact, half way down page 12 when yet another string of bombs fell across the playing fields. Four bombs burst at, I suppose, about two-second intervals. Each was closer than the last and when the fourth exploded the house shook and I heard the sound of shattering glass. I had a premonition that the fifth bomb was going to fall on the house and in the last few seconds of my life, as I supposed it to be, I thought of the Latin word 'igitur' which I had just translated and I saw momentarily, but clearly, the smile of Barbara Allen. The fifth bomb never fell.

When I recovered from the shock I became aware of the general hubbub of boys running downstairs to the shelter and I ran after them. Once I was seated on my bunk I began to think about what had happened. Three things seemed clear. First my premonition was not just fear, it was knowledge. If there had been a fifth bomb I was certain my existence would have ended there and then. Second, I had seen Barbara Allen's smile but not her face. This may seem a strange statement but it is true. For a moment the universe had become an all-embracing smile. Third, the Latin word 'igitur' means 'therefore'.

A boy at the age of sixteen, as I was then, can be very sensitive about matters which an older person would write off as coincidence or of no special significance. I could not get out of my mind the word 'igitur' which would have been on my lips at the moment of death and I got into such a tangle about the whole affair that I found courage to go and see the chaplain and give him a guarded version of what had happened. The chaplain advised me to read the Book of Job, which I did. This was a typical clergyman's way of not answering a question and it was only years later that I saw the connection.

It was about this time that I started my drift towards becoming a medical student. I had no special desire to be a doctor because the doctors I had met, like the one who had treated me for scarlet fever at Springwell, appeared to have no interest in children or young people and had this peculiar habit of grunting instead of talking. I thought them an inhuman lot. The school doctor was my enemy because of an unfortunate episode when, as a new boy, I had visited him for a check up.

He had looked at my feet, decided they were flat and told me I must have special exercises in the gym. This rather flustered me so when he handed me a bottle as he went out of the room, saying over his shoulder, 'I want a specimen of water in that', I filled the bottle from the tap. This was pure ignorance on my part.

He came back into the room a few minutes later and held the bottle up to the light, obviously surprised at its transparency. When I told him in all innocence what I had done he called me a bloody fool and said he would report me. Nothing came of it but I thought at the time he lacked both sympathy and a sense of humour.

All the other boys in the science fifth were starting work for their First MB, the initial medical exam, so I tagged along with them although my interest still lay in natural history and agriculture, especially forestry. I liked biology, found chemistry quite interesting and failed to understand physics. The great fascination was finding out how animals and plants worked. I could not have cared less about machines.

So I sat patiently dissecting worms, cockroaches and dogfish until I stank of formalin, and gazed in awe at the highly active world revealed by the microscope. The amoebae and hydra hunting their prey were almost as real to me as a tiger creeping through the jungle. The biology master encouraged me to make a special study and I chose water fleas.

This was not as odd as it sounds because the water flea is a beautiful creature, much maligned by being called a flea. The Latin name, *Daphnia*, is much more appropriate. I used to search for her in the nearby ponds and lakes, both at school and at home, using a special net with mesh funnelling towards a test tube. Then I would transfer my Daphnia to a jam jar and watch her with a magnifying glass or, in a drop of water, under the microscope. Daphnia is a tiny, shimmering transparent creature touched with the colours of the rainbow. Her speciality is to make sudden darting movements then hover with vibrating antennae, just as a humming-bird hovers in front of a flower. Daphnia was one of my loves.

I hunted her for her beauty rather than a desire to classify her, although this was interesting too, but I soon found I did not have the inclination for serious scientific study. I could not separate the beauty of living creatures from their mechanics and this made me an awkward pupil to the rather narrow-minded science teachers of those days.

I discovered, for example, that Daphnia appeared in many different colours. In one particular pond, its surface covered in green slime, she herself was bright green. In a disused iron tank where the water had a reddish tinge she was rust coloured. I thought of trying to change her colour by transferring her from one type of water to another but I was too lazy.

Daphnia symbolised for me the junction between science and art. The two, it seemed, were in conflict and this matter came to a head with the affair of the Shakespeare prize.

I had adored Shakespeare from quite an early age and was once, to my shame, caught crying over *Antony and Cleopatra* by two other boys and was teased mercilessly about this. The story of the play was so sad, I thought, that it was worth buckets of tears but that was not the way to earn respect in a public school. I decided to go in for the prize although I was a scientist and to everyone's surprise won the gold medal. It was about the greatest achievement of my life but my teachers did not think so. I was summoned before the chemistry master and told such things distracted me from serious work. This so upset me that I decided to give up science but fortunately father persuaded me to carry on and it did not take long to find that the conflict between science and the arts was only in the minds of puny people. In all fairness it must be said that many classics scholars of those days wrote off science as 'learning more and more about less and less'. Ironically I never received the gold medal because they were not made in wartime.

Thus it was that I found I had become a medical student almost by mistake but the more I thought of it the more I liked the idea. I invested in a copy of *Gray's Anatomy*, an enormous blue volume, which I carted round with me. It was far too complicated for me to understand but was in great demand amongst my friends because of the sexy bits.

The model public schoolboy was meant to ignore sex, which was an impossibility, as M. Furiosus found out. Most of us survived on fantasies and it was lucky for me that I had a strong romantic streak and a delightful dream figure in Barbara Allen who remained un-tarnished and was what mother would have called 'a good influence'. Soon, however, a rival appeared on the scene.

It was when I was in the sixth form and a senior boy in the house that I fell in love with Miss Wilmott. She was the new house matron, not particularly good-looking but very alluring. I was not the only one to fall in love with her but was way back in a queue of sex-starved youths who doted on her. My feelings for her were something new to me because this was the first time I loved someone without especially liking them. It was unusual for me too, because I thought of her general shape more than her face, which had rather a sulky expression.

I think she was in reality quite a good-natured person and it was perhaps her misfortune that she oozed sex from every pore, without having sufficient back-up in the way of good looks, kindness or attractiveness of personality. She was at that time fated to be desired but not particularly liked. And desire her I certainly did, with a rush of passion which coloured my life but gave me a feeling of uncertainty and, at times, guilt.

The only way I could get close to her was by feigning illness and I did this by producing a rash on the palm of my hand by rubbing it with a pumice stone. I would go to the surgery in the evening where she would hold my hand, look thoughtfully at it and turn it over to examine the back. This sent shivers of rapture down my spine. Various ointments were tried but of course the rash did not get better because I made sure it wouldn't so the hand-holding sessions continued. Finally she either got bored with the whole affair or, to do her justice, at last realised the game I was playing and talked of sending me to the doctor. I immediately allowed the rash to cure itself because I did not want to meet that particular doctor again. I thought he would see through my game and call me something worse than a bloody fool.

Although I no longer had an excuse to visit Miss Wilmott in the surgery I had erotic dreams about her as, I am sure, did many of the other boys. My feelings for her were incomparably different from my feelings for Barbara Allen yet they were both called love. I noticed Barbara Allen's image definitely faded when I thought about Miss Wilmott.

I desired her more and more and a short time later I had the good fortune to injure my back playing rugger. I was considered a fairly important member of the team, so for a whole wonderful week I used to go to the surgery each evening where I lay on a couch while Miss Wilmott massaged the tender muscles. It was my first experience of eroticism and Miss Wilmott knew what she was doing and it amused her.

She left soon after that and I expect she was later happily married, had lots of children and became a model mother. At school she had the ill luck to be a sex goddess and was probably glad to escape. Looking back at this incident makes me realise how very immature I was at the time. It was my first experience, long overdue, of the battle between love and passion which few people learn to resolve and thank heavens they do not. Where would great art be, and great literature and music, without the tyranny of unresolved conflict between the sacred and profane? This was a subject I did not discuss with the chaplain nor with my housemaster when at about this time he came to my study to give me a sex talk, which was presumably his statutory duty. He seemed rather ill at ease but came straight to the point.

'Do you know about sex, Binns?' he said.

'Yes, sir.'

'Good.'

That was the long and short of my second sex talk — with no mention of tulips or hockey, or of love for that matter.

It was about a year later that I left Harrow and surprised even myself with the intensity of 'the wild regret of the last goodbye'. I had been happy there and my chief sadness was that I had missed so much through my shyness and inconsequence and the growing-up pains which led to so many conflicts in my mind.

Was it worth it — this strange system of learning to grow up to which fate had committed me? I think it was. One lesson I learnt was not to give up too easily and another the habit of loyalty, a valuable possession so long as one is loyal to the right sort of ideas. I certainly did not become a snob but developed an intense dislike of snobbery in all shapes and sizes. The big disadvantage was that, being more or less segregated from women, I formed imaginative but unrealistic notions about them which coloured events of my later life.

PART II

VII

Craven A
1942–4

I went up to Cambridge at a time when the war seemed a never-ending struggle. The university was geared to wartime conditions with a limited number of undergraduates, many like myself medical students, and parts of the colleges taken over by various ministries and strange secret organisations. A sentry was posted on the Bridge of Sighs which separated one half of my college, St John's, from the other and we were required to show a pass when we crossed over. There was obviously a secret worth keeping in the college building on the far side of the river but what it was I never did find out. One of my friends tried to brush past the sentry and, according to him, nearly got bayonetted for his pains, which would have been a fitting end because the original Bridge of Sighs in Venice was a place where criminals met their doom. On the whole the university was curiously isolated from outside events and retained its charm which was something of a luxury in wartime. We had to wear gowns in spite of the clothes rationing and it was compulsory to dine in Hall with all the paraphernalia, including a long Latin grace, although the meagre helpings of food on our plates would not have been acceptable in a cheap café by present day standards. Other meals I ate in my rooms, the stand-by being peanut butter and dried egg, which could be scrambled or made into a reasonable omelette. Later a British restaurant was opened and I sometimes went to this because the food was cheap.

Cambridge, in those days, was even more a town of bicycles than it is today. Shortly before nine o'clock each morning they would emerge like shoals of fish from the colleges and flow down King's Parade and the side streets. I had an ancient, upright machine which had been handed down to me through Edward and Michael. It was so strongly built that it always came off best in the occasional collisions I had and so ugly that no one ever tried to steal it. Bicycle stealing was a serious problem and although it was customary to chain one's cycle to the railings many of my friends, who owned more graceful machines, found only the front wheel remaining when they came out of lectures, the remainder having been detached and spirited away.

We worked very hard. On the assumption that the war would go on forever and doctors, like tanks, should be turned out as quickly as possible the three-year course was compressed into two. So from nine to five our days were spent attending lectures or working in the laboratories or the dissecting room, while most evenings I was closeted in my own room with books scattered over the desk and floor, learning, learning, learning. There was a system then – and still is – whereby if you wanted to be left alone you closed your outside door or 'sported the oak' as the expression was. This ensured solitude and was nearly always respected. On the rare occasions when a party of drunken friends wanted you to join them the oak door was strong enough to resist their hammering.

Being imaginative rather than a true scientist I found the work difficult, anatomy especially. It is hard enough for medical students today, but in those days we had to master an enormous amount of detailed and largely irrelevant facts. We had a fierce anatomy tutor called Dr Davis, pronounced Davis-s-s, a small Welshman whose rooms were on the far side of the college. He was so fierce that we wondered if it was he who was the hidden menace on the other side of the river.

I used to dread Thursday evenings. Half a dozen of us would attend these tutorials and we sat round a large polished table while Dr Davis looked at us speculatively, trying to decide which of us was least likely to be able to answer his questions. It was a game of bluff. Those of us who had done some work, and felt reasonably confident, would sit with eyes averted, while those who had not the slightest idea of the subject we were going to discuss would look at him with a steady untroubled gaze. Dr Davis had an uncanny gift of reading our minds and if we played a game of double bluff and looked worried when we had every reason to be so he was not deceived.

He was not a sadist, and when I met him years later on a social occasion he turned out to be a rather shy man, devoted to his wife and children. I think he felt the only way to teach us anatomy was through fear and in this he was probably right.

After studying us closely he would start by asking someone a deceptively easy question and smile appreciatively when the correct answer came back promptly.

'Well, we are in good form tonight,' he would say, lighting a cigarette, and then ask a few probing questions until he had decided who the first victim was going to be. Then, like a hawk picking out a single bird from a flock of starlings, he launched a ruthless attack, following his prey through every twist and turn. He used to call me Bince and if it was my turn the conversation would go something like this:

'And now Bince, if it's not too much trouble, perhaps you would describe to me the blood supply of the heart.'

That being the one section I had omitted to read, I would look down at the table, hoping to see in its polished surface a diagram of the heart, and finally come out with some inane remark.

'Very interesting, very interesting. I can see Mr Gray will have to rewrite his Textbook of Anatomy. A pity he's dead. Now perhaps somebody would tell our friend Bince the more orthodox view of the matter.'

No one would speak because we had an unwritten law that if we all appeared unintelligent the true idiots would be less noticeable, but Dr Davis was wise to this and extracted the answers from those who knew them. It is, in fact, almost impossible not to give the correct answer if you know it.

'And now Bince, perhaps, in your gifted fashion, you would summarise the conclusions we have so painfully come to,' and as I struggled on he would add, 'Good, good . . . at least you seem to have become aware that the heart is usually situated in the thorax,' and so on. Within ten minutes we knew the circulation of the heart and remembered it and he then selected another victim. 'And now Walker, if you've recovered from your drinking binge last night – and I did manage to get off to sleep eventually – perhaps you would describe the anatomy of the aorta which, to give you a good start, is one of the larger blood vessels in the human body.'

Dr Davis was the best tutor I have ever had. The other tutors were to him as water to bitter wine and we sometimes treated them just as badly as Dr Davis treated us. Our pathology tutor took great trouble adjusting the slides under the microscope to illustrate different cells of the human body and we used to nudge them ever so slightly and say, 'But sir, I really can't see it.' He became quite upset and years later when I met him he told me he used to work all hours in the hospital before coming to give us tutorials and I felt ashamed at our behaviour.

I was not, on the whole, greatly impressed by the standard of lecturing and formed a general theory that the more brilliant and famous a scientist is the less able is he to pass on his knowledge to those who are ignorant of the subject. One delightful old professor used to wander haphazardly round the lecture theatre as he talked to us and on one occasion disappeared through one door and reappeared through another a few minutes later still talking.

The centre of our existence in those days was the dissecting room where we spent many hours exploring the human body. We were told to treat the cadavers, as they were called, with respect and we used to form a strange attachment to them, once we had got over the initial distaste. My first cadaver was a shrivelled up old man who looked rather like the mummy of Rameses III but he had a humorous face and I wondered, as I dissected the nerves and blood vessels of his right arm which was my allotted portion, what sort of person he had been. We worked in pairs and there were several pairs to each body so it became something of a social event, rather like a ladies' sewing circle, when we exchanged gossip. Medical students usually have a fund of funny stories and the wit thrown backwards and forwards across that old man's body must have made him laugh in his grave, as it were. I think ending one's days in the cheerful company of the dissecting room is much better than lying in a cold churchyard or becoming a casket full of useless ashes.

We had little time for outside activities but I was fortunate in being keen on games and played rugger on Saturday afternoons and squash in the evenings, sometimes at midnight or later. This was a good way of clearing the cobwebs of anatomy and kept me fit.

As a contribution to the war effort we were compelled to join the Home Guard which we took as something of a joke because the danger of invasion was, by now, non-existent. On Sunday mornings we drilled on Midsummer Common and in the evenings had instructions from elderly sergeants. We behaved rather badly towards them and used to play dumb. I remember it took us six weeks to learn how to dismantle a bren gun and put it together again and our sergeant remarked that we were 'the stupidest platoon he had ever had, begging your pardon, sirs', and went on to describe what would have been the fate of the British Army at Ypres if we had been about at that time.

We had various field exercises and camps but I never got beyond being No. 2 on the bren gun. My job was to wave a rattle in short bursts while the No. 1 pointed a wooden gun at the enemy. It was like the nursery in Springwell and I did not feel I had made a significant contribution to the war effort although I suppose my rattle might have frightened a parachutist into submission. I led a double life in the

Home Guard. The name Elliott-Binns was too complicated for the authorities to deal with so I was listed as Elliott in A Company and Binns in D Company. This led to impossible confusion which I turned to my advantage. Eventually the two characters were merged and I officially joined D Company as 'Elliott-bloody-Binns and why your father gave you a name like that God alone knows'.

During this time I had very little to do with girls. There were a few female medical students but I avoided them because, if they were pretty they were besieged by their male colleagues, and if they were not pretty I had no special interest in them, preferring the company of my college friends. I was fascinated by one girl whom we called the Duchess. She was a lot older than the rest of us and had a sort of ravaged beauty. I longed to ask her why she had become a medical student feeling sure she had suffered some terrible tragedy but I was far too shy to speak to her and felt ill at ease if I happened to sit next to her at a lecture. She used a bewitching scent, faintly herb-like, which made her seem to belong to the eighteenth century.

Because I was so bound up in work I had less and less contact with people outside my small circle of friends, or it may have been the other way round and I was using work as an excuse not to meet people. If I did go to a party I was quite capable of saying absolutely nothing all evening and I could become so tongue-tied that I was not able to bring myself to say goodbye and would slip out of the room unobserved. There were no angels singing for me and even the smile of Barbara Allen became hazy.

We used to go to the cinema fairly often, queueing for half-crown seats, and I had a passion for Ann Sheridan, the 'oomph girl' of that era, but my favourite was the girl with a large hat whose face advertised Craven A cigarettes. She was dark-haired and beautiful and gave the impression of having just come from Ascot but, at the same time, being homely enough to be sitting at ease by the fire in my college rooms. I began to smoke quite heavily to please her. This love of mine epitomised the strange withdrawn life I led but I was not alone in this. Most of my friends were exactly the same. They did not speak to girls and knew little about them and this was accepted as normal. Those who had girlfriends at Girton, Newnham or elsewhere were treated with envious suspicion and we did not approve of one young man who used to secrete shop-girls into his room. For all that we were not prigs. We were merely following the custom of those not so distant days.

In spite of this, life at Cambridge was far from arid. When we took time off work we used to enjoy ourselves canoeing up the river to Granchester and Byron's pool beyond, bicycling far into the country-side or sitting talking and drinking coffee until late into the night. The presence of a stranger, however, would make me unwilling to speak and if there was a girl in the room I would usually stay silent. If she was pretty I would pass the time weaving attractive little stories round her.

One of my joys was a green, portable gramophone which, like the bicycle, was handed down to me via Edward and Michael. I had a limited supply of records which I played over and over again. Metal needles were now out of date and we used wooden ones which had to be sharpened between each record. This made a horrid grating noise and rather spoilt the continuity of a long symphony. The reproduction was poor anyway but we did not mind because we were not used to anything better.

I developed a love for classical music and went to concerts fairly frequently. I can remember Myra Hess coming to the college to give a recital to our musical society. She made a mistake in the sonata she was playing, came to a halt and said 'Damn' then continued as if nothing had happened. I could not believe my ears but other people agreed it had taken place. I admired her already but she went up even further in my estimation.

A similar thing happened when I went to the Sadler's Wells Ballet touring company. The prima ballerina leapt through the air while her partner happened to be at the other side of the stage although he was obviously meant to be in position to catch her. She landed on the floorboards and *bounced* and I've seldom seen anyone look so angry. Again I had to confirm with someone else in the audience that it had actually happened.

Sometimes we got drunk. We found the cheapest way was to buy beer and lace it with 'absolute alcohol' from the labs. This made an effective combination but we were wise enough not to use it very often. Once I became completely comatose and woke up in the morning lying across two chairs. This strained my back quite badly and there was no Miss Wilmott to massage it for me.

But mostly it was work and I gradually mastered the workings of the human body even if I understood little of the workings of the human mind and I was fairly satisfied with my love affair with the Craven A girl.

I was not so satisfied with life at home. At about the time I went up to Cambridge, father became vicar of the parish of Newlyn East with Mitchell in Cornwall. This was a few miles inland from Newquay and I found the countryside rather desolate. Mitchell had two distinctions – it had at one time been a rotten borough, that is to say a parliamentary seat with a handful of voters, and it had the smallest railway station I have ever seen. I was not happy there. I missed the memories of Devon and the possibility of seeing Barbara Allen but most of all I missed our bull-terrier Bingo who had sadly been put down. This had happened while we were still at Newton St Cyres. I was taking him for a walk in the woods when quite suddenly he started howling in a mournful way. I thought he had been stung by a hornet and went to pat him but he turned and made as if to bite me then set off down the path at full speed. I ran after him all the way home and he did not stop until he was curled up in his favourite chair in the drawing room. I made a great fuss of him and when mother and father came back from a trip to Exeter I don't think they believed the story I told them because by now Bingo was his normal self. However, later that evening he had a fit and when the vet came next day he said Bingo was suffering from 'canine hysteria' which could not be cured and was a danger to humans because he might attack them. Father and the vet took him to the garage. I did not have a chance to say goodbye to him but he went jauntily thinking it was some sort of game. It is the only time I saw my father cry and as soon as I could I crept off to the garage where I hugged Bingo who was lying there apparently asleep. Then I went into the woods and sat on a tree stump where I wept and wept.

With Bingo walks had never been lonely but in Cornwall I wandered through the fields by myself. For a long time I used to forget he was now dead and would turn to say, 'Come along you silly old dog.' He was not there of course and I felt more lonely than ever. In particular I haunted a stretch of waste ground between the two villages. This was rather a dangerous place because it was full of unprotected mineshafts, long in disuse. In the middle was a broken-down tower where a pair of buzzards nested. Their wild angry cries suited my mood.

Joan was away most of the time, Michael was overseas and we rarely saw Edward who was by now married. His wife, Kay, came to stay with us, so for a time I had someone nearer my age to talk to. She brought with her their year-old-baby, Margaret, whom we used to take for long walks, sticking to the roads because of the pram. It was here that a strange phenomenon took place. I used to like positioning myself beside the front of the pram while Kay felt it more natural for us to walk side by side. As a result she was always trying to catch me up while I was trying to keep ahead so we went faster and faster until it became rather like the last scene of a Disney cartoon as we tore up and down hills arriving home worn out. I must admit I thought Kay's walking habits rather odd until one day we were both so exhausted that we had to stop and then the truth came out and we had a good laugh about it. But most of the time I was bored and lonely and because I was going through a natural anti-parent phase I would sulk fo days on end. I must have caused them both much unhappiness and, looking back, I feel ashamed. I could not decide if I was more irritated by father's apparent lack of interest or mother's obvious desire to help. The trouble was she was the sort of person who would say, 'I understand perfectly', before you had time to tell her what the trouble was, so I lost the ability to talk with her.

Eidy still lived with us in the nursery but it was for me a haunted place except during the time when Kay and Margaret were staying with us when it came to life again. I loved Eidy dearly but when I sat and talked with her it was out of kindness. The nursery was no longer a refuge and the skimpy nursery tea was a travesty with Eidy fussing about with the kettle, while I scraped the jelly mixture, which we used as a substitute for jam, on a single slice of bread.

My true refuge was my bedroom. For sentimental reasons mother kept Joan's room and Michael's room ready for their return and I slept in a converted loft above the garage which suited me well because I wanted to be independent and unsociable. Here I played my records, mused, read books and composed reams of sublimation poetry about waves beating endlessly on the rocks or sad figures wandering in eternal mists. It was mostly rubbish but when, the other day, out of interest I fetched the collection, still in the original ring folder, from the attic I found one poem which expressed my feelings at that period of my life. It started

> The moon is dead, I saw her ghost
> Last night up in the sky

and finished

> As pale as glass, as sick as death
> Far happier than me.

I think I really was unhappy, mainly through boredom and frustration, and I even used to dice with death. I climbed dangerous cliffs on the coast round Newquay and once swam out to some islands knowing it was an unwise thing to do. They did not look very far away but when I reached them they were so surrounded with seaweed that I could not climb on to the rocks. On the way back I was caught in a current and was lucky not to be drowned, reaching safety farther down the coast after a two-hour struggle. It was the second time I had faced the prospect of death and this time there was no smiling image of Barbara Allen or metaphysical speculation, only the consciousness of the dark sea and the depth of water beneath me, and the numbing chill which crept through my body. I was desperately afraid.

I think it was before this that I risked death in a different way. Newlyn East was a small village and, having once been a mining village, was not all that attractive. The church, too, was not especially beautiful but it had a 'feature', a large fig-tree growing out of the wall high up near the porch. It looked miraculous although obviously the stem penetrated many feet through the stonework to the roots in the soil beneath the church. Being in Cornwall there was a legend about it and I cannot remember exactly what it was but it was well known that anyone who cut off a branch would die suddenly. A previous vicar had collapsed soon after rashly pruning it because he thought it made the church look untidy and there were dark tales of similar incidents. So, like Hamlet, 'I defied augury' and cut off a branch with a penknife. I did not die suddenly but I developed a bad cold two days later so maybe the fates were making allowances for my adolescent humours and giving me a gentle reprimand.

I felt there was something sinister about that church and vicarage. It is the only house that I have lived in where I felt uncomfortable but this may have been due to my prevailing mood rather than anything inherent in the building. Certainly the house 'talked' at night and in my room above the garage I was often woken by creaks and groans.

One autumn night I had the most frightening experience of my life. I woke in the early hours of the morning with the wind blowing against the window, disturbing the curtains so that shafts of moonlight flickered through, making patterns on the floor. There was a feeling in the room of something wrong, rather as if the witch of my childhood had escaped from her place on the wall and was at large. My right hand was resting on the pillow and, as I turned over to look at the window, it came in contact with something that seemed like cold damp leather. As I felt it, still half in a dream, I realised with an inward scream of horror that it had fingers. The thing that lay on my pillow was a human hand.

To escape from it I leapt out of bed and stumbled across to the light switch. It was then that I noticed that I could not feel my left arm. My pyjama top must have become tight under the arm-pit and compressed the circulation causing the whole arm to become numb and cold and it was this I had felt. It soon came back to life and gave me 'hot aches' but I was grateful that there was a natural explanation of the incident, although the terror of that moment haunted me for weeks to come. I have mentioned this incident to many people and several told me that something similar had happened to them.

At that time, because of my interest in playing rugger at Cambridge, I was fanatical about keeping fit. I went for runs but, because I was shy of doing this in the daytime, I used to get up early and go out before breakfast. One of my memories of Cornwall is these runs in the early morning, especially in winter when it was dark, and I felt the crunch of ice under my gym shoes. As dawn was breaking I would get back home and really enjoy my breakfast. I don't suppose I went unobserved and I wonder if I started a legend about a figure in white flitting along the hedgerows and across the fields in the fading light of the moon. The phantom runner of Newlyn East!

I was curiously unimpressed by the beauties of Cornwall although I sometimes went for solitary bicycle rides to the coast and walked along the cliffs. Later I learned to love Cornwall because, after further moves, we settled there a second time and I like to think of my upbringing as being, at least in part, Cornish.

It was an unhappy time for mother and father, too. Mother was haunted by First World War memories of waiting for telegrams announcing death in action while father preached scholarly sermons to a tiny congregation who did not understand what he was talking about. I could have helped them a lot but preferred to remain isolated and sulky while, for my part, home life was no longer a source of the love I so much needed.

VIII

Kate

1944

At the end of my two years at Cambridge I passed my 2nd MB, the most difficult hurdle of all for a medical student. In comparison with the fierce Dr Davis the examiners in anatomy seemed charming and eager to please. I got most of the answers right. I did not do so well in the other subjects and was lucky to pass in physiology because I did a little cheating in the practical exam. In one experiment I had to attach the muscle of a frog's leg to a stylus which recorded the twitching on a rotating smoked drum. This sounds horrible but the frog was in fact dead. The results seemed to me to be the exact opposite of what they should have been, so when no one was looking I turned the drum upside down. I can remember glancing over my shoulder as I left the laboratory and seeing two examiners gazing at the drum with puzzled looks on their faces. I do not know what conclusion they came to but I imagine they decided I was an idiot rather than a cheat and being an idiot does not necessarily debar a medical student from becoming a doctor.

Having passed this exam my next step was to go to a London teaching hospital for three years' clinical practice before taking my finals. I did not feel ready for this. I was young for my age and knew almost nothing about people apart from having a fair knowledge of how their bodies worked. I felt I had missed out. The two years of intensive study had been necessary but there had been little time to 'hear the angels sing' and the singing of angels was something I could not go without forever.

Luck was on my side. Father's picture of Cambridge was obscured by clouds of nostalgia dating back to his own time at the university. He had the annoying habit of saying to me, 'Of course you've never known Cambridge', by which he meant, I presume, ladies with parasols floating down the Cam in punts with Rupert Brooke reciting poems from the stern. This was quite true because my Cambridge had been reading *Gray's Anatomy* with the oak sported.

However, father made this remark once too often and I suggested diplomatically that it would be a good idea if I stayed up at Cambridge an extra year to 'get to know it'. This caught him unprepared.

I think it was mother who persuaded him it was a sensible idea. She realised I was little more than a child in my outlook and would find it difficult to cope with the hurly-burly of hospital life, although others of my age were being thrown into the greater hurly-burly of the war whether they liked it or not. However, the war was drawing to its close and there was now no patriotic urgency in my becoming a doctor.

I decided I would take a second degree and chose history — shades of Miss Brownlees. The authorities decided I wouldn't. I was meant to be a scientist and after a lot of discussion I was put down for moral sciences (psychology) which was the nearest I could get to an arts subject. This seemed a good idea because I was under the mistaken impression that psychology would teach me something about people.

So I had another year at Cambridge but before that I had the Long Vacation ahead of me, nearly four summer months, and I decided to make full use of them. I had at that time become very friendly with a fellow medical student called Tom and we both decided it was time we 'expanded our personalities'. We were fond of coining such expressions because it made us feel important. 'It is time,' Tom said, 'that we became students of Life.' The three Lives I decided to study were those of unsuspecting fruit-pickers in Lincolnshire, blind men at St Dunstan's Home and 'the poorer classes' in a settlement in north London. The last of these places eventually became my home but the first two were transient episodes which had a considerable effect on my future outlook. Tom came with me to discover life with the fruit-pickers.

The fruit-picking camp was in a field on the banks of the Ouse — or so I believed — which seemed a very suitable name for the river because the muddy water oozed backwards and forwards, slowly but persistently. Only at very high tide would the salt water cleanse it and wash close to our tents, while at low tide the mud at the edges would dry and crack. Looking it up on the map I find it could not have been the River Ouse, so my memory has played me false.

The fruit-pickers came from the East End of London, cheerful, loud-mouthed families with members of all ages from newborn babies to grannies bent almost double with arthritis. They were housed in stables, one family to a stall, and lived in squalor, sleeping on palliasses or on the straw. It was cheap labour at its worst – or best. For them it was the traditional family holiday which they booked year after year. It was also an escape from London which was now being harassed by buzz-bombs, the most devilish of weapons. I had some experience of them and the pause between the engine stopping and the bomb tumbling to the ground, like a shot partridge, gave one enough time to face eternity but not enough time to do anything about it. It was a real conversation stopper.

The helpers' camps were reasonably hygienic. They were run by a religious order, my memory of the Franciscan Friars being tall, humorous men, eternally clad in brown dressing-gowns with outsize tassels on the cord. Most of the helpers were, like myself, students from Cambridge and our main job was to look after the children while their parents worked, and in the evenings to go round the various stables and hovels to apply our limited knowledge of first aid and try to do something about the hygiene. The first aid part they liked, the hygiene part they considered gross interference, if not an insult.

For the first few days I was a lost soul, too shy to talk much with my companions apart from Tom and not knowing what to do with the children. Then I was adopted by a little boy called Macky. For some reason he developed a devotion towards me and would follow me everywhere. If it was my turn to organise games for the children Macky would do it for me. If I was cooking the midday meal Macky would know just how much Cremona to pour into the hot milk and would stick his filthy thumb into the mixture until the consistency was just right. He made me a success.

After a week at the camp I was as happy as I ever had been. I even took part in the concerts we sometimes gave in the evenings. I still hated acting, remembering the disaster of Frankenstein's daughter, but I took small parts in sketches, sometimes even getting a laugh, and I sang in the chorus. The favourite was 'There's a hole in my bucket, dear Liza' and the audience would double up with laughter although they'd heard it a hundred times before.

Our day always ended with the evening service of compline said round the camp fire. I found this intensely moving although I was going through an anti-religion phase at the time. The language was curiously medieval and when I heard about 'the devil who, as a roaring lion, goeth about seeking whom he may devour' I imagined an evil beast circling round the camp just beyond the light of the fire.

We took it in turns to read the service and I dreaded my turn, being hesitant in speech on such occasions, and fate was very definitely against me. On the far side of the river was a railway line and two or three times a day a goods train, pulled by an old-fashioned engine, came puffing along the track. The driver knew us and would blow his whistle which was a signal for everyone, children and adults alike, to run along the bank, cheering wildly.

On my night for saying compline we were early and the train was late so the two coincided and when the engine gave a whistle there was no response. The driver must have looked out of his cab and seen us standing in a circle in a sort of mass sulk. He whistled again and, after a pause, a third time. Then the train disappeared slowly down the line, issuing a series of hurt whistles until it was out of earshot. By now everyone was finding it impossible not to giggle, apart from our resident friar who stood in his brown dressing-gown with head bowed and arms folded. Quite suddenly there was an explosion of laughter and with difficulty I brought the service to a premature close.

Strangely enough I got the blame. The friar, the only one on the camp without a sense of humour, was very angry – not because of the laughter but because I had cut the service short. 'The Church must go on,' he said, glaring at me from under his dark brows and I felt the hot breath of the Inquisition down my neck. I thus earned myself the entirely unfair reputation of being wicked which, as things turned out, did me a disservice later.

Of the twelve helpers in our camp, four were girls. One was an attractive medical student with grey eyes, called Celia. Following my personal law which decreed that the more attractive I found someone the less likely I was to speak to them, I hardly said a word to her. One day we were playing a game of chase with the children – Celia, myself and Tom. In the middle of the chase Tom, quite unexpectedly, did a superb crash tackle on Celia as she was running away. There was a flurry of long hair, skirts and bare legs and a moment later Celia was sitting on the grass, slightly dishevelled and very cross. She reminded me of the ballet dancer who had bounced. I was surprised and rather shocked at Tom's behaviour and that night in our tent I taxed him with the matter. He laughed.

'It just seemed a good idea at the time,' he said. 'There she was looking pretty and knowing she looked pretty so I thought it would do her no harm to be given a shaking up.'

'You certainly did that. She wasn't at all pleased.'

'She was really. The trouble about you is that you think women are there to be worshipped. It's about time you learnt they are there to be upended and dumped on the grass.'

This conversation, too, stuck in my mind. I found it disturbing. How could I correlate the picture of Celia, in a heap on the grass, with Barbara Allen's sweet, all-embracing smile?

In an indirect way it was Tom's fault I got into trouble with the friars. We were talking one night about our search for Life amongst the fruit-pickers.

'I think it's all wrong,' said Tom.

'What's all wrong?'

'The way we set about things here. We condescendingly look after their children and in the evenings we bicycle round with our little first aid boxes but it stinks of charity. You can smell it a mile off.'

'I think they like it.'

'Maybe they do but they despise us. What we are doing is slumming. It has always been one of the hobbies of the middle classes but we choose to do it in the healthy fresh air so we don't have to go to an awful place like Stepney to see what life there's really like.'

'I think they are far happier than we are.'

But Tom was not listening.

'And look at the way we work with them in the fields. We go from one to another chatting and perhaps drop the odd bit of fruit in their baskets as a favour so they can earn a penny or two more. 'Here you are, my good man – or woman. It's an insult.'

Tom's idea was that we should become 'one of them'. When I pointed out that this meant being at work in the fields at seven in the morning he did not look quite so enthusiastic but having committed himself to the idea he had little choice in the matter. So next morning we dragged ourselves out of our sleeping bags at 6.30 a.m., made a pot of tea and set off.

It was chilly at that time in the morning. We arrived a little late and through the mist we saw a line of pickers with their baskets. I cannot remember what crop we were picking but it was some kind of vegetable. Many of the women wore scarves round their heads and I remarked to Tom that it looked like a scene from a Russian novel. He grunted and while I found a space in the line nearby he went farther down the field. We agreed to work separately to prove our 'oneness with them'.

I found myself next to a girl of about seventeen who smiled and made a place for me. The middle-aged woman on my left turned away and made it clear she wanted nothing to do with me. I said good morning to the girl and conversation dried up before it started. I worked doggedly, picking the vegetables and putting them in her basket, it being Tom's theory we should not distribute our favours but stick with one person. When the basket was full I helped her carry it back to the lorry where we emptied it and her name was entered in a book so she could claim her payment – which I think was a shilling.

Although we had hardly spoken I felt a working companionship with her. Occasionally I glanced sideways at her. She was dark-complexioned with rather a thin face and though not especially pretty there was a certain grace about her movements which singled her out from the others, or so I liked to think.

She noticed me looking at her and blushed.

'What's your name?' I managed to get out.

'Kate,' and after a pause she added, 'I'm Macky's sister.' This gave us something to talk about. She told me she was one of eleven brothers and sisters. She was the second eldest and Macky was three from the bottom. Her mum had brought the two-month-old baby to the camp with the family.

We carried the empty basket back to the line of pickers and she continued to talk as we filled it with vegetables. By now the mist had cleared and the sun had come up so I took off my sweater and worked in shirt sleeves. She was wearing an old brown coat and when she took this off I became more aware of the grace of her movements as she stooped.

She told me a lot about her life in Stepney and spoke with unfeigned simplicity and no complaints, the reason being she found nothing to complain about. She had shared a room with three of her sisters for as long as she could remember and did not know what it was like to sleep in a bed alone. She had never eaten an entire boiled egg because when she was half way down she would hand it to one of her brothers or sisters to finish. This was the chief source of family quarrels. If one of the children accused another of eating more than half the egg there would be terrible rows which her mum would settle by laying into everyone with a coathanger. Many other things I learnt. It seemed to me the chief difference between Kate and me was that she had never known solitude. Yet strangely enough she read books. I found this out because in a pause in the conversation she said, 'Before you started helping me you said to your friend it was like part of a Russian novel. What did you mean?'

'You weren't meant to hear that.'

'In the mist voices carry a long way.'

'It was just that I read a book a few weeks ago which described

Russian peasants working in the fields. Seeing you in the mist reminded me of it. That's all.'

'Would I like it?'

'Like what?'

'The Russian book.'

I thought of seven hundred pages of Tolstoy and said, 'I think you would find it heavy going.'

'But I like reading.'

'With ten brothers and sisters? I don't suppose you have much chance.'

'It is noisy. But I can sit in a corner and shut my ears. Tell me about the book.'

I tried to give her a potted version of *Anna Karenina*. Kate listened attentively. I had reached the point in the story where Anna's lover takes a nasty tumble in a horse race and she cannot hide her feelings for him, when I realised Kate and I were all alone. Everyone else had gone back to the lorry while we had been pulling up the vegetables and dropping them in the basket in a natural rhythm of the kind Russian peasants, I am sure, could maintain from dawn till dusk. We stood up and smiled at each other. Then we carried our half-filled basket back to the lorry.

I noticed people were staring at us. When I caught their eyes they looked away and smiled to themselves. I felt embarrassed. Tom was standing, hands on hips, looking at me quizzically. We were at the back of the queue waiting to have the contents of the basket weighed so I said a hurried goodbye to Kate then went to join Tom and we walked back to the camp together. As soon as we were out of earshot he said, 'When I said we ought to become one of them I didn't mean it quite like that.'

'Like what?'

'Flirting in public.'

'I wasn't.'

'Another ten minutes and it was odds on you could have raped the girl.'

'Don't be ridiculous.'

'You should have heard what the others were saying. That old harridan who was working next to you – not that you probably even noticed her – was hopping mad about it. Anyway what were you two talking about?'

'Actually we were discussing Anna Karenina.' Tom looked at me in amazement then started laughing. He found it difficult to stop and when I tried to explain he started all over again. It was quite impossible to hold a conversation with him and by the time we got back to the camp I was in a sulk. Tom kept giggling to himself all through breakfast and once he nudged me and whispered, 'Try Dostoevski.' I thought his behaviour was quite unnecessary and rather stupid.

On the Saturday evening there was a 'hop' in one of the barns. We were asked to attend but Tom seemed to have gone off the idea of being 'one of them' and said he would stay at the camp.

'Not that you don't need a chaperone,' he remarked to me, 'you'll probably start teaching that girl Cossack dancing and strain a ligament.' I was finding Tom a bit of a bore. I had intended asking him exactly what a hop was but decided not to. It turned out to be a merry get-together of the fruit-pickers and helpers. We ate cheese rolls and drank lemonade and danced on the earthen floor to the music of a piano which was so deficient in notes that it might have been more correct to call it two-thirds of a piano.

The older children were there as well and it was a noisy, happy affair. I thought everyone would have been tired out after their work in the fields but they showed no signs of it. There were various dances but every few minutes the piano seemed to erupt spontaneously into 'Knees up Mother Brown' which we all performed exuberantly until the sweat poured off us because it was a hot evening. Kate was there but I avoided her. I amused myself imagining Miss Davenport standing by the piano chanting, 'Now boys and girls, a-one, a-two, a-Knees-up-Mother-Brown.' This started me laughing and, feeling a bit weary by now, I retired to the side of the barn where there were some chairs. I sat down and found I was sitting next to Kate.

'Why are you laughing?' she asked.

'I was thinking about Miss Davenport,' I said.

'Is she your girlfriend?'

'Good heavens, no. She isn't anyone's girlfriend.' But I was ashamed to tell her about the dancing classes.

I spent the rest of the evening with Kate. She was as exuberant as anyone else in 'Knees up Mother Brown' and I loved the happiness in her eyes. That evening I loved them all and wished I could have been as carefree as they were. The weight of my upbringing hung round my neck like an albatross. The only concession to the Miss Davenport type of dancing was to have a 'Last Waltz' although they couldn't resist having another go at 'Knees up Mother Brown' afterwards. During the waltz the lights were turned down and Kate danced with her arms round my neck. There was nothing special about this because a lot of other couples were doing the same but her body felt very close to mine, and I could feel her hair against my cheek. I wanted to kiss her but did not dare to. When the lights went on she looked up at me obviously wondering why I had not kissed her and I felt angry with myself. When we parted I said goodnight rather brusquely and went back to the camp with the other helpers.

I found Tom had not stayed at the camp but had gone off to the pub. He was moderately drunk.

'I needed a few drinks,' he said, 'all this torrid sex is too much for me.'

'I don't know what you are talking about.'

'Mind you, she's got style. I'll have to give you that.' We fell silent and then he asked me politely if we had found time to have a nice chat about the inner life of Rimsky-Korsakov. At this I lost my temper.

'Why the hell are you making such a fuss over it? Are you jealous because I've picked up a girl and you haven't?'

'Picking up is what you do to potatoes, not girls.'

'And what does that mean?'

'Oh, Christopher, you're a fool. This prince and the beggar-maid stuff never works.'

'I'm not a prince and Kate's not a beggar-maid.'

'Have it your own way. It's the poor girl who'll get hurt, not you.'

'I never knew you could get so corny.'

'You would have done much better to have come drinking with me.'

'I didn't know you were going drinking, did I? Besides I thoroughly enjoyed myself. They're wonderful people. All your talk about being "one of them" – that's just what I was doing and you don't like it. You're a hypocrite, Tom.'

'Think that if you like.' Tom seemed to have sobered up. He wandered over to the camp fire where he sat down by Celia and engaged her in conversation. At one point I saw them looking in my direction and I suspected they were talking about me. This made me even angrier.

That night I lay awake a long time. Through the flap of the tent I could see a cluster of stars on the horizon and, as my anger faded, I listened to the sounds of the night, the wind in the alder trees and the lapping of the water as the tide came strongly up the river. A dog was barking in the distance. Needless to say I imagined Kate's arms round my neck as I dropped off to sleep.

I next met Kate picking pears. Tom and I were friends again and had decided to put in a couple of hours in the orchards. It was very hot and we thought it would be cooler for us amongst the trees than helping with the children at the camp. I sidled up to an old lady in black and politely offered to help her because I noticed she was only picking pears from the lowest branches.

'I can go up the ladder if you hold the basket,' I said. She started chuckling or rather cackling, because she was witch-like in appearance.

'It's not me that needs help but that one over there,' she said, pointing with her thumb and, ignoring me, she continued with her work. I turned and went in the direction she had indicated and found Kate at the top of a ladder with her basket balanced on a branch. She looked down at me and smiled.

'The old lady over there told me you could do with some help,' I said.

'I don't mind.'

We took it in turns to climb the ladder while the other held the basket. The pears had to be handled carefully because their skins were easily damaged and Kate, who was deft with her fingers, showed me the best way to pick them. There were several wasps about but she did not seem to mind them, brushing them away and saying 'Gerrorf,' dropping into her East End accent. By rights she should have been stung. I am the sort of person who ducks and runs when a wasp is circling round me but pride prevented me. I thought I would rather have a sting or two than be thought a coward.

In the days when skirts were worn rather than slacks picking fruit with a girl was, as I soon found out, a pleasurable experience especially when Kate was up the ladder. My pulse began to beat rather fast and when I helped her down we would hold hands longer than necessary. It was strange that the other fruit-pickers seemed to drift away to another part of the orchard and I did not notice their sly but affectionate glances. I suppose I was being set up in a well-meaning way.

'Did you like the hop?' asked Kate, peering down at me through the branches.

'I liked dancing with you.'

'Oh, bother.' She had dropped one of the pears. 'It was a lovely one but it will be no good now. It's always the best ones you drop.'

'I liked Knees up Mother Brown', I continued, 'they didn't teach me that one at the dancing class.'

'You went to a dancing class?' She seemed surprised.

'When I was little,' I said apologetically. I found I was telling her about Miss Davenport and soon was giving her a modified account of my life at Springwell. She was so obviously absorbed in what I was saying that she stopped picking the pears and came down the ladder. She kept on pursing her lips and saying 'Ooh' because I was telling her of a world that she thought only existed in story books.

When I had finished talking she looked at me thoughtfully and said, 'But you're nice,' again with a slight suggestion of surprise in her voice. We changed places and as I picked the pears standing at the top of the ladder the juice ran down my bare arms. A wasp settled on my hand. I tried to brush it off and it buzzed angrily then stung me on the elbow. I gave a yell and half tumbled down the ladder.

Kate was sympathetic but a little amused and I had an overwhelming desire to take her in my arms. I looked into her eyes and knew she felt the same. Her chin was raised and her lips were waiting to be kissed – but not by me. I was afraid. She was a fruit-picker and I was a helper and others might be watching.

We decided I was likely to survive the wasp sting and continued picking pears. I did not want to talk about my family any more. Kate was such a joyous person, having had nothing, while I with everything, was cramped and stilted and had to think myself into being happy. So I fell silent.

'Go on telling me about Eidy,' she said.

'I'm boring you.' She seemed upset and her eyes filled with tears.

'I love it. It's more fun than that story about Anna and that bloke falling off his horse.' But I wouldn't go on. After a long silence she said, 'Well, tell me about your friends in college then. Do you have fun? I think it must be wonderful.' But I wouldn't talk about that either. How could I tell her I had a bedroom, sitting room and even a small kitchen, all to myself, and if I wanted solitude I could shut the door and be alone for hours on end? That there was a bedmaker who tidied and dusted my room every day? That we dined at long tables in a panelled hall? There was so much else too that would have been as foreign to her as the world of *Anna Karenina*. She lived in a small house with twelve other people and was never alone.

So I put her off with commonplace remarks whereas I should have told her everything and she would have loved it and not felt at all envious. How little I knew about people in those days.

The silence between us was, at first, strained then became restful because she seemed incapable of embarrassment or unhappiness for long. When it was time for me to go back to the camp to prepare the children's tea I helped her down the ladder and we remained holding hands with the sunbeams dancing round us as the leaves of the pear trees wavered in the slight breeze. Tom was nowhere to be seen.

'I ought to go back and help mum with the baby,' said Kate. She took her hand out of mine and we carried the basket of pears to the lorry parked at the edge of the orchard.

'I can give you a lift on the handlebars of my bike,' I said, 'the stable's on the way back to the camp.'

Carrying a passenger on a bicycle is quite a difficult technique and is hard work. Kate sat sideways on the handlebars with her bare legs dangling beside the front wheel. She leant back against me and my head was pressed against her side with my arms encircling her as I tried to steer the bike. I felt the warmth of her body and the pleasant smell of perspiration in someone who keeps herself clean. I wondered afterwards how it was that she, who lived in squalor, was always clean. I wanted very much to kiss her but the dusty road ran through flat fields and everywhere there seemed to be fruit-pickers. Some paused in their work to look at us as we went by, the bicycle wobbling from side to side.

We stopped immediately opposite the stable in the shade of an elm tree. Kate slid off the handlebars but kept one arm round me. I got off, too, and let the bike fall to the ground where the back wheel spun round as it lay on the grass. This, I knew, was to be my first kiss. For a moment I felt Kate's soft lips against mine, then she suddenly pushed me away. Behind me, and only a few yards off, stood a small wiry woman. She was scowling. In her hand was something which my memory tells me was a coathanger but I can hardly believe this was true.

Kate ran off and disappeared through the stable door. The woman stood looking at me. I picked up my bike and rode back to the camp. Tom was back before me and gave me one of his quizzical looks.

'I didn't see any point in waiting for you,' he said.

'You could have done.'

'People are talking, you know.'

'What about?' We went to the trestle table which stood by the tent and started cutting loaves of bread into thick slices and smearing margarine on them. Some of the children came to watch us, standing round the table with their mouths open. Macky stood close to me.

'Anyone who pinches a bit will get a wallop,' said Tom.

'Garn,' said Macky, and to me, 'I've found a frog. I've got it in a tin.'

'I'll come and see it later,' I said.

'I'm going to take it back to frighten mum.'

'I shouldn't do that.'

After we had given the children their tea we shooed them off and Tom and I washed the plates in a chipped enamel basin. 'There's going to be trouble,' said Tom.

'Why?'

'Because you're a fool. Not that our Stepney friends mind. I expect they're tickled pink.' In a poor imitation of a cockney accent, he added, 'but there's them as won't like it one little bit, old cock.'

I decided to confide in Tom. 'Her mum doesn't like it,' I said.

'You've met her?'

'Not exactly. She threatened me with a coathanger.'

'A what?'

'A coathanger.' Tom let this pass.

'You'll have to stop it, you know.'

'I don't want to.'

'Well, they'll put a stop to it.'

'Who's they?'

'That we'll soon find out.'

Tom was right. After supper that evening we saw the tall figure of Father Dennis striding towards the camp. He was the head of the friars, and one of the humorous ones, well known to many of my generation of students and much loved. He was six foot tall and against the skyline he looked like a giant. It was my duty evening and, with Tom and Celia, I was again doing the washing up. I kept my head down and pretended to be listening to the portable radio which we used to have on to encourage us to work our way through the piles of dishes.

Father Dennis spent an interminable time chatting with the other helpers but when he finally came round to us he made a jovial remark about some mutts being landed with the washing up.

'Why not give us a hand then,' said Tom.

He laughed. 'No, I actually wanted a quick word in private with Christopher.'

'I suppose we can let him off the rest,' said Tom.

I put down my towel and, for want of anywhere better, took Father Dennis to a tree trunk which lay close to the river bank. It seemed a suitable place to sit and talk out of earshot. The river was in its oozy phase and a pair of small birds were probing the mud with their beaks, dipping up and down like mechanical toys. Father Dennis started talking. I was watching the birds and half listening. 'Our relationship with the fruit-pickers is a delicate and privileged one,' was one of the sentences that got through to me. Why privileged I wondered. We were helping them and not being paid a penny for it. Incongruously my mind turned to roller-skating with Heather along the street by our house in Cambridge and I felt angry.

'Are you listening, Christopher?' said Father Dennis.

'I'm listening.'

'They trust us with their children,' he said, 'and they trust us in other ways too.'

'What other ways?'

'You know what I mean.'

'I'm afraid I don't.'

Father Dennis rubbed his hand against his chin and looked across the river.

'It's about this girl, Kate,' he said.

'I know her.'

'It's more than that. You've singled her out.'

'I've helped her pick pears if that's what you mean. I find her interesting to talk to. Oh, yes,' I continued with heavy sarcasm, wishing to give Father Dennis his money's worth, 'I gave her a ride home on the handlebars of my bicycle. Is that breaking the traffic regulations?'

'No, but kissing her is breaking other regulations.'

'Kissing her?'

'In public.'

I felt like laughing. It was all so ridiculous.

'Her father came to see me. He created hell.'

'What did he say?'

'Well . . . quite a lot and quite forcibly. I won't repeat it. The gist of it was that he thinks you're making a monkey out of his daughter. I've known Kate's family for years. They're very close-knit and half the other people here are aunts and cousins, or some other relations. Her father's a bit of a drunkard. I don't suppose Kate told you that. She's loyal to him but there has been trouble in the past.'

'Am I meant to be afraid?'

'No, but what I'm trying to get into your thick skull is that if you carry on with this affair, however harmless it is at the moment, there's going to be trouble and it will be Kate who'll come off worst.'

'Someone else said that.'

'It's true. And there's another matter. I saw you smiling when I said our position here was a privileged one, but it is. The farmers like us being here because, to be uncharitable, we are doing for nothing what they should be paying for. But one word of complaint and we're out. They wouldn't stand for it. We've worked hard here and you've got to realise that it's my job to teach these people a bit about Christianity. They respect us and the little bit of Sunday School we do with the children sows seeds.'

I thought of my conversation with Tom and wanted to say, 'They don't respect us. They tolerate us.' My mind wandered again and I half-heard Father Dennis talking about me being a medical student and when I was a doctor I would have to learn to keep patients at arm's length and not get too involved with them.

'So?'

'To me it's quite simple. This affair of yours with Kate has got to be nipped in the bud — for everyone's sake.'

'And if I don't agree?'

'I'm afraid you will have to leave.' He got up off the log and stretched himself. 'I'm sorry, Christopher, but that's what I came to tell you.' I still sat on the log looking at the river. He put a hand on my shoulder.

'I'm going to scrounge a coffee then I'll get back to my own camp for compline. Think about it. If you feel unhappy about it come and have a chat with me, any time, day or night.'

He strode back to the camp fire. His final words tumbled over and over in my mind. One's life is but repetitions of the same events and the same remarks. I heard the headmaster of the school in Sussex saying, 'If you feel unhappy . . .', and a ghostly wave of depression flooded over me. I must not love Kate. If one tries to love anyone it has to be stopped because loving people is inconvenient. If one loves home one has to be sent off to school. If one has a childhood friend one is forbidden to play with her. If one loves a smiling face it is unattainable. It is safe only to admire the picture of a girl on a hoarding advertising cigarettes. Of course my affair with Kate would have come to nothing but I was on the point of breaking through a barrier. I had waited a long time for that moment. In a fit of anger I picked up the log and half dropped it, half threw it into the mud where it sank gurgling. Bubbles rose from the slime and when they had ceased I walked along the river bank away from the camp. When I got back it was dark and everyone had gone to bed. I slipped into the tent, undressed and got into my sleeping bag. Tom was awake.

'Where the hell have you been?' he said.

I stayed on at the camp for a further ten days when I was due to leave anyway. I saw Kate at a distance a few times but only met her once face to face. I suspected there was a conspiracy between Father Dennis and Kate's family to keep us apart.

I kept away from the stable where she lived as far as possible but sometimes I had to go there with other helpers to do our first aid round. One evening Macky met me at the door with the news that the baby had spots. He dragged me over to their stall before I had a chance to resist and there was Kate, sitting on a box, holding the baby.

She saw me coming and quietly slipped off the baby's grubby vest. He was covered in spots, which I thought might be chicken-pox and I called for the other helpers to come and have a look. None of us knew for certain so we decided we ought to send for a doctor.

During all this Kate avoided looking at me but our eyes met once for a moment. Neither of us smiled and I could understand nothing from her expression. I wanted to say I was sorry and that it was not my fault, but there was no opportunity.

I left the camp with mixed feelings. Macky clung to me and cried and I promised I would write to him at Christmas. I kept my word and sent him a card showing Santa Claus tumbling out of a chimney covered with soot, which I thought might amuse him. I put at the bottom, 'Give my love to Kate and the rest of the family.'

I was disappointed he did not send me a card but soon after Christmas my own card was returned, unopened, with an official stamp on it — 'Return to sender. Address does not exist.'

Probably Macky, whose spelling and knowledge of the English language was limited, had given me the wrong street name or wrong number, or both. But that was the autumn of the V2 rockets which would destroy half a street at a time and I had a horrible vision of Macky, Kate and all the family buried in the ruins of their home. I had no easy means of finding out and I did not want to. That is why I so much regret the kiss that never happened.

IX

Blind Date
1944

A fortnight later I was on my way to St Dunstans Home for the Blind.
To say I was nervous would be an understatement. What on earth was
I letting myself in for? I had never met a blind man in my life apart
from the beggars and musicians one saw in London at street corners. I
remember them from my childhood, sitting with placards in front of
them. 'I served my country in the war.' Once I lingered behind mother
and father – we were being taken back to school – and dropped a penny
in the cloth cap lying on the pavement in front of an unkempt bearded
old man.

'Thank you, my boy,' he said in an educated voice and I wondered
how he knew I was a boy.

'What did you do that for?' asked father as I caught up with them,
'he probably has more money than we have.'

It was one of the mysterious remarks grown-ups make and I could
not understand why dropping a penny in a blind man's cap was not a
good thing.

Now, sitting in the railway carriage, I thought of the bearded old
man and through my mind, in rhythm with the train, ran the old
saying, 'In the country of the blind the one-eyed man is king.' There
was something eerie about it. At least, I thought, whatever happens it
will stop me thinking about Kate. For Kate had been on my mind and
I had been indulging in self-hate. What is more despicable than
cowardice and weakness? I had daydreams of what I might have done –
secret assignations in the orchard after dark, defying Father Dennis
and his system in a dramatic camp fire scene, even saying a few
spontaneous words in the middle of compline about the meaning of
love so that their heads hung in shame.

St Dunstans is normally situated in a large building on the Sussex
coast but during the war it was evacuated to Church Stretton in case of
invasion, which did not take place, and to avoid aerial bombardment,

which did. It was for this Shropshire town that I was heading and, because I had to take a cross-country route from Cornwall and had missed my connection, I was already three hours late. Not a very good start.

It was dark when I finally reached the station and got off the train. There was no one on the platform besides myself and the train hurried off as if it was not meant to stop there anyway. I found my way to the ticket collector's office and asked him where I could find St Dunstans. He looked at me as if I was mad.

'Which part, sonny? Half the place is St Dunstans.'

'I don't know.'

'Well, you go to the main square. It's straight down the street. With a bit of luck the office will be open and you can ask there.'

The town was brightly lit but whether this was moonlight or because the blackout restrictions had, by now, been lifted I am not sure. At times of anxiety one's mind is susceptible to beauty and I remember how lovely the stone buildings were on either side of the street as I lugged my suitcase towards the main square where the office might, or might not, be open.

The square, when I finally reached it, was less beautiful, being disfigured by various Nissen huts and temporary buildings. There was a light visible in the corner of one window. I found a door round the back and knocked cautiously. It was opened by a woman of about thirty in a smart blue uniform. I tried to explain who I was and what I was doing there but she obviously knew nothing about me.

'Come along in and sit down,' she said, 'I'll phone round.' She tried several numbers without success then shook her head and looked at me curiously. 'You're sure it's St Dunstans you want,' she asked, 'not St Pancras Station or St Paul's Cathedral because, if so, you are a bit out of your way.'

I felt like making a sarcastic retort but thought it wiser not to. I shook my head.

'Anyway have a bar of chocolate. This is about the only place in England where sweet rationing doesn't seem to matter. Have you eaten?'

'No.'

'Have two bars of chocolate then.' She pushed a cardboard box full of chocolates towards me. 'We even had bananas the other day. You know, those curved yellow things you have to peel.'

'I know.' She picked up the phone and tried another number. 'I've got a young man here who says his name's Elliott something-or-other.

Do you know anything about him? You do. Thank God for that. I'll send him straight up.' She put the receiver down.

'They were expecting you hours ago.'

'I missed my connection.'

She looked at my overweight suitcase and said kindly, 'If you hang on a tick I'll give you a lift. I've got to close this place down anyway and Brockhurst is near the top of the hill. It's on my way more or less.'

'Thank you very much. What's Brockhurst?'

'It's the home for officers. At St Dunstans we keep the ranks separate. God knows why. Tradition I suppose. The good old British Army.' She tidied up a few papers on her desk while I ate the chocolate then we went out into the square where, after locking up the building, she took me across to a battered-looking black Morris.

'Pile your suitcase on the back seat,' she said. It took some time to get the car started. 'Temperamental beast,' she said, 'ah, triumph at last.'

We jerked through the town then laboured up a rather steep hill. My companion looked round at me doubtfully.

'Have you had dealings with blind men before?'

'No.'

'Well, I dare say you will get used to it in time. What job are you doing?'

'They haven't told me yet.'

She hummed quietly to herself. 'By the way my name's Witney, Diane Witney. I'm a sort of dogsbody extraordinary.'

The Morris turned into a driveway then came to a sudden halt with a clatter of gravel against the bodywork of the car. In front of us was a large house and to the left what appeared to be acres of playing fields with a row of tall trees behind. It was so like my Sussex boarding school that a wave of panic came over me. For a moment Diane Witney became Miss Brownlees, whom she in fact resembled in appearance.

'We had better get out,' said Diane. 'Are you all right?'

'Yes, thank you.' She took me to the main door and pulled an old fashioned bell which jangled in the distance.

'You'll like it here,' she said reassuringly. The door was opened by another lady in blue uniform who shook me politely by the hand.

'One Mr Elliott something-or-other safely delivered,' said Diane, 'do I have to sign for him?'

'That won't be necessary.'

'All right. Be seeing you I expect.'

I was taken to a pleasant sitting room with a coal fire protected by a large fire-guard of a sort and I had not seen since my nursery days. The lady sat opposite me and looked at me closely.

I use the word lady intentionally because that is what she was. Her name was Mrs Irwin and she was about fifty, with beautiful smooth silver hair. She was very smart and very gracious but had a certain sadness about her which made me suspect she was a widow, probably of some high-ranking officer, but I never found out if this was so.

'I'm sorry you've had a tiring journey. I'm afraid the boys have gone to bed so you won't be able to meet them till morning. Have you eaten yet?'

'Yes.'

Her use of the word 'boys' reinforced the illusion of the house being a boarding school. I could not think of anything to say. Mrs Irwin chatted a little, while I remained almost silent. I could see she was disappointed. She looked tired and was probably hoping to find in me someone who would take part of the load off her shoulders. Obviously I was going to be another of her 'boys', a little extra work and worry. She gave a small sigh.

'I'll show you your bedroom. I expect you're worn out.' She led the way upstairs, me following with my suitcase, and opened the door of a large room with two beds in it.

'We hope to have another student with us in a few days. It's something of an experiment. We'll talk about it tomorrow. By the way the washroom is just opposite.' She went to the dressing table and pulled open one of the drawers.

'You should have plenty of room for your things,' she said, then, smiling kindly, she said goodnight and left me to my thoughts.

I was dreading the morning and took a long time to get to sleep. There was an owl hooting from the trees on the other side of the playing fields. Usually I love listening to owls at night then turning over to go to sleep again but this owl called every time I was about to drop off and woke me with a start. Finally I slept uneasily and the next thing I remember was the clanging of a bell, which made me imagine I was back at school and late for a class. I lay in bed for a while then got up and went to the washroom with my sponge bag.

When I opened the door I was met by a babble of voices. There were half a dozen men in pyjamas, washing and shaving and as I stood at the door the noise slowly drifted into silence. They all turned and looked at me. They were blind but they looked at me. I stood quite still hoping they did not know I was there.

One of them said, 'Who's that?' then, because I did not reply, 'It must be the student they were talking about. Come along in. There's a free washbasin here.'

'Good morning,' I said. They started talking again. I went to the washbasin next to the man who had first spoken to me. His face was deeply scarred with one eye completely obliterated. The other was a glass eye and he turned and seemed to stare at me with deep penetration.

'You needn't worry about us. We're an odd lot but you'll soon get used to it. What's your name?'

'Christopher.'

'We've been looking forward to you coming. Too many bloody women about here. I had better introduce you.' He pointed in turn to his friends, knowing exactly where each was. I shook them all by the hand which was, I realised, a mistake because I had to grope for their hands and this led one of them to drop his razor on the floor. I apologised profusely and picked it up for him. One man had only a left hand with three fingers but his grip was remarkably firm. Later, when I had got to know them well, one of them told me it had not been a mistake to shake hands. 'We could tell you were as nervous as hell and that reassured us. We don't like cocky people.'

I asked if I could do anything to help because that's what I was there for and they said, 'Yes, you can take us down to the pub tonight.'

It did not take me long to realise that one of their problems was that nearly everyone else, apart from themselves, was female. These were charming women, devoted to their work, and it wasn't their fault they were female, but the men I lived and worked with for six weeks sometimes wanted all-male company. 'Any women about?' they would whisper to me and if I said 'No' they would start using obscene expressions and tell filthy stories until I warned them one of the girls was within earshot.

They wanted very much to know what the girls looked like. 'Is she pretty?' 'Has she got big tits?' 'What colour's her hair? Bother, I only go for blondes.' Often I had to tell lies for the girls' sake because all the men wanted to be seen with pretty girls.

'She's an absolute stunner,' I would say, 'beautiful blue eyes and tits like blancmanges,' knowing that the girl in question was really rather plain.

There were quite a number of romances and eventually a few marriages which was, I suspect, one of the objects at St Dunstans at that time and the secret motive for some of those tender-hearted girls to work there. I knew when one of the blind men was becoming genuinely fond of a girl because he would take me to one side and ask me about her in great detail, not just about the size of her bosom but the expression on her face, how she walked, the sort of clothes she liked wearing, what made her look sad and so on. I became quite good at these descriptions and it taught me to study girls objectively without being overcome with embarrassment every time one was within a few yards of me. If I thought one of the men was serious I was serious too and gave as accurate an account of the girl as I could because there was no point in creating illusions.

Strangely enough many of them did not like Mrs Irwin, whom I greatly admired. I think this was because she epitomised the aristocratic Red Cross or VAD type, who were more characteristic of the First than the Second World War. I think Mrs Irwin realised this and it was one of the reasons she was always a little sad. I was loyal to her and if the men started making obscene jokes about her I would try to shut them up.

It was not only the girls they wanted to hear about. What cars were parked in the square? Were those Spitfires flying overhead? How many? Had the leaves started turning brown? Instead of being at a loose end I found I was becoming very busy and I was pleased when, after a few days, the other student arrived. His name was Charles and he was the exact opposite of me, being carefree and extrovert. We got on well together but I was glad I had come first because shyness was foreign to him and I think his presence would have prevented me from getting to know the men. As it was I think most of them preferred me and this gave me secret pleasure.

Most of our work was escorting the men from one building to another, especially the newer ones who had not had time to sense the geography. They were kept busy and there were classes in almost everything a blind man could be expected to learn.

Often in the evenings I would take a group down to the pub. Most of them were quite capable of finding their own way because there was a convenient wire fence all the way down the hill along the verge of the road but Mrs Irwin was worried they might have difficulty finding their way *back* and have an accident of some kind. She had a point.

One evening stands out in my mind. After dinner some of them said to me, 'Let's go down the pub. Gwen and Barbara will be there.'

'Who are Gwen and Barbara?'

'Wren officers. Give them a couple of gins and they sing like nightingales.' My throat went dry. I had a premonition that Barbara was the Barbara Allen of my Devon days.

'Well, are you coming or not?'

'Of course I'll come. What are their surnames?'

'Don't know. They're just Gwen and Barbara.'

I was very quiet on the way down and they began to tease me. 'Haven't you met a blind Wren before? They're the same as other Wrens except they can't see.'

It was not Barbara Allen. I did not know whether to be happy or sad. I had already built up a dream fantasy of marrying her and looking after her for ever and ever, gazing at her all-embracing sightless smile. Life would have ceased to be a problem.

Gwen and Barbara had their two gins and then sang for us. They had beautiful voices, one soprano, the other contralto. Their speciality was the barcarole from Offenbach's *Tales of Hoffman*, which they sang unaccompanied in perfect harmony. They had been pretty girls, both of them, but their faces were badly scarred. As I listened to them singing the tears ran down my cheeks. It was the first time I had wept since Bingo the bull-terrier died and it did not matter because no one could see me except the barman. I moved over to a chair in the corner and I could not stop myself crying. Gwen and Barbara sang several songs and then someone said, 'You had better stop now. We can't have Christopher upset.' They all knew I was crying.

My relationship with those men was a very sweet one and quite unexpected. I was naive and studious. They were hardened by the war and their blindness but somehow we seemed to understand each other. Not for the last time I realised that to be naive without being stupid can be an attractive combination.

I remember having a long talk with a lieutenant called Steve. He was about my age and I got him to tell me how he had been blinded — usually they did not want to talk about it. He had been blown up at Falaise in Normandy and lay in a ditch for two days before he was found. He told me, and I quote his words, 'Of course I knew I was blind. I had to decide whether I wanted to live or die. At first I wanted to die but after a bit I changed my mind so I stuck it out and eventually someone rescued me.'

'Are you glad now?'

'I'm not so sure. It's a funny thing to say but the novelty wears off. I will finish up one of the forgotten men.'

'I don't think so.' But I remembered the blind old man in the London street. He asked me to tell him about my life but I did not want to. My troubles were tiny and of my own making. 'The shadow is but a small and passing thing.' For Steve the shadow was forever.

It was after this conversation that I became quite suddenly depressed. I decided to seek out Diane Witney who had become, perhaps, my chief friend and confidante. Like me she was a fetcher and carrier and we had often driven together in her Morris to pick someone up or take a package from the station to one of the classrooms. Sometimes she surprised me by holding my hand which I found pleasant but, because she seemed a lot older than me, I took this to be the maternal instinct coming out in her.

On this occasion I wanted to get away from Brockhurst so I phoned up the office in the town square and asked if she was driving anywhere and, if so, whether I could come with her.

'I've got to go to Shrewsbury to buy some things. Come with me by all means.'

I got permission from Mrs Irwin to have the afternoon off, telling her I wanted to have a look round Shrewsbury, which was partly true.

'It's a beautiful town,' she said. 'You deserve a break.'

Diane was not ready when I arrived at her office in the Nissen hut in the main square. 'Submerged in paper,' she said. 'I'll shove it all in the waste paper basket.'

'You can't do that.'

'You watch me,' and she proceeded to do exactly what she said she would. I was amazed.

On the way out she called through the door of the next office, 'Marjorie, be a dear and rescue all the stuff from my waste paper basket. Keep anything that looks interesting.' I couldn't hear the reply from inside.

'I often do that,' Diane said to me as we walked across to the Morris.

'Why?'

'Childish pique. Marjorie does the same. We take it in turns.'

We drove through lovely wooded country and Diane talked a lot but as much to herself as me. After we had gone a few miles she said, 'What's wrong?'

I started telling her about my conversation with Steve. She slowed the Morris and we drove down a side road to the left where she brought it to a halt at the edge of the road, under some trees.

'Why did you do that?' I asked. She turned in her seat and kissed me. I felt the pressure of her lips on mine and kissed her in return as if I had been doing it for a thousand years and not for just about the first time. She kissed thoughtfully and affectionately. There was no great passion in it. This is wonderful, I thought. I had imagined kissing being something terribly exciting leading on to all sorts of other things which I knew little about and which worried me because I expected to be clumsy and ineffective. Diane's kissing was an end in itself. There was nothing to worry about.

After a time she pushed me gently away. 'What were you saying?' she said. I went on telling her about Steve while she took a comb from her handbag and tidied her hair.

'I don't see what you are upset about.'

'It was just that I felt ashamed.'

'For God's sake. If you start being sorry for yourself I'll boot you out of the car. It's not you who's deprived, you know, it's those poor buggers.'

'I don't feel ashamed any more.'

'That's what kissing's for . . . no that's an understatement. We'd better get on to Shrewsbury.' She backed the Morris, turned it and we drove on to the main road. We chatted casually and I kept on taking surreptitious glances at her, wondering if it had really happened.

In Shrewsbury Diane had a lot of shopping to do, and stores to collect. She looked smart in her blue uniform and was the sort of person who got instant service when she went into a shop. Not that she was officious. Almost invariably the person who served her would be smiling or laughing as he made a point of opening the door for her. I tagged along behind. By the time we had finished, the boot and back seat of the car were full. We were too laden with parcels and packages to walk hand in hand.

'Let's find some tea,' she said. We discovered a small café near the river. It had wooden beams and there was a pleasant smell of toast. We had teacakes and cream buns which, at that time of the war, were not easy to come by.

'Delicious,' said Diane, licking her fingers, 'have another cup.' I watched her pouring the tea into the cups from a flower-patterned teapot.

'Better than mugs,' I said for something to say.

'Once in a while.'

I insisted on paying for the tea and she laughed. Then we walked down to the river and watched the swans. A long, slender boat, a schools eight, came by at speed. The oarsmen were not very good and the spray from their blades was silver in the evening sun. The cox was shouting at them in a high-pitched treble voice.

'A mug's game that,' said Diane.

'I don't know so much.'

'There's no point. I can think of better ways of getting knackered.'

The river was very beautiful. One of the swans, disturbed by the boat, glided by, its wings half raised in anger leaving a trail of light in the water behind it. Another swan drifted towards us, had a good look, and backed away. The hanging branches of a willow touched the surface of the water. Diane and I were sitting on the bank holding hands. She said unexpectedly, 'You improve on acquaintance, you know. When I first met you in the office I thought you were something that had just emerged from a boys' magazine.'

'I just about have.'

'Don't change too quickly.'

'The quicker the better.'

She shrugged her shoulders. 'We had better get back otherwise Ma Irwin will be sending out a search party for her little boy.' She sounded cross and I could not understand why.

We did not say much on the way back. As we got near to the place where we had previously turned off I wanted the same thing to happen again but I did not dare suggest it. Diane put her hand on my arm.

'No,' she said, reading my thoughts, 'that was a once only occasion.'

'I don't see why.'

'Because I no longer harbour romantic notions. Besides what would people say? I don't want to get the reputation of being a cradle-snatcher.'

'I didn't think you would care what people say.'

'I do.'

'But I want to kiss you.'

She stopped the car on the verge of the main road and this time we kissed briefly but passionately. 'You see what I mean,' she said.

'I love you Diane.'

'Well, I don't love you. There are plenty here who do, mind you. That bitch in the Braille shop for one. But not me. Make the most of your time here but count me out.'

We drove back to the office to unload the car. Diane and I did not kiss again although we saw a lot of each other. Looking back, I feel enormously grateful to her. We could so easily have fallen into a sexual relationship of the kind I was not ready for. She knew this but she was such an unselfish and good-hearted person that our friendship continued without any bitterness or embarrassment, which must have been almost unique for a situation of this sort.

I think I was in love with everyone at that time. I was intoxicated with the female company and it was a new experience for me to be welcomed and liked. Wherever I went, especially on my escort duties, someone would say, 'Stop for a cup of coffee, Christopher,' or 'Stay and help me move some furniture,' or 'Don't rush off.'

The 'bitch' in the Braille shop was not a bitch at all. She was a Canadian girl who was considered by the men, obviously on hearsay alone, to be the most beautiful girl at St Dunstans at the time.

She had a lovely oval face with slightly slanting eyes and her complexion was what is described as peach-like, although I have never yet seen a peach which would match her skin in fineness of texture or colour. She wore a green uniform which, unlike most of the uniforms round the place, seemed specially designed to fit her figure. She was as beautiful as any film star and, of course, in those days film stars were the goddesses with which one compared lesser mortals.

She must have let slip a remark to one of the men because I was told gleefully that 'she had a thing about me'. I could scarcely believe this and as soon as the opportunity arose I went up to the bedroom to look at myself in the mirror. My acne wasn't too bad because the sun at the fruit-pickers' camp had burnt my face a dark brown, but there was nothing remotely good-looking about me with my glasses and serious expression. I certainly could not compare with Charles's fair curly hair and blue eyes. I wished I was like him.

I expect any attraction she felt for me was because I was so unusual to her, being 'an English public school type' with the varnish of youth not worn away by the war and other harsh experiences of life. Also I was, as I have said, in love with everyone at that time and when someone is in this state everyone is a bit in love with him too.

Because of her beauty she was, for me, in the unattainable class and after the men had teased me about her I felt anxious whenever I had to escort them to the Braille shop but I could not avoid this. As soon as we got there they would start on me. 'Let's leave those two together. We're not wanted here,' they would say, and I would look at the Canadian girl in a state of delicious embarrassment. Our eyes would meet and we would be the only people in the room who could see. It was like being alone together. 'Go on, give her a kiss,' someone would say, 'we won't look.'

I think she was quite distressed by the whole affair. Of course I wanted to kiss her but all I could do was stand amongst the Braille typewriters and other equipment, looking foolish. I could not find the courage to ask her out. I could tell she was a shy and very sensitive person and together what could we have said or done? Nothing. I had to keep her in a dream world because the light of reality was too dazzling.

So I never really met her and hardly spoke to her until almost the last day I was at St Dunstans when she came to a dance at Brockhurst. Then we did dance together once but I had a bad cold and that, together with my all-purpose shuffle, must have killed off any romance there was. We talked platitudes and I was worried in case my nose dripped over her dress.

It's a funny thing but I cannot remember her name. I see her as an oval face in an oval mirror. There is something symbolic in that. It is like Perseus looking at the reflection in the shield which the goddess Athene gave him. 'Let the shield take the image, the image shield you.'

Those days at St Dunstans should have gone on longer. In six weeks I grew up, but not enough. I was learning all the time.

One evening, not long after my arrival, I was talking to two of the men in the sitting room about happiness. I had been reading a small book by the philosopher Bertrand Russell, whom I admired and had heard lecturing at Cambridge. The book was called *The Conquest of Happiness*, and to illustrate a point I ran up to my bedroom to fetch it and read a passage to them. When I had finished they said, 'Go on' and, forgetting the hesitancy in my speech, I read on until I had finished the chapter. By now some of the others had come into the room and they had a short discussion about what I had been reading while I sat silently listening to them. It was after this that Mrs Irwin, whom I had not noticed sitting by the window, asked me to come to her office.

It is only on rare occasions in life that one is overjoyed by things people say but when she told me how much I meant to the 'boys', and how much they liked me, I could have wept with happiness. For almost the first time in my life I had attained something. I had not been shown or told what to do, I had done it all on my own. It was me, Christopher.

After that I read to some of the men fairly regularly in the evenings after tea. They preferred this to the wireless or the trivial conversation which flitted backwards and forwards, sometimes good-humoured but at other times a cover for boredom or despair.

Mrs Irwin asked me to take special care of one particular man called Iain who had arrived the same day as myself. He was an officer in one of the famous Highland Regiments and was still a part of it. He would often wear a kilt and when he found out that most of the others did not want to talk about the army, or not very often, he used to sit silently in a corner. He had not yet come to believe he was blind. Everyone was worried about him and when he broke silence he was often quarrelsome and rude.

'He needs taking out of himself,' said Mrs Irwin, stating the obvious.

One of the finest tools we had at St Dunstans was the tandem bicycle. Iain did not like going for walks because he was ashamed of his visible dependence on others, but on the back of a tandem nothing was expected of him except that he should do his share of the pedalling. So whenever I had the opportunity I took him for a tandem ride.

Usually we set out in the afternoon. I would describe the countryside as we rode through the lanes but on the hills we were much too out of breath to talk. I made a point of not sparing him or myself, thinking it would do him good to get tired out.

We always stopped somewhere for tea and I would tell him about the other people in the café and any detail which I thought might interest him. The waitresses were kind and usually stopped to chat with us. Sometimes they refused to let us pay. They would call Iain 'dear' and he seemed to accept it from them although if anyone at Brockhurst showed they were sorry for him he became resentful.

He talked a lot about the army and I enjoyed listening to him as well as thinking it would do him good to get it out of his system. Poor Iain! He was a sort of latter-day Picton, the toy soldier of my nursery days at Springwell and about equally in touch with reality. His family had been bound up with the Highland Regiment for generations and he was very knowledgeable about military history – Talavera, Quatre Bras and Waterloo, the 'thin red line' in the Crimea and so on, right up to the surrender of the 51st Highland Division at St Valery a few years previously. He talked about his own fighting experiences but always stopped short before he came to the point where he lost his sight. If he can once tell me about that, I thought, he will be all right. But he never did and I do not know what eventually became of him.

There was another man whom I found more worrying than Iain. He was an RAF officer who had been blinded early in the war and was partly paralysed on one side. He was not a full-time resident at Brockhurst but came twice a year for rehabilitation. I did not have much to do with him and was quite surprised when, one day, he asked me to take him for a walk. I asked Mrs Irwin if it would be all right.

'By all means,' she said, 'but not too far because he gets tired easily.'

We set out soon after lunch. I had by now learnt the art of leading the blind rather than pushing them and we got on pretty well, with him holding my arm with his weaker hand. He seemed to know exactly where he wanted to go, which surprised me, and when I thought it was time to turn back he insisted we should go on.

He said he would like to skirt the hill and get to the other side because, he said in his half teasing way, 'the view's good from there.' It took us a long time but when we finally rounded the crest of the hill I found we were at the edge of a gorge which cut deeply through the countryside. Later I discovered it was a well-known beauty spot but to come across it unawares was a wonderful experience. We sat on the grass and he asked me to tell him exactly what I could see.

I told him about the jutting rocks and how the trees clung to the side of the gorge, about the deep purple heather and patches of gorse. There were storm clouds on the horizon and above a kestrel hovered for several minutes before turning and gliding through the air out of sight. Far below was a group of people following the path along the bottom of the gorge.

'I've been here before,' he said.

'I know that. There's no need for me to describe it all to you then.'

'I like to be reminded about things. Take me near the edge. I want to feel the wind blowing in my face.'

I helped him to his feet and we shuffled over to where the ground fell away steeply to the gorge below. I had a feeling of *déjà vu* and then the scene came back to me in a flash. Blind Gloucester in *King Lear* standing at the edge of the cliff near Dover. I was Edgar the demon or guide who was his means of escape. A pair of jackdaws flew below us, tumbling in the wind, and it was this that made me see it all. 'The crows and choughs that wing the midway air,' Edgar had described them to old blind Gloucester.

I gripped my companion's arm tightly. 'It's time we went,' I said, 'there's a storm blowing up and anyway we will be late for tea.'

I felt his muscles tighten against mine and he took a half step forward. I held him firmly and he seemed to slump so that I had to support him. We stood for a minute with the wind blowing in our faces then made our way back along the side of the hill. Neither of us mentioned that moment which had come and gone and was best forgotten.

We were late for tea and both wet because the storm caught us a few hundred yards from Brockhurst. Mrs Irwin told me to help him up to bed because he was obviously exhausted. When I came downstairs she was angry with me.

'I told you not to take him too far,' she said, 'you should have had more sense.'

'I'm very sorry.'

She questioned me as to exactly where we had been and I wondered if she suspected what had happened. I did not tell her because I was not sure if it was all in my imagination. I was expert at confusing fact and fiction and maybe the chance appearance of the two jackdaws had set a train of thought going through my mind. Or maybe my love of Shakespeare had saved a blind man from injury or death. Saved? I found the matter confusing. Mrs Irwin saw I was upset. To my surprise she gave me a hug and said she would send a tray of tea into the lounge for me.

The matter remained on my conscience and it was natural I should ask Diane for her advice the next time we did our fetching and carrying in the Morris. She thought for a minute then said, 'Leave well alone. That's my opinion. If the poor sod wants to do himself in that's his affair. Better luck next time.'

'Shouldn't I tell Mrs Irwin?'

'God, no. Mention it to her and she'll get all righteous about it. Duty and conscience and all that. He'll have to fight off hordes of psychiatrists and finish up being locked up somewhere.'

As always Diane was right. The RAF officer seemed his normal self next day.

'Mind you,' he said at breakfast, 'Christopher half killed me. Never go for a walk with him. He'll take you miles.' I let it go at that.

Many years later I heard, quite by chance, that he had married and was doing well in a career in industry.

The time at St Dunstans came to an end. On the last day we had sports. I was given the job of helping with the racing. These were hundred-yard sprints. The men had to run individually and were timed with a stop-watch because if they ran together they would obviously bump into each other. Charles stood at one end of the field and clanged a bell and the men ran towards the sound. I positioned myself half-way and ran with them to the finishing line, guiding them by voice and catching them if they went too far. There was a lot of enthusiasm and the winner was so fast I had a job keeping up with him in spite of my being able to see. He nearly finished in the bushes.

It was after the sports that I said goodbye to Diane.

'Shall we write to each other?' I asked.

'No. I'm not a writing sort of person.'

'But I don't want never to see you again.'

'That doesn't sound very grammatical.'

'You know what I mean.'

There was no more to be said. I kissed her on the cheek, because others were watching, and whispered, 'Thank you.' As the Morris disappeared down the drive I saw a hand raised momentarily in farewell and a feeling of dereliction came over me. There were few people in my life to whom I have owed more gratitude. She had been my teacher and if only I had remembered more of the lessons she had taught me I would have saved myself a lot of wear and tear in the years to come.

Sadly I lost touch with all my blind friends. Six weeks is such a short time and I do not suppose they would even remember me now. I remember them but that's fair because I, not they, was the gainer.

I exchanged Christmas cards with Mrs Irwin for, I think, a couple of years and that was the end of it all.

My last memory of St Dunstans was leaving Brockhurst on the back of Charles's motor-bike. I was waving goodbye until we were out of sight knowing that few of those I was waving at could see me.

X

In Wonderland
1944–5

After leaving St Dunstans I spent two weeks at the Mary Ward
Settlement in London, then a week later I was back in Cambridge for
my bonus of an extra year. I was determined not to do very much work
and I mentioned this to Tom when he arrived uninvited to tea the day
after my return. I now had rooms overlooking the river. The water
lapped against the stonework a few yards beneath the window and,
when I had nothing better to do, I could watch the shadow-like fish
lying motionless, apart from their gently moving tails. We sat on the
window seat, looking across the lawns towards the Fellows' Garden.

'That's forbidden territory,' I remarked to Tom, who came from
another lesser college a short way down the street. 'It's where the dons
walk round thinking great thoughts.'

'Nonsense. They probably go there to spend their pennies behind
the trees when they can't make it back to the college. Most of them are
senile enough to have trouble that way. So you've decided not to work?
Good for you. Let's have a pact. I won't either.'

'You never do.'

'I know that, but sometimes the odd bit of work slips through
without my realising. I'll have to clamp down on it ruthlessly. How
did you get on after the fruit-picking fiasco? I suppose you've forgotten all about that poor ravished girl?'

Kate. Yes, it was true. I had almost forgotten her. I remembered
her now and did not want to talk about it.

'The whole affair was stupid,' I said, and I went on to tell him about
St Dunstans.

'That Diane sounds interesting,' he commented, 'you missed your
chance there. But I forget, that's not your way of doing things.'

'It wasn't her way either. Nor is it yours.'

'I'll let that allegation pass.'

It seemed impossible to get my feelings about St Dunstans across to

Tom but I thought I might as well try. I wanted to tell someone.

'It wasn't just Diane I was in love with. It was everybody.'

'That's nonsense. If you say "everybody" in that tone of voice what you really mean is nobody. Let's extend our pact. We'll get ourselves a couple of nice girls and do things properly. Eh?'

'That sounds a bit calculating.'

'It is. Love, as you would call it, needs working out like any other equation. $L + M \times F = S$.'

'I know what M and F are but what's S?'

'Ah.'

We lapsed into silence, then Tom said, 'At any rate the war will soon be over.'

'Why do you say that?'

'I suppose I'm wondering what peace will be like. It's odd isn't it? We were children when it started and now we are sort of grown-up. I know we haven't been that much involved but we are sort of scarred by it all.'

'I don't think we are "sort of" anything.'

'Exactly. We're a missing generation, neither one thing nor the other.' We watched a punt party trying to negotiate the bridge and making a hopeless mess of it, a couple of soldiers on leave with their girlfriends by the look of it. The one with the punt pole had little idea of what he was doing. The other was necking ferociously with his girl and he obviously did know what he was doing.

'Peaceful spot this,' said Tom and *sotto voce* he quoted a little verse that was doing the rounds at that time:

A boy and girl went boating
A-sitting in the stern
And she was holding his'n
And he was holding her'n.

The punt went straight into the bank and there was a lot of giggling. I closed the windows with a slight feeling of disgust. 'It's getting chilly,' I said.

Tom laughed. 'To get back to the burning question of sex, we've got to do something about it. Have you any contacts?'

'I know a judge's daughter at Girton.'

'Sounds promising. She's probably a nymphomaniac.'

'And there are some girls in the psychology class. I called in to look at the list this afternoon.'

'Well . . . yes. I doubt if we would have a jolly time with that lot.

I'll see what I can do and we'll compare notes.'

Tom left soon after that and I was glad to see him go. His conversation had struck the wrong note. I had no wish to go hunting with Tom like a couple of greyhounds coursing a hare. What I was going to do I would do on my own. I needed someone to love and someone who would love me. I was nearly twenty and I had never had a girlfriend, sweetheart, inamorata or whatever expression one used. A few dreams – that was almost the sum total of my experience apart from the short episode with Diane which had been an unequal sort of relationship. I wondered if Tom was any more knowledgeable than me. Probably not, although he pretended to be.

So I sat musing. Then I put a record on the gramophone and sat looking across the gardens as the sun set and the room became darker. A face was forming in the gloom but I could not see it clearly. It was compounded of faces I had seen in the past built up from memories, almost like a police identikit. Barbara Allen's smile, Miss Brownlees's common sense, Miss Wilmott's sulky sensuality, Kate's simplicity, Diane's good humour, the Canadian girl's slanting eyes, even a touch of childhood remembrance of mother and Eidy as they then were, many other faces too. Somehow they seemed to fuse together but the essence was missing. An identikit picture is never more than a framework.

I went to the window again and opened it. The river was now dark, with the lights from the college reflected on the surface, moving to and fro with the water. The sun was just strong enough to throw long shadows across the lawns and touch the top of the trees along the river bank with its dying light. The trees were dying too, some in half-leaf like ragged garments, others fully clothed but I knew the leaves were shrivelling and going brown. An infinite sadness came over me, not dereliction but a welcome sadness, a sense both of loss and comfort. Soon, I thought, I will find what I am looking for.

Tom was right of course. We had to find girlfriends. My psychology class was fruitless in this respect. We were a mixed bunch and included, amongst others, a gentle Turkish doctor of philosophy, a good-hearted Presbyterian minister, an actress, a Polish squadron leader and, when his other duties permitted, a Roman Catholic priest. Conversation amongst ourselves was complicated but sometimes interesting when the various lines of approach happened to meet over an issue. Then everyone started to get cross. But on the whole we got on well although we struggled with the course whose object seemed to be to convert human beings into statistical phenomena. The only occasion I can remember actually meeting a living person as an object of study was when I was required to do intelligence tests on three local schoolgirls. They giggled and I felt embarrassed. I got so angry with one of them that I managed to give her an IQ of 88 and I hope this did not ruin her future career.

There were four girls in our class but all were already attached in one way or another. The only one whose face came near to my dream was married. She had a madonna-like beauty but I could sense a hidden turmoil behind the face and this proved to be true so it was lucky that my instinct, as well as my strict moral standards, prevented me from becoming fond of her. 'Fond' is perhaps not the right word because, in our little group, we were all fond of each other in spite of our differences in outlook.

So it was Janet, the judge's daughter, or nothing. We suffered the great disadvantage of knowing that our respective parents were old friends and I had, in fact, been asked by mother to 'look her up', which is about the worst start to a relationship that could be imagined. It took my mind back to the tennis parties when I was a child and used to glower at other children under the parental gaze.

It was said of Girton girls that they were easily identified by their powerful calf muscles because they seemed to spend most of their time bicycling to and from Cambridge with long scarves trailing dangerously against the back wheel. Janet was an exception, being definitely petite. I invited her to tea in my rooms, where we did not know what to say to one another, and it was a relief when she got up to go. In return I was asked to Girton one Sunday afternoon. She wisely arranged for a couple of her friends to join us, otherwise we would probably have sat in silence, or had a re-run of our previous conversation for what it was worth. Being on my own with three girls made me at once tongue-tied and I could see by the glances passing between them that they realised they were in for a sticky time.

Fortunately Janet produced one of those lengthy quizzes beloved by Sunday newspapers and we all became so absorbed in this that I forgot about them being women. When we had more or less finished the quiz we drifted into a discussion about Jane Austen and because we were all four 'Janeites' there was no further problem with maintaining the conversation. I have never worked out why Jane Austen, like bird-watching or stamp-collecting, acts as an enzyme between like-minded people in a way that no other author, apart from Shakespeare, is able to do. I have a theory that what she *doesn't* say is her chief attraction.

Janet's two friends eventually looked at each other and decided they had to do some studying, so Janet and I were left together in the pleasant aura of tea and conversation. We talked of this and that and sat looking at the fire in easy silence. The magic began to work. She and the others had earlier mentioned a dance which was being held in aid of something or other, and I cannot remember if I invited her or she invited me. Whichever way it was the invitation was made and accepted and I cycled back to Cambridge in the warm glow of tea and cakes, Jane Austen and intellectual chat, by the fire, in the intimacy of a girl's room in college.

The dance was nothing special. It wasn't a formal dance and it wasn't a hop, somewhere between the two. Some people dressed casually and others were in full evening dress. We were dressed casually because there seemed no practical way for Janet to get back to Girton except on her bicycle.

I invited her to dinner beforehand and, because it was the first time I had ever taken a girl out, I was worried sick. What would we talk about? How much should I tip the waiter? Would she mind me not being a very good dancer? What would happen if it rained? In fact anything that it was possible to worry about I worried about. I had worked out the exact route to the restaurant and inspected it as closely as if I was planning an armed robbery. I also had in my top pocket a list of fifteen conversation pieces for use as a reserve. It was ambitious to take Janet out on my own but Tom had already broken our pact and was very much involved with a Newnham girl and I could think of no one else to make up a foursome.

Janet seemed nearly as nervous as I was – or maybe I made her jumpy – but she was a pleasant kind-hearted girl and tried to help.

'We'll have a lovely time,' she said, 'I know several people who are going so there'll be someone to talk to if we don't feel like dancing.'

This made matters worse because I hated meeting people I didn't know, and if she knew them already it would be worse still. 'This is Christopher,' she would say, and that would be the end of it as far as I was concerned. All the confidence I had gained at the fruit-picking camp and St Dunstans had slipped away from me and I was almost back to the Miss Davenport era. I knew it was going to be a disastrous evening.

The dinner turned out better than I hoped. My companion was pleased to be taken out and that evening she was bright-eyed and pretty. By chance some undergraduates I knew were having a bachelor meal at the next table and the occasional envious glances they cast in our direction made me feel important. My confidence came back and I found I was beginning to enjoy myself and forgot all about the list of fifteen conversation topics in my pocket.

Janet took me by the arm as we walked through the market square to the dance hall. Our talk by now came easily and when we were on the dance floor I found she was so light on her feet that she neutralised my clumsiness like a skilled matador well able to handle a not very intelligent bull. She would just skip to one side and avoid trouble. Dances at that time consisted basically of quickstep, foxtrot and waltz, with occasional exotica such as the tango or Gay Gordons. My all-purpose shuffle was based on the quickstep with variations which often took my partners by surprise. It was a funny thing because I was an agile person, especially on the rugger field, but on the dance floor I lost all co-ordination. I was also unable to communicate, to use a modern term, and if I decided to turn right my partner would have the impression that I was going to turn left. I often cursed the tradition that boy-meets-girl episodes in those days involved going to dances – or the back seat of the cinema – but at least the music was soft and it was possible to talk with one's partner.

There were not many couples dancing so we decided to go to the bar and joined the back of the queue. In front of us was a burly young man with sandy hair in a dress suit, and next to him his partner, a slender girl in a long white dress. Her hair was nut brown in colour and cut rather short showing a thin gold chain round her neck.

Janet nudged me. 'That's Alice,' she said and touched her on the shoulder. The girl turned towards us and when I saw her face I fell completely, overwhelmingly and, as it turned out, disastrously in love with her. It was as simple as that.

'This is Christopher,' Janet was saying, and we shook hands politely. Then, equally politely, the girl introduced her partner whose name was Charles. It was a relief to talk with him while the other two chatted together. They were obviously good friends. I listened to what Charles was saying but I felt as if I was coming round from an anaesthetic. His face was blurred. When he had worked our way to the bar he said to me, 'Look, I've had enough dancing. Let's bag that empty table and make a foursome of it.'

'I feel just the same,' I muttered, trying not to show by the tremor in my voice how I really felt. He must have thought I was an odd person. It was thus that a few minutes later I was sitting opposite the girl whom I had already decided I would love forever.

How can one explain what had happened and why? Of course it's impossible and only those who have experienced the same thing will understand the extremity of emotion which had taken me over. It would be nice, and it would fit in with the theme of this book very well, if I could say the face I was looking at was the compound face of my dreams, but this would not be true. It was the face of Alice. There was no part of any other person in her and all those other faces were quickly forgotten. Later I remembered them.

And how can I describe what she looked like? Again this is an impossible task but at least I still have a photograph of her so what I put down is not an image blurred with nostalgia, but the truth.

Her face was beautiful, the most beautiful face I had ever seen. Nothing else about her mattered very much. Her hair was swept back behind her ears and rightly so because, although lovely in colour, it was an intrusion. She bore a resemblance – and, as I have said before, in those days film stars were our yardsticks of feminine beauty – to Ingrid Bergman, but she was not Ingrid Bergman. Her lips were fuller, her expression sadder, her eyes touched with green, her eyebrows so finely chiselled that they looked sculptured. I am talking of her as a work of art. She was not, she was an ordinary person. And this was the one blemish of her beauty although to me it was a delight. She had not the slightest conception that she was even good-looking and when I knew her better and said the usual things that those in love say she would look at me with smiling disbelief.

Apart from her face nothing mattered. She was tall, about my own height, and slender. Her figure was not striking and she had a very slight stoop which became noticeable when she was tired. Nor were her movements particularly graceful. She was at her best sitting quietly and that is how I remember her.

My reaction that evening in the dance hall was extraordinary. Because I could not say much to Alice I tried to flirt with Janet in the strange desperate hope that something of it would be deflected from her to the girl who sat opposite me and whose gaze rested on me thoughtfully from time to time.

We drank quite a lot but Alice had one glass of sherry, then stuck to orange juice. Janet put down several gins and became talkative. We other two drank beer and it developed into what one would call a good party, although I was conscious that only a bit of me was involved. Part of the conversation I can remember word for word.

'What's it like being a judge's daughter, Janet?' I asked. 'Are people frightened of you?'

'It's a position of respect and don't you forget it. You needn't actually bow each time you speak to me but I want you to bow in spirit.'

'You make it sound like a preservative,' said Charles, 'peaches in wine.' Janet was puzzled and I came to her rescue.

'You said "bow in spirit". I don't want to spend the rest of my life in a bottle with my back bent at right angles.'

'That's just how it's going to be. I'll keep you on the mantelpiece.'

She started giggling and I said, 'I know my father's only a clergyman but it does seem rather extreme to me.' I noticed Alice glance at me quickly and it was an opportunity for me to speak to her.

'What does your father do?'

'He was a clergyman, too, but he died five years ago.'

'I'm sorry.'

'I live with mother now.'

She smiled at me charmingly and was going to say more but Janet took the conversation away from us. She pointed a finger at me and said, 'I would take you down from the mantelpiece once a week to dust you.'

'I know, and one day you would drop the bottle and that would be the end of me. Shattered glass on the floor, swept up and put in the dustbin.'

'I might try to stick you together again.'

'Like Humpty-Dumpty,' said Charles, 'all the king's horses and all the king's men.'

'But,' said Alice gently, 'they weren't very successful in their attempt, if you remember.'

It was the first general remark she had made for some time and I looked at her face which was half turned from me and said, 'Perhaps they didn't try very hard.' She smiled. 'None the less I think Humpty-Dumpty would have done better not to have climbed on the wall in the first place.'

Janet was laughing over a secret joke. 'I'm thinking of those poor horses,' she said. 'How the hell can they stick things together with *hoofs*? Terribly difficult. Have you ever tried fixing something with a hoof?' I noticed a flicker in Alice's eyes. She did not like Janet swearing.

Charles said, 'I haven't got a hoof so how could I try?'

'Ask Christopher. He's got two, one on each foot.'

Obviously Janet was referring to my dancing and I couldn't help feeling upset. It was a sensitive point with me. This must have shown on my face because there was an awkward pause. I saw Alice look at Charles. He stood up and asked Janet if she would like a dance. She jumped up with alacrity and they whirled away amongst the other couples.

I was alone with Alice. I felt her eyes on me but I could not look at her. The feeling of unreality came over me again and with difficulty I managed to say, 'Janet's a very good dancer.'

'Have you known her long?'

'We sort of met when we were children. That was a long time ago. We've only just met again.'

'Would you like to ask me for a dance?'

I looked up. Her expression was solemn but there was a touch of mirth about her lips. She was trying not to tease me.

'Hoofs and all?'

'You couldn't be a worse dancer than me. We can tread on each other's toes as much as we like.'

We stood up. I was afraid to touch her. She was so lovely. So we held each other awkwardly and it was true that, like me, she was not a very good dancer. We tripped over each other's feet and I said, 'Sorry.'

'Don't say that.'

I gazed at the profile of her face as she watched the other couples over my shoulder. Then she glanced at me and smiled.

'Left or right?' she asked.

'Left this time.'

'Janet was exaggerating, you know.'

'No hoofs?'

'No.'

'Me Big Foot. Me Indian chief,' I said, trying to be funny.

'Me Nokomis. Daughter of the moon Nokomis,' she replied and her words were a fragile echo from the past.

The subject of hoofs led to the subject of horses and I found myself telling her about the shire horses in Devon and how they stood under the trees in the evening, facing towards each other as if in conversation.

'Maybe they were,' said Alice.

I asked her about herself and she told me she was not in the 'proper university' but was a student from one of the several colleges evacuated from London to Cambridge for the war.

'Very convenient too. It's my home town so I live with mother.'

'Do you like that?'

'Of course I do.'

'I don't think I would like to live at home all the time.'

'Why not?'

'One outgrows it I suppose.'

Remembering that evening is like remembering the sea or a forest of tall trees. Apart from this conversation there were no landmarks, just as each wave and each tree is much the same as the next. It is the general awareness of beauty that I remember. At first I could not look Alice in the face. Later I could not look away. It was like trying not to look at the wallpaper witch in my bedroom at Springwell, except that there was nothing of a witch about Alice. Apart from her having cast a spell over me. She was friendly and humorous and even if I had not been in love with her I would have loved being with her.

The dance ended at about eleven and the four of us stood outside wondering what to do next. I could not invite them to the college because having girls in your rooms was a mortal sin. I think Alice would have liked to ask us back to her house but it was late and I don't suppose her mother would have appreciated our slightly alcoholic state. So Charles said he would take Alice home and I offered to escort Janet back to Girton which seemed the correct and gentlemanly thing to do.

I liked Janet immensely but when the moon is shining the stars become invisible and I scarcely listened to her friendly chatter as we cycled down the long straight road to Girton. When we drew near to the college entrance she asked me what I thought of Charles and Alice.

'I liked them very much.'

'They're a nice couple aren't they?'

Couple. Charles and Alice were a couple. Janet had said that deliberately. I knew they weren't engaged because Alice did not wear a ring, but was I being warned off? Humpty-Dumpty sat on a wall.

Next morning I woke late. Sunshine was pouring into the room and I sat on the window seat to eat my breakfast. I had never seen the lawns and trees in such splendour. Even the slow moving Cam gave the impression of tumbling like a mountain stream. In a moment of madness I consumed almost my entire butter ration on two pieces of toast and finished the tin of Australian marmalade which I had got with the points from my ration book.

The fact that I did not know Alice's surname or where she lived did not bother me nor, at that moment, did the existence of the likeable Charles. At that time of my life I had no definite beliefs but, having saturated myself in the novels of Thomas Hardy, I understood there was a thing called Destiny. The President of the Immortals, if he existed, was a callous being and I could not ask him for help even if I had wanted to, but I knew I was destined to meet Alice again very soon. Whether Destiny would be kind-hearted or take a swipe at me did not matter. My love for Alice was so immense that nothing else was very significant.

The only tiny cloud, an inconvenience rather than a coming deluge, was the unfortunate fact that I had allowed myself to be caught climbing into the college the night before. Climbing in was not permitted, although nearly everyone did it because it was less trouble than seeking a special pass to stay out late. Usually we would climb the wrought iron gates at the back of the college – looking in our gowns like bats against the night sky – but on this occasion I was so full of inexpressible feelings that I had taken the direct route over the gate by the chapel and one of the porters had seen me. I had managed to dodge him by darting into the bicycle shed but I heard him call, 'I know who you are, sir.' He would probably report me and the punishment was usually to be gated for a week, that is to say one was not permitted to leave the college in the evening. It would make it that much more difficult for me to meet Alice.

In the afternoon I had to play in a rugger match and I remembered little of the game. It was as if I had been concussed in the opening minutes. It was getting dark as I came in through the college gates and one of the porters called after me. Here we go, I thought, but he did not mention the escapade of the night before, and in fact I never did get into trouble over it.

'A young lady left you this note.' He handed me a blue envelope. I dropped my rugger boots with a clatter on the paving stones and as I bent down to pick them up I knew the letter was from Alice. I took it back to my rooms before opening it with trembling fingers.

It was from Janet, thanking me for a lovely evening and would I come round next Wednesday, after dinner, because they were going to have a party? Also would I bring a friend if possible? I was terribly disappointed and did not want to go because Alice was the last person I would expect to meet there and besides I had no wish to double-deal Janet because I liked her very much. But she was my only contact with Alice and if that was what Destiny decreed . . . I asked Tom if he would like to come and to my surprise he said he would. His Newnham affair had gone into the doldrums quite suddenly and he was on the hunting-in-a-pair-theme again. I did not disillusion him.

Destiny decided I was worth the odd favour. As Tom and I pushed open the door of Janet's room at Girton the following Wednesday, the first person I saw was Alice. She was sitting alone and seemed at a loss because she did not know many of the others. When she saw me she was pleased and smiled. I sat by her and for me, that evening, there was no one else in the room. Her beauty and her closeness overwhelmed me. I tried to conceal this because a lovesick young man is nobody's favourite, also my conscience pricked me over Janet. Then it struck me that she had invited both Alice and me because she *knew*. It did not matter much anyway but I was glad to see that she and Tom got on well together and when, after the party, she said goodnight to me, there was no coldness in her expression. She seemed amused.

Those of us who had to go back to Cambridge, and this included Tom, collected our cycles. There was room to ride two abreast and I had to be beside Alice. One of the other men had the same idea. She started a little ahead of us and I deliberately forced his bicycle into the middle of the road. I had no choice. I can remember that moment so well. His bike veering away into the darkness and the surprise on his face as he hung desperately on to the wobbling handlebars. Alice looked at me in her strange half-humorous way as I drew up alongside her and the dimmed headlights of an approaching car reflected for a moment in her eyes.

This was the first time we had been alone together. My chance had come. I had to commit myself because I loved her so much. The words stuck. I could not bring myself to say anything. The two circles of light from the beams of our bicycle lamps bobbed about on the road ahead of us. Sometimes they touched, sometimes they parted and still I said nothing.

Alice seemed content with the silence. We were drawing near Cambridge when, in desperation, I blurted out, 'You know Charles.'

'Yes,' she said, looking straight ahead.

'Well, you've got to tell me. You and him. I want to ask you out, you see.' Suddenly I felt like cycling madly away leaving Alice and everything else behind. She turned her face towards me. She was laughing.

'You know *you*,' she said.

'Yes.'

'Well, I wouldn't mind at all you asking me out.' There was so much warmth in her voice and my relief was so great that once again I was robbed of the power of speech. Alice was obviously perplexed.

'Aren't you going to invite me then?' she said at last.

'Of course I am.'

'I thought you had changed your mind already.'

'No.'

'It would have been a bit quick.' She was teasing me.

The plan I had in mind was to invite her to the medical students' dance, generally known by the odd name The Med Sock Ball. I had already bought tickets because – and it seemed a long time ago – this had been part of the grand strategy Tom and I had thought up to catch our imaginary girls during the hunting-in-a-pair phase. It was to have been a bait but now it seemed out of place, like dangling a piece of bread on a bent pin in front of a leaping salmon. I said in a jumble of words, 'I was going to ask you to the Med Sock Ball but what I really want is for you to come and have tea in my rooms.'

Alice thought about this.

'Couldn't we do both?'

'I suppose so.'

She was still puzzled and allowed her bike to free-wheel while she considered the matter. By now we were in the town and our privacy had gone. The others were close behind us. She said, 'I'll have to turn off at the next crossroads. I'm sorry, I didn't mean to invite myself like that. I just didn't understand. Tea in your rooms sounds a lovely idea.'

While we slowed the other bicycles caught us up and surged round us. All I had time to say was, 'Next Friday at about four?' She nodded and a few seconds later swung away down a side road raising a hand in farewell. I had made a fool of myself but at least I was going to see her again. Tom was beside me.

'You certainly specialise in bicycle romances,' he said.

'Do I?'

'You were a bit rough on that poor bloke behind us. Nearly knocked him flying.'

'I didn't notice.'

'Is this serious?'

'Yes.'

'Well, in that case I will try to curb my native wit. She's certainly a bonny lass,' which were about the last words I would have used to describe Alice.

'Janet's not too bad either,' he added as an afterthought.

That was how it started. By cutting a lecture and joining a queue I was able to procure a cherry cake from Fitzbillies, the tiny shop opposite the museum and for tea we sat and ate this delicacy in front of the fire. It was a cold, damp day so we could not, as I had planned, sit on the window seat and look at the beauty of the river and college grounds. It was Alice's beauty I looked at and for the first time in my life dream and reality came near to being the same thing. Alice was there and I was no longer alone. So we sat and munched the cherry cake and when we had eaten half we decided it wasn't worth keeping the rest so we ate it all. We cleared up the confusion about the Med Sock Ball.

'I was terribly embarrassed about it all,' said Alice. 'I thought you had invited Janet already and I had put my big foot in it.'

I did not tell her how close I had been to asking Janet. Shyness had prevented me. So I made no comment and Alice said, 'Mother would like you to come to our house first and have a drink.'

'I'm being vetted?'

'Oh, definitely.'

'Are the standards very high?'

'Very high indeed.' She was laughing but I felt an undertone of seriousness.

'What's the pass mark?'

'Ten out of ten of course. I suppose you've got about five points already. Let's see. Three for a clergyman's son, three for a medical student, minus one for being a psychologist.'

'I'm not a psychologist. I'm only doing it because I wasn't allowed to do history.'

'Pity. History would have been an extra point.'

'I bet your mother goes about thinking "Freud is not respectable", but that isn't the sort of psychology I'm doing.'

'I thought psychology *was* Freud nowadays.'

'He's a dirty word in our department.'

I tried to explain what we did, but it sounded dreadfully uninteresting. Statistics, time and motion study, the behaviour of rats in mazes – although we never actually saw a rat in a maze – trying to measure things that couldn't be measured, like cleverness, beauty and happiness. The only aspect of the work I found exciting was a project which was meant to be Highly Secret and I should not have told Alice the details of it but, to impress her, I did. It was connected with wartime bombing, the idea being that a pathfinder bomber would drop flares as accurately as possible over the target and the following aircraft would aim for the middle of the group of flares. Fine, but what was the middle? If there were five flares close together and another at a distance, should the outer one be counted? I was flattered that I, a student, had been asked to collect 'guinea pigs' and show them cards marked with arrangements of black circles in various patterns so they could mark what they considered to be the centre on tracing paper. I had already asked most of the undergraduates I knew and still had a long way to go so I suggested to Alice that she might do it for me. Our heads were close together as we examined the cards and in the middle of the experiment I became acutely aware of her and my voice faltered. Alice coloured up and pressed the marker hard on the tracing paper so that it tore slightly. I wanted to kiss her but she turned her head away.

That particular set of cards caused speculation in the department because the results were considered inconsistent. I explained to the professor that it had been done by a female whereas all but a few of the others had been done by males and this led to speculation as to whether women perceive patterns in a different way from men. There was some talk of following the matter up but it came to nothing.

'I expect,' the professor commented, 'no. 39 lost concentration. We will have to include it for statistical purposes. It shouldn't affect the overall result.'

So that was my positive and Alice's negative contribution to the war effort.

My memories of the Med Sock Ball are confused. I collected Alice from her mother's house and stayed for the vetting and a glass of sherry. Alice was wearing the long white dress she had worn the first time I met her but the sleeves had been altered and she had about her waist and over her shoulder a chiffon sash. She looked lovely and I said so spontaneously. Her mother had done the alterations and was obviously pleased. This must have counted for an extra mark or two. My dress suit, handed down from Michael, was shabby and I had touched up the lapels with Indian Ink the night before.

I liked her mother. She resembled my own mother in some ways but was rather more severe. This was because, as I found out later, she had suffered a lot. She seemed to quite like me although I was too shy to say much. As we left the house I asked Alice what my score was. She reckoned it was about eight out of ten with some room for improvement. She spoke lightly but I had a slight feeling of unease.

We did not go to the dance in a party so mostly we were alone together as indeed two people can be alone in a crowded room and this is how I wanted it. Tom had invited Janet, having remarked to me that he wasn't going to make a habit of picking up my rejects. I could see he was really very attracted to her. When we met on the dance floor Janet said, 'Wheels turn fast,' but she gave Alice an affectionate kiss and Tom put his tongue out at me. We had supper together.

The quicksteps and foxtrots followed one after the other and sometimes we danced and sometimes we sat and watched the others. We
did not talk much. Some of my happiness was pride. Alice was, I
thought, the loveliest woman there and I wanted everyone to know she
was mine. I have an odd little memory of meeting one of our
department lecturers in the mens' toilet and he told me what a lucky
chap I was. He added, 'The professor is very pleased with your work on
Pathfinders.' My cup was full. Humpty-Dumpty had climbed on the
wall.

The last waltz came with unexpected suddeness and after Alice had
collected her wrap we walked slowly back to her house, our arms
round each other's waists. Alice's eyes were bright and, for the second
time in my life, the stars were tipped with steel. We kissed in the
porch of the house and it was with surprised joy that I sensed that this
was her first love affair. Our lips touched tentatively at first and then it
was of such rare beauty that I kept on thinking to myself, 'This cannot
be happening to me.' I could have gone on kissing and talking quietly
all night but Alice pushed me gently away and hunted in her evening
bag for the latch key. I was a little disappointed but she threw her arms
round my neck and gave me a final kiss – then she was gone. That kiss
lingered as I walked slowly through the streets of Cambridge.

I did not want to return to the college straight away so I took a long
circuitous route back. Human behaviour is inexplicable. I had a
strong desire to see Dalberg, my childhood home, which was so far
removed from my university life that if I happened to pass that way I
did not bother to recognise it. That night I stood in the fens by the
stream where I had fished for sticklebacks and newts as a boy and
looked at the ugly building against the night sky and I thought of the
Japanese Garden, Eidy, mother and the fat merchant from the East
with his thin wife hiding in the wardrobe. Life had come full circle.

For the next nine months or so this first love affair dominated my
life in a way that first love affairs do, bringing me great happiness and
great unhappiness.

The undercurrent of unhappiness started, I suppose, the day after
the dance when I phoned Alice at lunch time.

'Can I see you this evening?' I said.

'I think that's a bit soon. Mother says will you come and have dinner
next Friday?'

I was bitterly disappointed. Was that all? Love is not love that
knows any bounds.

'Have I got to knock up a few more points?'

'I think that's a horrid thing to say.'

'But I want to see you today.'

There was a pause at the other end of the line.

'No, Friday will be better.'

That, I think, was more or less the end of the conversation. I was plunged from the heights to the depths and when Tom called round to see me later that day I told him about it, feeling as soon as I had said it a great sense of disloyalty to Alice. Tom was not very helpful. He, too, was suffering from an emotional hangover and sat at the window smoking cigarettes and throwing them, half finished, into the river where they floated away sodden and obscene. He made various lugubrious remarks and finally admitted he thought he was going to fall in love with Janet.

'Hell and damnation. A judge's daughter.' I found this amusing. 'Her dad can always help you out if you get into a scrape.'

'It's not funny. You and I are in dead trouble. Do you realise that? Love is nothing but trouble.' I remembered how carefree he had been when he knocked Celia flying at the fruit-picking camp and wondered if he was right.

I could not settle to anything that week and when Friday came I was torn between a longing to see Alice and a sense of foreboding. I need not have worried. Alice, I think, felt some remorse and she was pathetically anxious that her mother and I should like each other. She was shy in her mother's presence and at first the conversation was stilted but when her mother realised how genuine my feelings were, I think she awarded me the extra two marks bringing the score to ten out of ten. Then we relaxed and chatted and I smiled at Alice and she smiled back. When at last I said it was time I went her mother asked me to come again and tactfully left Alice to show me to the door. We kissed goodnight in the hall.

'When do we meet again?' I asked.

'A week today.'

'Why not tomorrow?'

'Christopher,' she said, 'you will have to bear with me. It's not that I don't want to see you sooner but we mustn't rush things.'

'But I want to see you every day. I want to rush things.'

'You don't understand.'

'All right. I'll be tied up with lectures in the morning. Shall I come round after lunch and we'll decide what to do?' She stood in the porch and watched me cycling down the short driveway.

There are only a few occasions, I think, in everyone's life when joy takes over completely and those few occasions are not usually associated with love between a man and a woman. I have described one such an occasion already. Another, I can remember, was when I was lying in bed one morning and heard a bird calling from the garden. There was nothing special about the day or the occasion but I had a feeling of immense delight in the world. The older one gets the less this happens because it is really a child's joy in being alive and it is a long time now since it has happened to me. But that afternoon, at Alice's house, it did happen.

We were sitting on the floor, looking at magazines and playing the gramophone, putting on records at random. Outside there was a drenching rain so we could not go anywhere and Alice's mother was out for the afternoon. Then it came about.

Alice had put on a record – and it is so vivid to me that I must describe it in detail – which I at once recognised as Beethoven's Seventh Symphony. Very quiet and expectant to start with, it leads at last to music of supreme beauty. We were both sitting on the floor with our magazines and, as the music started, I looked at Alice and she looked at me. We sat there and the rain beat against the window-pane. Inside the room the music went on and on until, and this is how Beethoven wrote it, it came almost to a stop, with single repeated notes like the call of a bird. The bird ceased its calling and the music came flooding in with joy, sorrow, laughter, tears and everything else. Alice and I sat looking at each other. I forgot even the music. I watched Alice's face, and all kinds of other images came and went. It became a dream. The world was unreal and Alice and myself and something indefinable were the true reality. It seemed that this strange actuality would go on forever but gradually I became aware of a faint grating noise. It was the needle of the old 78 record going backwards and forwards, backwards and forwards, in its groove.

We continued to sit on the floor and after a while I told Alice that I loved her and that I wanted to marry her. She looked at me and said nothing. I told her that nothing else in the world mattered to me and never would and still she said nothing. We did not touch hands and we did not kiss. The grating of the record became louder as the wooden needle wore down. Alice got up slowly and lifted the arm of the gramophone so the noise stopped. She went to the window and knelt on the sill, looking out on the rain-drenched laurel bushes. Over her shoulder she said, 'It's too soon, Christopher.'

'But sometime?'

'I don't know. I can't explain.'

I was silent, not wanting the moment to slide away into nothing. Alice was silent too. Then she turned, climbed down from the window sill and knelt in front of me. She put her hands on either side of my face and looked straight into my eyes. There was no kiss. Nothing but the touch of her fingers on my cheeks.

'You had better go, Christopher.'

And I went. Through the pouring rain I bicycled back to the college where I sat in my room alone for a long, long time.

It was thus that I proposed marriage and was not accepted. And it was thus that my love for Alice, and I think her love for me, reached its climax and was never the same again because it could not be sustained. Alice was right. It had been too soon.

Every week, more or less, we met. Sometimes we went to concerts together but we both made sure one particular piece of music was not played. Often we walked to Granchester along the river. We never talked a lot because we both liked solitude. It was enough to speak occasionally. At Granchester we would have tea, sitting out of doors looking across the fields towards the Cam as it wound its way from Byron's pool and Trumpington Mill. Sometimes, if we had enough money, we would hire a punt and Alice would lie looking at the colleges as we passed under one bridge after another and under the willow trees. I did not go to her house often. I felt a little ill at ease with her mother and also with Joy, her sister, who was often there. She was almost as shy of me as I was of her and on one occasion when we were left alone in the sitting room we sat in complete silence. I suppose I really wanted Alice to belong to me, not them. So it was easier when she came to my college rooms. There we could talk or listen to my small collection of gramophone records. Sometimes we were content to read books. I loved to watch Alice with a book. Her lips would be pursed in concentration and when she realised I was looking at her she would glance up with a smile.

So it went on. In the vacation we would write to each other once a week. I would take her letter to the solitude of my room and delay opening it for a long time because I knew in my heart I would be disappointed. Her handwriting was thin and rather untidy and she put down what she had been doing in a factual way as if she was writing about someone else. I could not love her writing as I had once loved the sensual curves of another woman's hand and her letters didn't bring her close to me as they should have done. Because she was so kind and uncomplicated there was no spark to leap between us. It was her presence I needed.

Our love came to nothing. We rarely kissed and, apart from an embrace of fondness on meeting and parting, there was no physical contact. The love that had been supreme for a few minutes while we listened to a symphony could not be rekindled. It was no more than 'the horns of elfland faintly blowing', faint indeed but clear enough to destroy all other possibilities of love. It had to end, and end it did.

There were three particular reasons this happened, or rather three scenes which I remember. The first was walking back, we two and her mother, from their house to the market square. Alice and her mother had linked arms and talked with each other about things which meant nothing to me and when we parted they hardly noticed I had gone.

The second scene was in the chapel of King's College. Alice had a beautiful voice but was too uncertain of herself to sing solo. She belonged to a choral society and on this occasion – it was Verdi's *Requiem* – she sang in a trio with two other sopranos. I was sitting with my arm resting on a carved wooden figure on one of the choir stalls and I watched Alice and her two companions as they sang the short passage. The music was so beautiful, the chapel was so beautiful and Alice was so beautiful that I thought, 'I cannot stand this any longer.'

The third reason was that, a little later, I met another girl. I cannot explain this, nor will I try. Her name was Stella and she was a secretary in one of the science departments. She was pretty and her hair was untidy so she was forever sweeping it away from her face. We used to meet in the forbidden Fellows' Garden in the late evening when, if Tom's theory was correct, we would be unlikely to come across dons spending their pennies behind the trees. The fact that we were trespassing made it all the more fun. Stella was carefree and had not the beauty of body or mind to overwhelm me.

So it was that my love for Alice withered and nearly died. It was one of the everlasting flowers, the immortelles, on Miss Brownlees's desk in the classroom, beautiful from a distance but, when seen too close, dry and dusty. There was no substance to it.

I wrote Alice a letter saying it would be better if we did not see each other again and found room to include the Shakespeare sonnet which begins,

Farewell, thou art too dear for my possessing

and ends,

Thus have I had thee as a dream does flatter

In sleep a king, but, waking, no such matter.

I received a sad letter in return and avoided meeting her for the rest of the term.

Stella was good company but I was too strait-laced and solemn for her so she quickly tired of me. We parted company and I thought of Alice and was heartbroken.

PART III

XI

Through the Looking Glass, Darkly
1945–6

The European war was over when I finally left Cambridge and went to the Middlesex Hospital in London to learn how to be a real doctor. This transition was not easy. University is an extension of school life with a little extra freedom of thought and action. It was a shock suddenly to be faced with real people, mostly suffering people too. Our training had not prepared us for this and my course in psychology proved almost worthless.

The system for teaching medical students at the Middlesex and other teaching hospitals was quite a good one and has not changed much since then. On our first morning we were taken to the wards on the second floor where we met the surgical registrar who gave us a short talk then allotted us about eight patients each to 'clerk', as the expression was.

'Get to know them,' he said, 'you haven't a clue and don't pretend you have because patients, believe it or not, are human beings like us, and most of them will see through you straight away if you try to be clever.'

This was one of the best pieces of advice I was given in my entire medical career. He then introduced us to Sister who looked at us with unconcealed contempt. I heard later that she was notorious for her dislike of medical students but we all found it disconcerting because we were frankly terrified and a little motherliness would have gone a long way towards easing the situation.

'Don't sit on the beds and don't interfere with my nurses,' were the only instructions I can remember her giving us. When we discussed the matter in the canteen later we could not decide whether interfering with the nurses meant interfering with their work or doing wicked things in the linen cupboard. Probably both. There was little chance of the latter because on those wards nurses were creatures we hardly dared speak to and they were drilled to ignore us.

So, wearing a short white coat with the unfamiliar feel of a stethoscope round my neck, I went to see my first ever patient. He was a small Jewish man with a thin face who looked at me with some hostility.

'Are you a student?' he asked, somewhat unnecessarily.

'Yes. I've been told to look after you.'

'Are you any good at taking blood?'

I thought of the registrar's remarks and said, 'Not yet.'

He pulled up his right sleeve and showed me his arm covered with bruises.

'That's what the last student did to me. Bloody mess. Sticking needles in all over the place.'

I took the folder from the end of the bed and pretended to understand what was written on it.

'I'm going upstairs tomorrow.'

'Upstairs?'

'For my operation.'

'Everything will be all right.'

It was a stupid thing to say because it was quite obvious I knew nothing about him or his case and it produced something of a reaction.

'All right, he says, all right. How the bloody hell does he know it's going to be all right? Half my bloody guts chopped out and he says it's going to be all right.'

Several other patients glanced up to see what the fuss was about and I was almost immediately aware of the tall figure of Sister standing behind me.

'I hope you are not upsetting one of my patients,' she said to me haughtily, 'If you want to rest, Mr Jacobs, I'm sure doctor will leave you in peace.' She had a nasty way of saying 'doctor' when referring to medical students. She moved on and Mr Jacobs said 'Bitch'.

This remark made us friends and allies. I put the folder down and asked him about himself. He lived not far from the hospital in Soho and had a fat wife whom he complained about almost continuously. When I saw them together his usual remark to her was, 'Stop fussing, you old cow.' They were very fond of each other.

The first patient is the one you remember all your life. Mr Jacobs had his operation next day. I stood for two hours, feeling sick and pouring sweat, while the surgeon removed a tumour from his bowel. I did not understand what was going on and was afraid I would do something wrong. My task was to hold an instrument called a retractor whose function was to pull the liver and other tissue away from the site of the tumour so as to give the surgeon a clear view. I hung on to this desperately until I had cramp in my fingers. Sometimes the surgeon would say, 'Pull harder,' or irritably push the retractor into its correct position.

That was my first memory of the romance of the operating theatre. I did not feel faint, like some of the other students, nor excited. It was blood, sweat and toil. I was lucky, however, that it was my case being operated on because the others stood in the background unable to see what was going on. The only two moments of excitement, one of my friends told me, were watching the thin red line made by the scalpel in the initial skin incision and the moment of triumph when the surgeon lifted the tumour up like a tombola prize then tossed it into a metal dish held by one of the nurses.

Mr Jacobs was too ill to talk to me for the first two days after his operation and I could not get close to him because I might interfere with the nursing treatment. So he lay there like a corpse and I looked at him from the end of the bed. Once a busy staff nurse literally pushed me out of the way.

On the third day we had the big ward round when Mr Patey, the surgeon, went round with his entourage, including various visiting doctors and us students trailing behind like the tail of a comet. I remember standing in the corridor between the two wards waiting for the great man to arrive. We were all intensely nervous and one of the other students, who is now a famous doctor in his own right, was literally shaking with fear. It was customary for the surgeon to be met by his registrar, house surgeon and others, at the main entrance of the hospital and to be escorted up to the ward. I had a moment of panic when the lift came to a halt, the gates opened and the priestly procession emerged to be received with formality by Sister. The registrar was a very kind man and he found time to come over to our group.

'Not to worry,' he said, 'this is your first week. No one will expect you to know much about the patients.'

I stayed well to the back but when Mr Patey reached Mr Jacobs's bed and the house surgeon presented him with the folder, like an acolyte holding the holy scriptures for a priest, he said the words I had dreaded.

'Who is the clerk of this case?'

A path was made for me and I found myself standing by the surgeon looking down the bed at Mr Jacobs, who by now was propped up on three pillows, but looked ghastly. 'Tell us about this patient,' said Mr

Patey, not unkindly. My mind was empty and I looked for inspiration at Mr Jacobs' pale face. He gave a little nod and I think he winked.

'He's Jewish,' I finally managed to get out, 'and he lives just down the road from here. He used to be a tailor but he had to give up his job. His wife visits him every day. Their son was killed in Tunisia. He was in the army and . . .'

'All right,' said the surgeon. He turned to the registrar and said, 'You will have to teach these students how to present cases properly.' Someone tittered.

I slunk to the back filled with the most unutterable shame while I heard the house surgeon saying, 'Mr Jacobs is a carcinoma of the colon presenting with disturbed bowel action four months ago. We have the barium enema pictures here.' A nurse pushed forward a portable screen and all eyes were directed at the X-Rays which the surgeon demonstrated before going on to describe the operation. I was forgotten.

Mr Jacobs made a good recovery. I had to take samples of blood from him and made a mess of his other arm and he complained bitterly about this. When he was discharged he asked me to visit him, which I did. His fat wife fed me with weak coffee and slabs of inedible cake and they showed me photographs of their son. I did not know what to say but this did not matter much because Mrs Jacobs talked incessantly. They were very pleased I had come.

Mr Jacobs was readmitted three months later, by which time I was less green as a medical student, and was able, on the ward round, to describe the secondary spread of cancer to the bones. He died a fortnight later and, because he was an Orthodox Jew, no one was allowed to touch his body. His wife literally screamed with grief when he died. I was on the ward at the time. She threw her arms round me and almost smothered me. Sister was cross at what she called 'this ridiculous scene'.

I have written in some detail about Mr Jacobs because, as I have said, one's first patient, like one's first love, has a unique quality and also because it shows some of the stresses in the life of a medical student at the start of his clinical work. I was not a very good student.

We were all very susceptible to praise or blame and a harsh word could upset us for days. It took me some time to regain confidence after the ward round fiasco although, in retrospect, I think I was right. The surgeon had asked me to tell him about the patient and I told him about the patient.

Small incidents come back. I remember the first time I put up a blood drip which was then a fairly new technique. The operation was arranged for nine o'clock so I had to go to the ward before breakfast. My hand was shaking but I felt the needle slide easily into the vein and I was filled with pride when I saw the blood dripping through the glass tubing. During the operation the anaesthetist said, 'I like this blood drip,' a casual remark which, for me, had the value of a gold medal. On another occasion I was put in charge of the tourniquet while Mr Patey amputated a leg. When the operation was completed he turned to me and said, 'Thank you for saving the patient's life.' It was a joke but it pleased me.

Life at the hospital was not too bad. Apart from work on the wards, which I learnt to enjoy, we spent hours standing in the operating theatre which was a waste of time, a relic from the previous century. We also spent a lot of time in the Outpatients' Department but there were too many students so we did not get as much benefit from this as we should have done. Formal lectures were not very helpful and I learnt most from talking with the registrar and house surgeon, both of whom were delightful people.

Our small group from Cambridge were outsiders because most of the students had been in the hospital from the beginning of their training. We stuck together and gradually got the hang of things. On Sister's day off we got a poker school going in the linen cupboard and used to chat up the nurses who had to climb on the table to collect piles of sheets. They loved it and the requirements of bed linen went up considerably. So we had our fun.

For me the trouble lay outside the hospital. London, after the war, was a drab place. The bomb sites remained and no one seemed to be doing anything about them. Everything was shabby and there was a dreariness about the people too. Many of those who, for years, had dreamed of coming home to their wives and families found their dreams had not come true. People, I think, genuinely missed the war. The excitement was over and life was like washing up after a dinner party.

For students in those days it was particularly bad. There was no place for me in the hospital or at the Mary Ward Settlement and after spending a few weeks with an aunt in Westminster I found 'recommended lodgings' in Camden Town. I think the word 'recommended' implied that the landlady had paid a small fee to an agency so that she could put an advertisement in a duplicated form to send round to the colleges and hospitals. I would not have recommended it to anyone.

It was a terraced house backing on to a canal, and some half dozen houses in the street had been obliterated by the bombing. I had a tiny room, facing directly towards a bomb site, with a bed and a chair. There was no table. At ten o'clock the lights were switched off to save electricity and people nowadays do not believe me when I tell them that much of my studies were done by candlelight. This was all right for reading but writing, with no table and one candle, was difficult.

Breakfast was served at eight and a high tea at 5.30 p.m. This was always sardines or tinned meat with chunks of bread followed by an apple, and because I found it nauseating and anyway it was difficult for me to get back from the hospital in time, I gave up attending. Instead I would go out later in the evening to a mobile canteen where, for a few pennies, I bought a cup of tea and sausages with bread and butter. This was my one happy memory of Camden Town – standing at the canteen, on a frosty starlit night, eating sausages, sometimes alone, sometimes with a tramp or strange people who did not belong to my world.

The landlady insisted on payment for the coming week each Monday at breakfast and would stand at the dining room door to collect it. The residents, of whom there were about a dozen, were either naturally unsociable or the place made them so. At Cambridge I had become used to at least politeness but here no one spoke to me. I was not a person who found it easy to enter a conversation and I expect they thought it was I who did not want to speak to them but during my stay there I made no friends. I hated going back in the evenings in the dirty tube train to the dirty station and then along the dingy poorly lit streets.

It was almost in desperation that I thought of Alice.

Her college had, I knew, moved back to London. I looked the number up in the directory but it took me a week to summon up courage to telephone the secretary's office from the kiosk in our hospital entrance. I gave Alice's name and said it was important that I contacted her. The secretary at first refused to give me her private number but I invented some story or other and she relented.

That evening I phoned. It was a student hostel of some sort and a girl's voice said, 'Hang on. I'll see if she's in.' I could hear a distant shout, 'Alice, phone call for you,' and I nearly put the receiver down there and then. At last I heard Alice's voice, rather out of breath.

'Hello,' I said.

'Christopher. I knew it was you.'

'How?'

'The secretary said a man had phoned the college and wouldn't leave his name. He said he was my cousin just back from North Africa. I haven't got any cousins who've been to any part of Africa, north, south, east or west. It had to be you.' She laughed and I knew everything was going to be all right.

We met at Lyons Corner House, near Marble Arch, the following evening. She was there before me and I stood for a minute or two content just to look at her. She was the same Alice. Illogically I thought she would be different in some way – more beautiful, less beautiful or not beautiful at all. She was standing alone, not glancing anxiously up and down the street, as I would have done, but placidly waiting for me.

I crossed the road to her. She smiled when she saw me and we shook hands rather formally. Then we kissed and arm in arm went down the stairway to the Salad Bowl. Her first remark was, 'I always come here because you can eat as much as you want for half a crown.'

The Salad Bowl at Lyons Corner House was not the most romantic spot in London and there was nothing especially romantic about our meeting. It was as if the months had fallen apart and we had never stopped seeing each other. Conversation started where we had left off.

But there was a difference. We were in London and, as I soon found out, we were both lonely and she was homesick. London presses in on you and even in the Salad Bowl we felt tightly drawn together.

'The hostel's not too bad,' she was saying, 'and I go to choral singing at least once a week but how I hate London. Don't you?'

'You miss your mother, I expect.'

'Yes, and I miss Cambridge too.'

'Well, I'm a bit of Cambridge for you.'

'Why did you write that letter?'

It's funny but I was not expecting her to ask that question. She was watching me closely and I did not know what to say. Having found her again I was desperate not to lose her.

'Because, at that time, there seemed to be no future.'

'Is there now?'

'There could be.'

'What do you mean by future?'

That I could not answer so I said lamely, 'Just going on seeing each other, I suppose.'

'That's not a future. It's the present.'

'What's the difference? The future becomes the present.'

'Please don't be clever, Christopher. I really want to know.'

'What do you expect of me?'

'Love.'

'Didn't I give you love?'

'Yes . . . and no.'

She rested her chin on her hand and tilted her head to one side. For a moment I was reminded of Miss Brownlees but when she looked at me it was Alice, nobody but Alice. The immortelle. But no longer dry, no longer withered. Warm and beautiful. The same soft lips, the same smile I had loved.

The moment passed. She picked up a piece of lettuce and chewed it thoughtfully. I laughed.

'Why are you laughing?'

'The piece of lettuce.'

'Do I look like a rabbit then?' But she wanted to be serious.

'I'm going to tell you a bit about myself,' she said.

'Why now?'

'You never asked me before.'

'I was afraid to, I expect.'

She shrugged her shoulders. 'Anyway, I'll tell you. When father died, that was six years ago, I was away at boarding school. I did not have a chance to say goodbye to him. That was the really dreadful thing about it all. When they told me he was dead I thought my world had come to an end. It was the end of the world for mother, too, but she kept us going, Joy and me. Then two years later Margaret died. . . .' I knew her elder sister had died but she had not said much about it and I had not asked her.

'. . . when Margaret died mother kept me going again. I was only sixteen at the time. It broke mother. Can you imagine it? Her child, just grown up and dead. In spite of this she saw me through it while I could do little to help her. No, I don't suppose you can imagine it because you've never known real grief.'

'Not grief like that.'

Alice continued. 'I'm not sure what I'm trying to say. I suppose mother, Joy and I share this thing and you can't be part of it. Father and Margaret belong to it too.'

'It's in the past.'

'No,' she shook her head and, for the first and last time, I saw Alice crying. I wanted to comfort her but I felt to touch her would be intrusive. So I let her cry but as well as feeling unhappy on Alice's behalf I was also filled with sudden hope. To be able to cry with someone is the greatest intimacy there is and, watching her, I felt we were together. She dried her eyes and I was expecting her to continue but she surprised me by saying, 'What do you think of me?'

'I think you are a sad person.'

'Do I really give that impression? I don't mean just now. I mean all the time.'

'Yes, but I like sad people. I love you.'

'This is where we come full circle. I want you to love me.' There was a burning issue that lay between us but neither of us could mention it. It flickered along the horizon like the bomb flashes of long ago, but there were no blazing fires, no thunder of guns, only thin columns of smoke as the flickering died away, a phantom light, the *ignus fatuus*. I was lost in my thoughts and when I paid attention again Alice was saying, 'It would be nice to meet once a week. Together we could learn to enjoy London perhaps.'

'Perhaps.'

But I was not prepared to let those flickering lights die out completely nor did I want a plan of meeting once a week. It had been like that before.

'What else came between us?' I asked. Her answer was unexpected.

'Belief.'

'Belief in what?'

'God, of course.'

'Are you certain I don't believe in God too?'

'Do you?'

'Not as far as I know. I believe in Destiny and I believe in a lot of other things but I cannot give them a name. I don't see why this should come between us.'

'It has to.'

'Why, Alice? Everyone is searching for something in life. We can help each other.'

'I don't think of it like that.'

'All right then, you can help me. I will follow you wherever you go.'

'That sounds like a bribe.'

That made me angry. I had never spoken angrily to Alice before.

'You're conceited. Just because you've had the advantage of real sorrow why should you take it out on me? You sit there and say, 'I believe in God,' and I don't know what you mean and for all I know you don't either. Then when I ask for your help you decide you've found what you want and I am no part of it so you talk about bribery. I'm not sure I believe you anyway.'

She leant forward and put her hand in mine. 'I'm sorry, Christopher. I should never have said that. But you must understand. I've seen religion *used* in that sort of way too often. It's wrong. I suppose I must ask you to forgive me.'

What could I say? Her face was close to mine. Her eyes, still wet from her tears, shone so brightly they were tipped with steel. Her lips had, as always, a suggestion of mirth in spite of the seriousness of her expression. She was so beautiful. I should have said, 'It is you that is bribing me,' and stood up and walked out.

Instead I said, 'At the moment the only thing I care about is you.' I squeezed her hand and we both laughed.

So we met once a week. It was autumn. I thought of Alice at that time as an autumn girl and she dressed in brown like the leaves scattered about the parks of London where we often walked together. Sometimes we went farther afield, to Hampstead or Epping Forest, where the leaves lay ankle deep. I no longer minded the squalor of Camden Town because once a week I knew I could get away from it.

We bought season tickets for concerts at the Albert Hall because that was the cheapest way to listen to music which was the chief thing, apart from loneliness, which kept us together. The London Philharmonic was our orchestra and Beecham our conductor. If possible we would sit above and to one side so that we could watch Beecham as well as listen to the music. Sometimes he scarcely moved his baton and often he muttered to himself, or threw remarks at the players which we longed to hear but seldom could. Once in a quiet passage of incredible beauty we heard him say distinctly, 'God, I could do with a brandy.'

With Beecham it was Mozart that counted. Of course all music was alive under him but often the things we expected to move us most, such as the Beethoven Symphonies – the seventh was still banned – moved us least. But Mozart . . . I remember saying to Alice, 'If I listen to Mozart and it means nothing to me than I'll know the end has come.'

After the concerts we would walk across Kensington Gardens, skirting the edge of the Serpentine to Marble Arch, where Alice caught the tube train to her hostel. We would talk about the music we had been listening to and, before we parted, have a cup of coffee in one of the many cafés round the Marble Arch end of Oxford Street.

I can remember little of our conversations because we did not often talk deeply about things, as we had done on our first meeting at the

Salad Bowl. There was a bargain between us, made at that meeting although not put into words, that ours was to be a companionship. There was no sex in the sense one would use the word today. We walked hand in hand and we kissed in affection when we felt like it. No more than that.

Just occasionally the lights flickered along the horizon. Once, I remember, we were on a crowded tube train. There was an old man standing up, swaying as he clutched the straps, so Alice offered him her seat and came to sit on my knee. There was nothing unusual about this. She had often sat on my knee in a tube train before. But on this occasion physical desire flared up in me and in her too. We both knew it. I suppose the very situation made emotion free from danger and for the only time in the two years or so we had known each other I felt submerged in her passion. My arm was round her waist and her arm rested on my shoulder and that was all. A few stops further on I had to get off the train while she continued the journey.

'Come with me,' I whispered, but she shook her head and it could not have been otherwise.

On another occasion, and this was a November evening, warm and cool in turn, we were standing looking at the Peter Pan statue which is not far from the Albert Hall, when she suddenly said, 'Tell me about Stella.'

I had no idea she knew anything about Stella and I was in complete confusion.

'Janet told me,' she continued, 'and Tom told her. It was after you wrote me that letter and I was upset. She was being kind and trying to make you seem unimportant. "He's got another girlfriend anyway," she said. What was she like?'

'Nothing really.'

'Don't be silly. No one's like nothing.'

I could not tell Alice that Stella was a pretty girl with large blue eyes, dark red lips and hair which was always a little untidy, nor that she was very sexual and that was why she had tired of me so quickly.

'She was OK,' I said, 'but it didn't last long. It was only because I was unhappy about you that I went out with her at all.'

'Were you thinking about me when you kissed her?' Alice asked.

Christmas came and we medical students had three weeks' holiday, while Alice had rather longer. Father and mother had now moved to Buckden, a village near Huntingdon, father having bought the house on the spur of the moment, without even seeing it first. It was a pleasant place, rather like Springwell, and I remember there was a hand pump in the kitchen and everyone who was not too fragile, guests included, was expected to take their turn at it every morning because it was our only source of water. There was a large garden with an elderly gardener called Frank, who 'went with the house'. I formed an immediate friendship with him and we spent much of the holidays sawing logs. We hardly said a word but enjoyed the rhythm of the double-handed saw as it slid backwards and forwards with very little effort on our part. Eidy was still with us in the nursery on the first floor, which was preserved largely for Edward and Kay's small daughter Margaret. They were frequent visitors. Eidy, of course, was very old but she still served nursery tea and, having grown out of my antagonism to childhood, I loved it. It became for me, once again, the best part of the day.

I was by now well past my anti-parent stage and when I was on holiday at Buckden I managed to recapture some of my boyhood happiness. Michael, back from the army, and Joan were about much of the time and we had a lot of fun. Joan maintained her passion for goats and at long last seemed to have found the knack of looking after them. They produced milk by the gallon. Father was more cheerful than he had been for years and mother was no longer afraid of the postman arriving with a telegram. They at least had no regrets about the war being over.

Mother and father of course knew about Alice, and were anxious to meet her. I had a photograph of her on my bedroom table and mother remarked that she looked just like great aunt Bess, but as I could not remember what great aunt Bess looked like I did not know if this was a compliment.

Buckden is only about twenty miles from Cambridge and that Christmas I arranged to bicycle over to Alice's house. Her mother received me kindly but it was quite obvious that I was no longer a recognised suitor and my score had dropped to about three out of ten. This did not stop me liking her and, knowing what I did, I felt great respect for her. I am sure she felt it would have been better for us all if I had not come back into Alice's life. I did not enjoy my visit very much. Alice was ill at ease and the gulf between us was unfathomable although we talked brightly. As I cycled home, past Girton and down the long road through Godmanchester, dusk was gathering and even with two pairs of gloves on, my hands were frozen. I was ice-cold inside too and for several days afterwards I was ill in bed with flu.

It was quite nice to be at home to be looked after. I lay in bed dozing and when I felt a little better read book after book, catching up with the modern writers of those days — Evelyn Waugh, E.M. Forster and their like. I looked at some old favourites too but put them to one side. Jane Austen mocked me and Hardy was too near the truth. Mother tried to pump me about Alice, obviously wondering if there was 'anything in it'. I was reluctant to tell her there wasn't so I made non-committal replies. Alice had arranged to visit us and, because she would have to come by bus, it was agreed she should stay overnight. However, she phoned to say she would catch a late bus back to Cambridge because her mother did not think it proper, under the circumstances, for her to spend the night. This made me angry but I didn't say anything.

It is, I have found, hopeless trying to unite two different parts of one's life. Home and school had always been separate compartments and so, too, was my life in London of which the medical school and Alice were a part. How could Alice be anything but a stranger in our house at Buckden?

It gave me an odd sensation introducing her to mother and father and watching her seated on the sofa in the nursery talking with Eidy. The two got on famously. Alice was genuinely interested in my childhood and Eidy liked nothing better than talking about it.

'He was a dear little boy,' said Eidy, 'but, ooh, he used to tuck me up sometimes,' and she beckoned Alice over to whisper in her ear the terrible secret of how I undid her apron strings and would not wash my hands before meals and as often as not forgot to take a clean hanky with me when I went out to tea.

'I don't know how you put up with it,' said Alice. 'I would have given him a jolly good spanking.'

'I daresay he deserved it, but you couldn't, could you?'

'I would have done.'

'Ah, but you didn't see him as he was then. He's different now.' I hated being talked about like this but could do nothing to stop them. Alice looked at me with the half-smile round her lips but there was no mockery in it. It was a look of tenderness.

'I hope you look after master Christopher in London,' Eidy continued, shaking her head to indicate that there was no need to describe the dangers of city life.

'I do my best.'

I showed Alice round the garden too, although there was not much to see because there was a thin mantle of snow on the ground. Frank was in the woodshed and he presented her with a potted plant from the greenhouse, a hyacinth just coming into bloom and smelling like a bluebell-carpeted wood. It was a kind thing to do but he treated her as a bride-to-be which she was not.

Mother and father had the same idea and I could sense them assessing her as a possible daughter-in-law. Alice had such charm that I think her rating must have been quite high. She was able to talk with father who was usually self-absorbed, sometimes to the point of rudeness, when we had visitors. I found I had become a spectator and decided I must get into the conversation somehow. Partly as a joke, partly as retaliation for Alice's talk with Eidy, I said, 'Mother thinks you look like great aunt Bess.'

'So she does,' said mother, taking it seriously, 'she's got the same chin.'

'But didn't great aunt Bess have floppy ears?'

'Of course not. The Irish side of the family had very nice ears.'

'He's teasing you,' said father but mother was well away and gave a long discourse on the Irish part of our ancestry.

It was snowing quite heavily by now and Alice decided she ought to catch an earlier bus home. We went up to the nursery to say goodbye to Eidy but she was asleep by the fire. Alice kissed her gently on the forehead without waking her. I thought it was a lovely thing to do and I envied Alice her lack of self-consciousness. We went downstairs and she shook hands with mother and father. They invited her to come again, and she said, 'That would be nice,' but I knew she never would. We walked up to the bus stop on the main road, carrying the hyacinth in its pot, and flakes of snow settled on our clothes and faces. The sky was grey and it looked as if there was a lot of snow to come. As it turned out there was a heavy fall throughout the night and many roads were blocked next morning.

Alice said, 'I'm sorry I've had to leave early. I didn't want to be trapped.'

It was after the Christmas holidays that everything went wrong. The hostel in Camden Town seemed even more dismal because I had been reminded of the comfort of living in a good home. The weather was atrocious, drizzling rain and when there was not rain there was fog. I love high winds and storms but this was just bleakness and in post-war bombed London it was the bleakness of a tundra. I did not feel very well because the flu germ seemed to hang about me and at night I was kept awake coughing. Often in the evenings I didn't bother to eat. I would work long hours at my textbooks but had little concentration and found I was often turning the pages over without taking anything in. The electricity was now left on until 11.30 p.m., I expect because someone had complained, and this was a help.

At the Middlesex, too, things were not going well for me. Our group of students had moved from surgical to medical wards where one of the consultants was lazy and the other bad-tempered. I think we all lost some of our enthusiasm. I used to dread going into the wards to take histories from the patients and became sensitive to any possible slight. I felt deep sympathy for those who were really ill and suffering but there is, in a London teaching hospital especially, a class of patient who treats illness as a hobby or profession. These were highly critical and preyed on the ignorance of the medical students, and I found them difficult to tolerate. In Outpatients I would sit as far back as possible hoping no one would ask me questions. We tried to start another poker school in the linen cupboard but were told bluntly we were there to work, so even that little pleasure was denied us. Of course we still had our fun and in the canteen we would laugh and joke but I felt more and more withdrawn from my friends. I would have preferred, some-times, to sit by myself but I knew this would be folly.

Alice was a comfort to me. She knew I was unhappy and had the sense not to put on an artificial act of cheerfulness for my benefit. I don't suppose it was much fun going out with me but she was a very kind person and in this, the last throes of our love affair, there was more tenderness on her part than there had been from the time we first met in Cambridge. We continued to meet once a week.

We had planned to 'explore London' but because of the atrocious weather this came to nothing. There was nowhere for us to go. Walking in the parks was no fun and when we went to a café we could not sit drinking coffee and talking endlessly as we used to in Cam-bridge. In London one drank coffee, paid the bill and went out into the joyless streets.

So we always had to be *doing* something – going to our concerts which lost some of their charm because Beecham was away on tour, sometimes going to the cinema or looking round museums. To escape from the rain we occasionally went to the National Gallery and here we learned to love the paintings of Michelangelo and Leonardo da Vinci. In particular Leonardo's *Virgin of the Rocks* fascinated me. This was before it was cleaned so the rocks and distant sea were visible through a dark haze which formed a sinister background to the serenity of the faces. It was while we were looking at this picture that Alice took my hand and said, 'I'm going to bribe you to come to church with me next Sunday.'

'I don't think that would be a good idea.'

'There's a reason. I've never been to a Catholic service, being a staunch Anglican and all that, and I want to go to a service at Westminster Cathedral. I've heard it's beautiful.'

'Your mother wouldn't like that. Nor would mine for that matter.'

'I certainly won't tell mother. I'm asking you to come because I want a nice agnostic escort.'

So we went to an evening mass in Westminster Cathedral and the lights were so dim and the roof so high that it was like sitting under a starless sky. I felt the mystery of a ritual I did not understand and the beauty of the music but it gave me no comfort and Alice said afterwards that she did not like it.

'I'm too fixed in my ways,' she said, 'I think I'm a commonplace person at heart.'

It was not long after this time that I began to get really depressed. Alice wanted me to look for new lodgings and I kept saying I would but did nothing about it. I remember once when I was having my hair cut the barber mentioning casually that his mother had a spare room and was on the lookout for a student to come as a lodger. It sounded ideal and was close to the hospital but I couldn't be bothered to call round to the address he gave me. Alice was cross with me about this.

To tell the truth I didn't care about anything very much and as the weeks went by I looked forward to my meetings with Alice less and less. This was partly because I knew my unhappiness made her unhappy and partly because her new-found tenderness irritated me. At times I felt a deep anger towards her. At other times I loved her. I did not know what to think. Winter turned into spring and the March winds blew away the damp squalor of the London streets.

The Albert Hall is a place of moods. It can fill an audience with rapture, sometimes amounting to the hysteria one sees at the Proms, while at other times it can say, 'No one is going to enjoy themselves tonight.' At that time it was the only major concert hall in London because Queen's Hall had been destroyed by bombs and the Festival Hall was a thought in the minds of architects. It was an evening in mid-April that Alice and I went to a concert there for the last time. The hall was half-empty and we sat high up near the back where there was an unpleasant echo effect, another trick the Albert Hall likes to play on people. The conductor was someone we had never seen before and the music was sterile. The last piece was Schubert's *Unfinished Symphony* which never fails to delight but that evening it meant nothing to me. I remembered my remark to Alice that if one could not love Mozart the end was near. This was not Mozart but it was much the same thing. I looked at Alice, sitting beside me, and thought, 'This is the end.'

The orchestra played the final sad notes and there was a formal round of applause. Alice turned to me and said, 'That was lovely.' It had not been lovely and I thought she was being insincere. We left the building and, as usual, walked across Kensington Gardens towards Marble Arch.

Oscar Wilde once wrote that each man kills the thing he loves: 'some do it with a bitter look, some with a flattering word; the coward does it with a kiss, the brave man with a sword.' I did it with bitterness.

We were standing at the edge of the Serpentine looking across the dark water towards the bridge and the distant lights and suddenly the frustration and anger I had stored up for months, probably years, came to the surface. I could hear myself speaking and, although I knew what I said was untrue even as I said it, I could not stop the words coming out. I told Alice that our love was a fraud, that it had brought us nothing but unhappiness, that all along it had been she who held the reins and used me for her own convenience. She had taken a lot and given little and I could stand it no longer. It would be better, I went on, if we said goodbye here and now and never met again.

She said nothing in reply and because she turned her face from me I could not see her expression. A water bird croaked on the lake and there was a background of the noise of traffic from Park Lane. Still she did not speak. I felt I was emerging from a dream and in desperation I started to say I was sorry for what I had said. I didn't mean it and so on – but I had said it and something inside me *had* meant it.

I don't know how long we stood there but finally Alice said, 'I'm sorry too. Goodbye Christopher.' She did not look at me but walked away slowly towards the lights of Marble Arch. In a little while I followed, and the last I saw of her was the slightly drooping figure disappearing down the steps of the Underground station.

When I say that I had killed the thing I loved I do not mean that my love for Alice was something that should have gone on forever. We could never have married or, if we had, it would have been a disaster because we were quite unsuited for each other. It could perhaps be dismissed as a first love affair that went on too long and which I romanticised at the time, and even more afterwards.

What I had killed was something in myself, a dream of a kind which could never be revived in any other form or with any other person. To make matters worse I had killed in cruelty and if there are such things as devils it was a devil that spoke from deep inside me that night. I know now that there are many other interpretations which can be applied to what had happened between Alice and me but I do not think reasons are important. To put it bluntly I had treated, with great cruelty, one of the best and kindest people I have ever met and for this I could not forgive myself. Alice, as I found out later – for this is not quite the end of the story – was upset largely on my behalf.

At the time I was filled with horror and a sense of complete isolation and desolation. Alice was the one thing in the world I cared for and she had gone forever. I looked at the blank entrance of the tube station hoping a miracle would happen and she would come back to me. Then I turned away with the intention of killing myself, not later that night but there and then. It was quite clear in my mind. It was not the self-indulgent idea that many people have from time to time, that is to say sorrow for oneself and a desire to make other people feel sorrow too. It was for me, at that particular moment, a logical and necessary act.

The Serpentine was the obvious place, dark deep waters and plenty of it. 'How easy a thing it is,' someone once said. But is it easy? How could I, who was able to swim the length of the Serpentine twenty times over, allow myself to sink without struggling to save myself? I might just as well try to suffocate myself by not breathing.

So logic, and a sense of proportion, came back to me and also a tiny hint of comedy, like the trace of a smile on Alice's lips when her face was sad. There was something trite about being drowned in the Serpentine, like jumping off the Eiffel Tower or throwing oneself on to the rocks below Beachy Head. In front of me was Park Lane with its stream of traffic. I stood on the pavement and watched the cars, lorries and buses hurrying by. The air was full of noise, hooting horns, occasionally the squeal of brakes and behind it all a dull roar which seemed to get louder and louder. A taxi slowed in front of me and I remember the driver's face as he looked at me curiously, wondering if I was a likely customer. I shook my head and he drove on. The noise was getting unbearable. I closed my eyes and stepped off the pavement. Time became a blank.

Later, and I do not know how much later, I was standing on the far side of Park Lane. No car had touched me and I had not been aware of the sound of brakes or slithering tyres. I stood at the edge of the road, angry and deprived. It would be foolish to walk back again. I stayed where I was.

Did I really attempt to commit suicide or was I throwing a gauntlet at the feet of Destiny? I don't know – it is so long ago that it is impossible to revive the emotions of that moment nor do I want to. They are dead and gone. I walked to Camden Town. It took three hours. Next morning I was back at medical school.

XII

The Settlement
1946

Destiny which had taken a swipe at me, or rather sat back and watched me taking a swipe at myself, now came to my aid. On the following Monday I received a letter from the Mary Ward Settlement where I had spent two weeks after my stay at St Dunstans. There was a vacancy for me and I could move in at once. I paid the landlady a week's rent, packed my bags and left Camden Town.

The Mary Ward proved to be my salvation. It was a centre for social work of various kinds, a boys' club, night classes, free legal advice, a drama school and many other activities. These were co-ordinated by two faithful secretaries, one enormously fat and the other painfully thin. Whenever I looked in at the office and saw them sitting at opposite ends of the long table where they worked, I imagined it as a see-saw with Cissie, the fat one, bumping on the floor while Trudy, the thin one, was thrown up to the ceiling. They were a delightful pair.

The building harboured about thirty residents, mostly students like myself, but there were some older people and a continuous flow of guests, many of them foreigners, which added to the interest. Occasionally quite famous people would stop for a day or two and these were friends of the warden, Mr Walkinshaw, who was a leading magistrate of that era.

We paid a weekly rent of thirty shillings, very cheap even in those days, on condition that we took part in the activities of the Settlement. I already knew the youth club leader, so one evening a week I would look after the canteen and sometimes keep an eye on the club for him. At weekends I often took some of the boys by bus to Parliament Hill Fields to play football or cricket. There was a spirit of co-operation amongst the residents so we chopped and changed our duties at will. Often I would find myself involved in evening classes or helping at a night hostel for servicemen near Euston Station.

Although the war was over, demobilisation was slow and there were still weary soldiers, heavily laden with packs, arriving late in the evening with nowhere to sleep. It was our job to check them in, give them two blankets each and direct them to their bunks.

The chief bonus of the Mary Ward was the good will amongst the residents. We were, for the most part, young, intelligent and still idealistic. It took me a little time to get used to the carefree enjoyment of the place, having recently come from the tomb-like Camden Town hostel, but once I did I felt I was in my element.

Apart from my evening on duty in the Youth Club the usual routine for me was to retire to my room after supper to work – because medical students then and now have to work hard – and about ten o' clock there was a general drift to the sitting room where tea was served from a large brown teapot. Conversation and wit flowed and we often stayed up late for the sheer enjoyment of each other's company. At weekends, too, we had great fun because there were always plenty of people about. We would have expeditions and anyone who wanted to come on these did so. Hampstead Heath was one of our favourite places, Kew Gardens another. London is a wonderful place when you have company and although few of us had enough money to go to the theatre we loved exploring the town and in the evenings wandered along Regent Street or Oxford Street gazing at the shop windows.

I was at first in mourning for Alice and because I did not want to be personally involved with anyone this 'gang life' suited me ideally. There were about equal numbers of men and women as residents and although fondness often grew between individuals, there was an unwritten law that sexual activities should not take place in the building. Laws are made to be broken and, of course, they sometimes were, but when I talk to young people today I find it difficult to explain how much freedom this attitude gave us. People of the opposite sex visited each other's rooms to sit and talk but there was no question of 'Shall we finish up in bed together?' This prevented much of the tension and quarrelling which is built in to student hostels of today. It also encouraged light, easy flirtations. This may seem a contradiction in terms but it did not feel so to us then.

To give an example: after I had been at the Mary Ward for a few months and the shadow of my affair with Alice had almost passed, I found myself one Sunday evening in the sitting room with a girl I knew, as the saying is, like a sister. Everyone else seemed to have gone out and quite spontaneously we started kissing and talked and kissed the best part of the evening. Next morning our relationship was the same as it always had been and the matter was never mentioned between us and was, in fact, forgotten. It was the unique atmosphere of the Mary Ward which permitted this sort of thing.

Mr Walkinshaw, or Walks as everyone called him, was a delightful elderly man who loved the company of young people. I was not one of his special favourites because I tended to be ill at ease with those in authority. I got on well with Mrs Shaw, the housekeeper. She was a strange person who ran the domestic side with a kind of inefficient efficiency. On my original visit there, before I had become a resident, it had been one of my jobs to help her in the kitchen and this was a time-and-motion expert's nightmare. The cups and saucers were kept at opposite ends of the kitchen and when she made pastry the various ingredients were as widely dispersed as possible. An added hazard was a large dried fish which hung from a hook in the middle of the ceiling at head height. I kept walking into it in my diagonal journeys across the kitchen and once nearly broke my glasses. This fish was quite a feature of the Mary Ward and we used to take guests down to have a look at it. Mrs Shaw had cared for the Settlement during the difficult days of the war and the fish was a sort of symbol, the last resort if we faced starvation. She was a terrible stickler over rather trivial matters and would go into a rage if someone brought a milk bottle into the sitting room. Milk had to be in jugs and seeing it on display in a bottle was like seeing it in the nude. Mrs Shaw was very kind to me when I first came to the Settlement but I imagine she was impossible to work with.

It was inevitable that I should fall in love again. Clarissa was quite a lot younger than me, being only seventeen when she came to the Mary Ward for a few months before going up to Oxford to read English. I was by then accepted and generally liked and she, who was new to the place, looked to me for support. She was romantic by nature and created an image which was impossible for me to fulfil to her satisfaction so our brief affair was doomed from the start. It was a novel situation for me because in the past it had always been I who had worshipped from afar. I felt flattered.

She was very pretty with a pale, rather ethereal face and long golden hair hanging in coils down her neck and on to her shoulders, a poet's 'dream of fair woman'. She came, in the first place, to help Mrs Shaw and I felt sorry for her because she was obviously unsuited to the work. She used to come with the rest of us on our various outings when she was not too busy and there seemed to be no special affinity between us until one evening coming back by bus we happened to be sitting next to each other and started talking about poetry. She had two tickets, she told me, for a recital by T.S. Eliot of some of his own works and asked me if I would go with her. This was an opportunity not to be missed – rather like watching Bradman in a Test Match or Joe Louis in the boxing ring.

I remember that recital well. T.S. Eliot had a dry, unattractive voice and he spoke the lines of his own poems rather as if he was reading from a textbook, but the effect was quite extraordinary. The words took control and I was more moved by him than I would have been by a skilled orator such as John Gielgud or Laurence Olivier because one would have been thinking more of the performance than of the poetry. When we got back to the Mary Ward Clarissa came to my room to borrow a book and when I saw her kneeling in front of the shelves examining the titles, and picking the books out one by one to look at them, I had an irresistible desire to touch her shining hair.

I did. She closed the book she was looking at, put it carefully back in its place, then stood up and in a moment her arms were round my neck and I knew I was involved in something I had not sought. I was glad. Who could fail to be glad?

Over the next few weeks I was carried on a tide of romance, knowing it was unreal but not caring. We tried to conceal our feelings in the dining room and sitting room and did not, in fact, have much opportunity of being alone together but when we were, the moments were precious. Although we sometimes met in either her room or mine we preferred to spend our time wandering together through the London streets. One of our joys was to walk to the nearby main-line stations where we would watch the trains coming in from the north. The giant engines glided alongside the platform with white steam and sparks pouring from the funnel and also around the wheels which slowly ceased their turning until the engine gave a great sigh and came to rest. Then the train disgorged its passengers and we watched them, as years before I had watched my imaginary train on the lawn of Springwell. We sometimes picked out certain people – a man with a bowler hat, a beautifully dressed lady – and wove stories about them. Once a group of Highlanders in kilts, with bagpipes under their arms, emerged from one of the compartments and there and then gave a spontaneous performance of Scottish music. They stood in a half circle with puffed red cheeks blowing into their clumsy looking bagpipes while the crowd flowed by and a few, like ourselves, lingered to watch and listen. It was the sort of occasion, we decided, which made life worth living.

Two incidents I remember in particular. On an afternoon in autumn Clarissa suggested we went to one of the street markets which, in those days, abounded and I believe still do. She led me straight to a stall where there were rings on display, pointed to one – I think it was an imitation ruby – and said she wanted me to buy it for her. It was very cheap and I could just about afford it and in the gardens of one of the nearby squares I placed it on her finger. I didn't know if this meant that we were engaged. The affair confused me. It was a symbolic act but more like that of children playing dolls than a true plighting of our troth. Later that afternoon we went to a book-shop where she bought me a book of poems. In the shop she marked a passage before handing it to me. It read

> Who then devised this torment? Love.
> Love is the unfamiliar name
> Behind the hands that wove
> The intolerable shirt of flame
> Which human power cannot remove.

I have this book still, and inside the cover is written October 2nd 1946, so I know the exact date of this incident. The book and the marked passage were again symbolic but I have since come to learn that the word Love in that poem was far removed from the romanti-cism we were trading in. It demonstrated, however, the ethereal nature of our feelings.

A few weeks later Clarissa took me to see her parents. Again I did not appreciate the significance of this nor would I have cared. They lived in the suburbs, I don't remember where, except that it was on the edge of a golf course.

Her father was a traveller in fountain pens. His behaviour was vulgar and he told coarse jokes to upset Clarissa and her mother who timidly tried to restrain him. I am sure he was putting on an act but I did not understand his reason. Maybe he was rebelling against his daughter's cultural refinement and her dreams of the spires of Oxford. He told us long crude stories about his travels round the towns of the Midlands and the North, while Clarissa sat clenching her hands until the knuckles were white. Strangely enough I rather liked him but the contrast between him and his daughter was too marked to be anything but painful. As we walked back across the golf course to the tube station Clarissa was crying. She had been stripped of her poetry and did not realise I loved her at that moment far more than ever before. I tried to explain this but she couldn't understand.

Shortly after this she left the Mary Ward to go to Oxford. We swore an eternal bond of affection but I knew this would be quickly broken. From Oxford she wrote beautifully composed letters describing her new life and the famous people she had met. Lord Cecil, C.S. Lewis, Tolkien and others and although she ended each letter with delicate expressions of love these read like exercises in English composition and left me strangely disconsolate.

I had promised to visit her in Oxford and near the end of her first term I went for a weekend. It was a disaster. We met on the station platform and I knew at once she had changed so much that there was no chance of rekindling the fires. She took me to her lodgings to meet her friends where I cut a sorry figure because, I suspect, I bore no resemblance to the picture she had painted of me. I was awkward and tongue-tied. There was only one moment of that evening I remember with any pleasure. One of Clarissa's friends had been watching me with amused interest and when the others were engaged in conversation amongst themselves she leant over and whispered in my ear 'Bad luck!' She had obviously sized up the situation and that gave me a feeling of support.

Next morning I was to meet Clarissa outside Balliol, where I was staying because I could get free lodgings on an exchange system with St John's College, Cambridge. She arrived over an hour late and we spent a sad day together. She had planned it so carefully, the places she was to show me, the intimate matters we were to discuss. But it was all meaningless and it was only in the evening, shortly before I caught the train back to London, that we agreed we did not love each other in the slightest. It was such a relief and we hugged each other with so much affection that I thought we were going to fall in love all over again in a different way.

We said goodbye and I don't think we ever saw each other again although we wrote for a year or so. I have often wondered what became of Clarissa. I expected to hear of her as a famous lady novelist or poet and, with her inspiration, she merited this. Maybe she has, under a different name. Life is strange and she could equally well have become the mother of a large family and lived a happy, secluded life. Either way I wish her well.

After this I returned to my hard work as a medical student and to the companionship of the others in the Mary Ward who had, I think, watched my affair with Clarissa with some dismay. They welcomed me back.

During the war it became customary for medical students in London Teaching Hospitals to spend part of their time in what were called sector hospitals. This was partly to escape the bombing and partly to gain experience by being of practical help in overcrowded understaffed wards. It was such a good idea that it was continued after the war and ever since. My small 'firm', as a group of students is called, stuck together throughout our clinical training and had three spells in sector hospitals. The most notable of these was the Central Middlesex Hospital, conveniently situated next to the Guinness Brewery in Acton, North London, which, in spite of its name, had no direct connection with the Middlesex.

Here we found medicine in the raw, very different from the refined atmosphere of a teaching hospital with its selected patients, and students and junior doctors tumbling over each other to get a look at them. For the first time we came across people with common illnesses – bronchitis, pneumonia, strokes, alcoholism, old age and so on. Because the actual diseases were often of no remarkable interest, we learned to study the patients themselves and I found that the feelings I had expressed about my patient, Mr Jacobs, on that first dreadful ward round were relevant and not a subject of scorn.

We were lucky in that Horace Joules, the consultant in charge of our ward, was a brilliant and famous teacher, as well as having a touch of humanity which was sadly lacking in many of the leading doctors of that time. His Friday afternoon ward rounds were renowned and doctors from all over London and sometimes from abroad made a point of coming to them. To be a clerk on his firm was a privilege and an ordeal because he expected us, without reference to notes, to know everything about the patients. By this he implied not only the results of the latest blood tests but the way of life of the patients, their work, their families and what they enjoyed doing.

Once Dr Joules asked me, 'What morning papers does this man read?'

'I don't know.'

'Well, you should.'

And on another occasion he gave me a severe ticking off because I had not realised a patient came from a mining community in South Wales.

'How can you expect to understand his illness if you don't know the man?' he said.

All this would happen in front of an audience of about thirty doctors on the Friday ward rounds so we students had to know the patients by heart, and condense what we knew into a short concise statement. Fear was the spur and we all dreaded Fridays but the training was invaluable. Dr Joules was over six feet tall and when we showed our ignorance his anger was dropped on us from a great height, as they say.

I was able to travel to Acton each day by tube from the Settlement but I became so absorbed in the study of medicine that I used to linger at the hospital. We students formed a life of our own and this made the warm support of the Mary Ward less essential for me and also helped me to forget quickly my brief but sparkling affair with Clarissa.

Before Christmas we organised a show for the hospital staff. I was in charge of the lighting and borrowed from the Mary Ward an old-fashioned spotlight, a black metal affair into which one could insert discs of coloured glass. I amused myself making the stage blue, green, yellow or any colour I wished and because I did this in an entirely irrational way, the audience became somewhat bemused. The show itself was the usual sort of hospital skit. I remember one scene of a casualty department in which the first patient came in dressed in a leather jerkin, holding an arrow to his face and exclaimed,

> *It happened that as I was passing by*
> *A Norman arrow caught me in the eye*

and of course we had Anne Boleyn with her head tucked under her arm and various other difficult surgical emergencies. This was the first full-scale show the hospital had put on since before the war and it made us very popular with everyone apart from the consultants, most of whom turned up with their wives, because we devised incredibly personal and vulgar rhymes about them. For this we were hauled over the coals and disapproval was poured on to us from an even greater height.

Everyone was too busy to bother about hospital etiquette so we were actually allowed to chat with the nurses and we enjoyed this although I was careful not to form any attachments. Before we left, the ward sister told us we were the best lot of students they had ever had. It was remarks like this that kept us going through the days of hard work and fear of authority which was the hallmark of medical training at that time. Our ultimate goal was the Finals which were seldom out of our thoughts and we all had nightmares of being asked impossible questions by enormously tall examiners. Beside this, matters like women and love affairs were trivial.

Shortly after I had returned to work at the Middlesex I was asked by

Mr Walkinshaw to move with five others to help set up a daughter settlement in Islington where a youth club had been opened. I was a little reluctant to leave what had become my home but was finally persuaded by John Kirkwood, the leader of the youth club, and his wife Pat who was to act as housekeeper. He was an army officer who had taken up youth work for altruistic reasons, while Pat had been an officer in the ATS and, being efficient, they had found it impossible to work with Mrs Shaw at the Mary Ward. They brought a mixture of army efficiency and humanity to their work. Our party of six moved into Canonbury House, a beautiful Georgian building, which must now be worth its weight in gold although at the time we did not appreciate it and used to knock nails in the wall, chip the plasterwork and do all the things one should not do to an historic building.

Life here was pleasant and more homely than at the Mary Ward, although the area was at that time pretty rough and members of the youth club could be insulting or even violent but there were none of the knife threats one would expect today. As we got to know them we liked them more and more. Today Canonbury is a different place, an area of sought-after residences with little trace of the squalor I knew.

Canonbury House was some way from the Middlesex so I brought my old bicycle into action again and weaved my way through the London traffic, skilfully avoiding the tramlines. I often called at the Mary Ward on my way back from the hospital and because of this became involved in a very much longer and more serious love affair.

XIII

Lene

1947–8

It started for me as a rumour. I had not been to the Mary Ward for some three weeks but, as often happened, I came across one of the residents as I was cycling back to Canonbury from the hospital.

'How are things?' I asked.

'Pretty bloody, but at least we've got a smashing new Danish girl.'

'A student?'

'No, one of Mrs Shaw's aides.' I knew he was going to add 'like Clarissa' but he changed his mind abruptly. I pictured a tall, long-legged Nordic beauty with blue eyes and blonde hair but the news did not merit a visit. I was too busy working for the Finals. I heard her name mentioned two or three times after that. She was called Lene, pronounced Lena.

About a fortnight later I was invited to join a party from the Mary Ward going to Kew Gardens. It was daffodil time. There were about eight of us and Lene was one of the party. Her appearance was not at all what I had expected. She was rather small and dark-complexioned with rounded cheeks and beautiful white teeth. Because she smiled so much one remembered these. Her eyes were soft and brown, her hair dark and rather short. She was beautifully proportioned and my first sight of her was when she walked briskly into the sitting room at the Settlement, very upright in posture, with her hair bobbing up and down. Someone introduced us and she held out her hand like a child who had been taught good manners. She could speak very little English and on the few occasions I spoke to her that day she did not understand what I was saying and looked puzzled.

'You talk much too fast,' said one of the other girls.

'I can't help it,' I said, and indeed this was true, because in those days my words used to tumble over each other. If my speech lost

177

momentum I was afraid it would stop altogether and I would not be able to start again.

'You ought to pronounce each syllable separately, like this – "Do you like daff-o-dils, Lene?" '

'Yes, they are yellow I think.'

This was the sort of remark she would make. Her broken English and appealing, puzzled expression made everyone a little in love with her. I was no exception. She showed childlike pleasure in the gardens and this put us all in a good humour. She knelt on the grass to touch the flowers and the breeze lifted her hair slightly, showing the soft brown skin of her neck.

'You must not pick them, Lene,' someone said.

'Pick, what is pick?'

'Pull them, lift them,' and whoever it was did a mime of picking a flower.

'Oh, pick. You mean like this?' and she broke the stem of a white narcissus and held it up to us.

'No, Lene. That's wrong. If they see you doing that they will cut your head off.'

'Cut my head off? Do they do that in England?' She was irresistible but as she knelt amongst the flowers of Kew Gardens that afternoon I said to myself, she is utterly charming but I wonder what she's really like?

After that I visited the Mary Ward quite often. I was captivated by Lene, but so was everyone else. She was the darling of the Settlement. I was too shy to speak to her and certainly too shy to ask her out but, after a few weeks, that is just what I did. It had been a warm day and I called in for tea. I was considered an honorary resident and Mrs Shaw did not mind me doing this.

Everyone was saying how fed up they were with London and how much they would like to get out into the country. Lene, who had been pouring the tea, came and sat next to me. She smiled and in her deliberate way said,

'Your English countryside, it is very beautiful?'

'Some of it.'

'Sadly I have not seen much.'

'You ought to see more.'

She shrugged her shoulders and, to my own surprise, I heard myself saying, 'Look, I'm going to Epping next Saturday. Would you like to come with me?'

'Epping? What is Epping?'

'It's a place. A forest. I love trees.'

'Sadly I am working on Saturday.' And she looked sad.

'Sunday then. It would do just as well for me.'

'I am happy to come with you to Epping on Sunday, Christopher.'

We met outside the tube station at the Angel, Islington. She wore a tartan skirt and simple blouse. She was very pretty. I was overcome and did not know what to say but her smile was warm and she seemed not to notice my gaucheness.

'Angel. Why do they speak of it as the Angel? To me it is not like an angel.'

'I can see what you mean,' I said, looking round at the dirty and unkempt streets, with, here and there, unrepaired bomb damage. I felt like apologising for the sordid place I had brought her to.

'It's like this because of the war,' I said.

'The war, yes?'

'Was Copenhagen bombed at all?'

She looked across at a stretch of rubble partly covered with weeds which had once been a street before it was flattened by a land-mine.

'Copenhagen was not nice. Not I think as nice as this.' Her eyes clouded for a moment then she smiled brightly and chatted gaily about other things. I was content to listen. We caught a trolley-bus near the station and, as I sat close to her, I thought, 'How lucky I am. Of all the people connected with the Mary Ward I am the one she has chosen.' For I was sure, even at that stage, that she had chosen me.

Later we walked amongst the beech trees of the forest. The newly formed leaves were so transparent that the sun shone straight through them. She was fascinated by everything and I looked at the trees, the grass and the flowers through her eyes. We rested for a time amongst the bracken at the edge of the forest with the fields stretching in front of us.

'Look,' she said, 'sheeps.'

'No, Lene, sheep.'

'But there are more than one.' She pointed at a group of ewes with their lambs. They ignored us, grazing contentedly, while two of the lambs leapt around after each other then flopped down in the grass.

'See, lots of sheeps.'

'We still call them sheep.'

'Well, I think they are sheeps,' she said obstinately, 'I am going to call them sheeps.'

How could one argue? I laughed and she laughed too and that moment was the beginning of our intimacy.

Lene was the first person to bring gaiety into my life. I was not bothered about the future because the present was enough for me. It did not take me long to realise her charm was not superficial. Her delight in life was genuine and her simplicity was no pose. I knew I was going to fall in love with her.

It was not long before I wanted to be with her the whole time but this was not possible. I had to spend the evenings labouring over my textbooks so the best I could do was to call at the Settlement for tea whenever possible. This was for the pleasure of watching Lene briskly push in the trolley with a rattle of cups on saucers and her obvious pleasure when she saw I was there. Her eyes would light up, then be quickly dimmed because we both pretended we were only a little fond of each other. No one was fooled.

Mrs Shaw, who had known me a long time, took me to one side and in a clumsy way tried to give me a warning. She talked about Lene's Scandinavian charm and muttered something about 'an unfortunate entanglement'. I was very angry and could not help showing it.

'What right have you to say that, Mrs Shaw?'

'Lene's my responsibility. She's alone in this country.'

'Well, all I do is show her around.'

'Lene takes things very seriously. Besides she's a lot older than you.'

'You needn't worry, Mrs Shaw, I'll look after her all right.' Interfering bitch, I thought. Going out with Lene was fun for both of us. Why do people always make a point of stopping enjoyment? Maybe Lene was a bit older than me but she was like a child and it didn't matter anyway. I tried to ignore what had been said but after this I went to the Mary Ward less often. I had a feeling that some of the residents, like Mrs Shaw, did not want me to take Lene away from them.

The weekends were ours. Lene's favourite place was the zoo at Regent's Park, where she liked to gaze at the animals. I was the kind of person who wanted to see everything at once and rushed from cage to cage but Lene would stand for ages watching one particular animal. Once we stood looking at a leopard, lying asleep on a tree stump which had been put in his small cage to make him think he was in the jungle. He did not move, apart from an occasional twitch of the tail, but every now and then he opened his yellow eyes and stared at us. After about ten minutes Lene said, 'He is very fierce, I think,' and we moved on. From anyone else this would have been a trite remark but for Lene it was a carefully considered summing up of her feelings and had more meaning than a lengthy description.

Lene was a devout Roman Catholic with strong feelings of morality and this gave a kind of ease to our love. It also made nonsense of what Mrs Shaw and some of the residents of the Mary Ward were probably thinking. Ours was a low-key affair and the attraction was the tranquility we felt when we were together. She was always happy and to share in her happiness was enough for me.

By now I knew my way about London and took her to places I had often visited in what was, for me, a forgotten era. Once, purely by chance, I found we were standing on the bridge over the Serpentine which had marked a very sad moment of my life. But Lene was laughing and leaning over the rail to watch the ducks who were splashing about in the water beneath us.

'You'll fall in,' I said.

'Then you will rescue me, no? You are an English gentleman and that is what English gentlemen are for, I think.' She pretended to lose her balance and I seized her round the waist. We kissed and I felt I had laid a ghost. Had I?

Later that evening, or it may have been on another day, we were standing looking at the Peter Pan statue in Kensington Gardens. Lene, after her usual lengthy inspection, said with an air of finality, 'He is pretty, I think.' It was at this moment that a soft voice behind me whispered, 'When you kiss her are you thinking of me?' I was startled and turned round quickly. Of course there was no one there. It was all very odd. The voice had seemed real enough. Lene noticed something was wrong. She held my arm tightly as we walked across the park.

'Why are you suddenly so sad, Christopher?' she asked.

'I'm not sad.'

'I cannot understand. There is nothing to be unhappy about.'

'I'm not unhappy.'

'Sometimes you are so solemn,' she said, shaking her head dolefully. She held my arm tighter but, for once, I was glad when we said goodbye and I caught a bus back to Canonbury House. The voice had come from deep inside me. This, too, I tried to forget.

Not long afterwards we had a strange adventure. We had been to the cinema and, because it was hot and stuffy, we decided to walk back across Regent's Park. It was a fairy-like night, with a half-moon shining through the branches and casting long shadows across the grass. In fun we chased each other through the trees, allowing ourselves to be caught so that we could kiss – in other words we were playing a lovers' game which dates from time immemorial. In a moment of abandon I leapt on a tree stump in imitation of the statue of Eros in Piccadilly Circus, but my foot caught in the roots jerking me forward so that I hit my head against the jagged wood of the stump.

When I came to, I was lying with my head in Lene's lap. She was kissing me passionately and I could feel the blood running down the side of my face. She was saying over and over again, 'Christopher, I do not want you to be dead.'

It was like a dream. The concussion made me feel drunk and robbed me of shyness so for a long time we kissed with the blood running between us. It was madness. Then, although I was in a daze, Lene helped me to my feet and soon afterwards I found myself in the casualty department of my own hospital, lying under the spotlight of the operating table.

'You're lucky,' said the casualty officer, as he stitched the wound. 'It's a deep gash but it's along your eyebrow so you won't get much of a scar. How did you say it happened?' I told him again that I had fallen against a tree stump, but he did not believe me. It was not a very convincing explanation of how I had come to arrive at midnight in my own casualty department with an attractive Danish girl, both of us covered in blood.

The whole matter caused something of a scandal. Word of what had happened spread round the hospital and gave me a notoriety I did not deserve. My friends could not resist making sly remarks and I noticed the nurses looking at me speculatively. In the Mary Ward there was a mixed reaction. People were protective towards Lene and the incident put me in a bad light which was rather unfair because it was I who had been injured. I was no villian. In a strange way it made Lene and me emotionally bound together, almost in a blood bond. Lene did not say much about what had happened but I could not forget the wild moment of abandon. I would have fallen over a hundred tree stumps to feel again the passion of the kisses and her tenderness. We were, by now, very much in love but the constraint between us was still a part of that love.

A month later I took Lene home for a weekend. She had often said she wanted to meet my mother and father and I wanted them to meet her. They still lived at Buckden but were already talking of moving back to Cornwall. Father wanted to do something practical. It was part of his two-year cycle.

The visit was not a success. Neither of them understood Lene and her charm did not impress them. At breakfast on the first morning we had boiled eggs and Lene scooped the contents out of the shell on to her plate. This was the Scandinavian way of eating eggs but to father it meant she had been badly brought up and I felt embarrassed on her behalf. Lene, of course, was not embarrassed because she sailed gaily through life assuming that everyone was as happy as she was.

Eidy still ruled the nursery upstairs but it was by now an empty kingdom. She was short-sighted and very old and she confused Lene with Alice. I could see Lene was puzzled but, when she understood, her bright eyes clouded over for a moment. Once Eidy had established that Lene was a foreigner she treated her with suspicion. It was not a happy meeting. The only person she got on well with was old Frank, the gardener. They had a natural affinity and conversation between them was not necessary.

On Sunday Lene decided to go to mass and I went with her, partly because I wanted to and partly because it was polite. I could see mother was upset. She must have felt I was being torn out of the family circle. Matins, for her, was still the Elliott-Binns church parade.

Even Lene realised all was not well. We went for a walk along the river in the afternoon, the only really pleasant part of the weekend. She said, 'Your mother, I do not think she likes me.'

'Of course she does.'

'Your father too, he does not like me.'

'You are just imagining it.'

'I do not think so, Christopher.' After a pause she added, 'I think it will make things very difficult for us.'

It was about a week later that I got a letter from mother. She always wrote in a rather florid manner, dating back to the time she used to read out loud to the family, and scattered clichés like confetti. She was warning me against Lene. 'I feel like a mother hen whose chick is in danger,' she wrote. This infuriated me. It was partly the triteness of the expression but more because I did not think they had given Lene a chance. She was a foreigner and a Catholic and this made her unacceptable. I think it was stupid, or at least bad tactics, for mother to write like that. I remembered Lene's words, 'It will make things difficult for us.' Until then I had not even considered the possibility of marriage because in those days medical students just did not get married. We were too hard-worked and too out of pocket. Mother and father had treated Lene shabbily under a veil of politeness and it would serve them right if Lene and I did something mad like dashing off to Gretna Green. It was all a dream of course and I said nothing of it to Lene.

We did visit Gretna Green but this was part of a bicycle tour we planned together. My Finals were looming closer and I was beginning to feel jaded. I had worked hard and thought I probably knew enough to pass if luck was with me but I was finding it difficult to concentrate. Once again I found myself turning the pages of textbooks without remembering a word I had read. I wanted to get away from London and I wanted to be with Lene, not just at weekends but the whole time. There was a fortnight's holiday due to me and I got permission to extend this to three weeks. Lene wanted very much to go north because she was fascinated by the kilts and bagpipes, lochs and mountains and all the other paraphernalia of Scotland. So we decided to take our bicycles by train to Darlington and from there cycle to Edinburgh and stay a couple of days with Edward and Kay. Then we would visit the Highlands and come back through the Lake District. It was an ambitious programme.

We could not really afford it but there were youth hostels all along the route and we felt we could manage with the small amount of money we had between us. Lene, with her Catholic scruples, wanted to keep it secret because in those days it was considered daring, if not immoral, for a boy and girl to go on holiday together, although the youth hostelling part gave it an air of respectability. Only healthy, clean country types went to youth hostels.

I had no such scruples. It was one in the eye for mother and father and I ran into just about as much parental opposition as I expected. Father behaved as if he was quite prepared to 'cut me off with a shilling' but, apart from anything else, this would not have been a sound economic proposition because I was nearing the end of a long and expensive education as a medical student. Mother, I think, accepted the inevitable. I got rid of my faithful old bike and bought a lighter second-hand machine and we borrowed cooking utensils and other equipment from the youth clubs. Until the last moment I thought something would prevent us from going but when we were at last sitting together, holding hands, in the train going north with our cycles in the luggage van, I had a sense of freedom such as I had never experienced before.

Three weeks is a long time when you are with someone all day and every day, a very different matter from weekly outings, and we soon ran into difficulties. Cycling out of Darlington towards Barnard Castle we passed a large ugly building on our right, which I think was a warehouse.

'What is that, Christopher?' Lene asked.

'Oh, that's one of the famous cathedrals of the north.'

'But it does not look like a cathedral.'

'I meant it as a joke.'

'You should not make jokes about such things.'

The remark had not been a clever one and, for Lene, was in poor taste but it suddenly struck me she had very little sense of humour. It also soon became clear that our cruising speeds on a bicycle were incompatible. I knew we had to cover a lot of ground each day but Lene liked to drift along, sitting upright and taking in everything she saw.

'Look, Christopher, some cows with long horns. Let's stop and talk to them.'

'But we've still got ten miles to do and it'll soon be dark.'

'Please, one of them has a carve.'

'A calf, you mean.'

'You are always correcting me.'

'You might as well get the words right.'

'Well, I am going to stop and look at the carve.'

'If you want. I'm going on. You can catch me up.'

This conversation took place on the third day of our trip and it ended in tears and reconciliation, so what did it matter that we had difficulty in finding the youth hostel in the dark and were late arriving?

I also realised that Lene and I had very little to talk about. She was a tourist through life, enjoying what she saw but forgetting about it almost at once. She expected everyone to share her delight and see everything through her eyes. What had attracted me so much to her and made her 'the darling of the Mary Ward' now became, at times, a burden. She was a child and sometimes I wanted a grown-up to talk to. I knew so little about her. She scarcely mentioned her family and, if I tried to get her to talk about the past, she appeared not to understand, or changed the conversation quickly. Only once did she tell me of an incident from her life in Denmark and this was one evening when we had wandered away from a particular youth hostel in Yorkshire and were sitting on the bank of a tiny stream which ran through the sloping meadows towards the town.

Just before the war, she said, she had met a Swiss boy who was on holiday in Denmark. 'We were, how do you say, very much in love.' The war came and they had no chance of meeting. They wrote, of course, but after the German occupation the letters did not get through.

'Did you think of him much?' I asked.

'I did at first, but later . . .' She shrugged her shoulders.

'So that was the end?'

'No, after the war he walked all the way to see me.'

'You mean all the way from Switzerland?'

She nodded.

I was amazed. Europe was in turmoil at the time. It must have been exceedingly difficult and dangerous but eventually the Swiss boy found his way to Copenhagen. It took him a long time to trace her but he was finally successful. At this point Lene stopped talking and, as if to escape from the conversation, took off her sandals, dipped a foot into the water, and said, 'Ooh, it is cold, Christopher. But I think I will paddle.'

'But Lene,' I said, 'what happened next?'

'We were not in love, not a little bit. He walked back to Switzerland.'

'Did you mind?'

'It was very sad.'

She did not seem upset and told me this story in a matter-of-fact voice. She paddled upstream holding her skirt high to stop it getting wet, then she turned and smiled. 'Come and join me, Christopher. It tickles between the toes.'

'No, I think I'll stay here a bit.'

Was her story true? I knew she had left Denmark soon after the war and worked in a camp in France before coming to England. She never talked of going back to her own country. Was it because of the Swiss boy? I didn't think so. Something had gone wrong. Had her family treated her badly or suffered badly themselves under the occupation? She was a very pretty girl – had something dreadful happened to her, something she could not bring herself to talk about? Watching her paddling in the stream I could not bear to think of it. Or had it been the other way round? Had her family been collaborators and was that why she had left the country? I couldn't believe this to be true. There was some mystery and she would not tell me about it. But one thing was certain. She had had a life before the war while I was still a child. She had never told me her age but she must be several years older than me. That did not matter because I loved her. I sat on the bank while she wandered a long way up the stream. When she came back she stood barefoot on the bank and we kissed. Then we clung to each other with her head pressed against my cheek. She was sweet and honest. I hated myself for doubting her. Her unhappiness, whatever it was, was buried and it was better left like that.

We continued our journey. There were times of exasperation and boredom but most of the time I loved her and I think she loved me. We had moments of great tenderness and great beauty. I remember pushing our bicycles up a steep hill on the Yorkshire moors near St Johns Chapel with the curlew calling around us. Lene was a little ahead of me. She was happy, not at all put out with the steepness of the hill and the effort of pushing the bicycle, and I wondered at her prettiness and my good fortune at being with her. She turned, smiling, and said, 'We will kiss at the top?' and continued to push the bike doggedly uphill. On the other side we sailed down the long winding road, holding hands for as long as we dared, then I let her ride ahead of me to enjoy the pleasure of watching her. When we finally reached the valley below she stopped and got off.

'Now we kiss at the bottom,' she said.

There were many moments like these . . . Once we stopped at a farm to ask for a drink of milk and were chased out of the farmyard by some furious turkeys. We rode away with them still gobbling angrily and shouted at them, 'You wait till Christmas.' At the next farm an old lady gave us as much milk as we could drink in tin mugs and insisted on us taking a bag of buttered scones when we rode off.

We enjoyed the youth hostels. In those days the two sexes slept in different rooms so we would say goodnight and meet to cook breakfast in the morning. In some hostels the facilities were good, in others we had to use our small primus stove. We met many nice people and because of Lene's transparent charm we had no chance of isolating ourselves even if we had wanted to. I did not always enjoy sharing her with other people and sometimes I sat silently while she smiled and listened to their bantering. I couldn't make myself smile when I did not feel like it and she would often call me solemn.

'I'm not like you,' I said.

In one hostel, I forget which, we were alone together. We kept expecting other people to arrive but no one came. We both felt ill at ease but I knew Lene's moral code was unshakeable. We said goodnight rather formally but when she had undressed and lay under her blankets I came and knelt for a long time by her bunk and we kissed. Then I went back to my own bunk. Later she called.

'Are you asleep, Christopher?'

'No.'

'Why not?'

'Because of you.'

'I am not asleep either.'

'Because of me?'

'Come and sleep by me.'

I could feel my heart banging in my chest until it was painful. I went to her and she kissed me firmly on the lips.

'Bring your bed in here,' she said. 'That is right.' So I pulled my mattress over the wooden floor and lay it by her bunk. We were together but apart and we went to sleep holding hands. Next morning when I woke Lene was up and had already made tea. She sat on the edge of the mattress as we drank from mugs. She said,

'We love each other very much, I think.'

I knew what I was meant to say, and wanted to say, but the words were never spoken and emptiness hung in the air.

It was quite impossible for us to cycle as far as we had hoped. The road seemed endless and the lowland hills made us feel tiny creatures in a vast country. There was little traffic in those days and we were alone. We spent some of our precious money on a train journey to Edinburgh. Here, in Edward and Kay's flat, we had baths and became civilised. We spent two days enjoying ourselves looking round the city but I know Edward and Kay found Lene a strange girl and difficult to talk to. The conversation always had to be directed towards her. Also they knew of mother and father's opposition to the affair and felt a little uneasy at being 'allies'. It was a difficult situation for them.

I borrowed money from Edward and we set off along the road to Glasgow, then headed north. We got as far as Loch Lomond and spent three days in the youth hostel there. We met some Danish boys and Lene was delighted to talk to them in her own language. I felt sad and wandered down to the edge of the loch by myself where I sat on the grass and watched the wind ruffling the surface of the water. Small clouds blew over, one after the other. I hummed to myself a song which was in vogue at the time. The words were trite but the tune so haunting that it is still a popular favourite.

'Good night, Irene. It's time to say goodbye.' Over and over again I hummed it.

Lene found me there and lay her cheek against mine.

'You are cross because I talk to those boys?'

'No, it's not that.'

'Why are you cross?'

'I am not cross. I'm sad. Looking at the water makes me feel sad.'

'Why should it make you sad? It is beautiful, I think.'

'Let's ride along the loch and stop for supper somewhere.'

'That will cost money.'

'It doesn't matter.'

We cycled a few miles and had a cheap meal at a small inn. That was as far north as we got.

The road down to Carlisle and the Lake District was a long one and for part of the way we got a lift on the back of a lorry where we sat on sacks with the bikes lying in front of us. The sun was hot and it was a pleasant way to look at the countryside without the effort of pedalling. The feeling of sadness evaporated. We chatted and dozed in turn.

I think it was at Cockermouth that the hostel was an old mill with the river running underneath the floor boards and we were happy there. We continued our journey, skirting the lakes of Bassenthwaite and Derwentwater where we ate corned beef sandwiches under the pine trees on a promontory. We climbed one mountain, I forget which. I had taken a camera with me, an old box Brownie, but it was faulty. The only photograph to come out, and that hazily, is of Lene on the top of the mountain with other mountain peaks behind her. She is standing with her head to one side, squinting into the sun, her body straight and her slender arms hanging by her side. That is the only thing left of our bicycle tour.

By now we were desperately short of money. We managed to get a lift across the Pennines on the back of another lorry but when the driver stopped at Penrith and asked us to join him for lunch at a café, we had to refuse because we could not afford it. He thought we were stand-offish and I was ashamed to tell him why we could not eat with him. We stayed on the lorry and shared our last bar of chocolate.

We got back to London two days earlier than expected, tired and hungry. I said goodbye to Lene outside the Mary Ward and she wheeled her bicycle into the yard. I continued through the noise of the traffic until I reached Canonbury House where Pat gave me an enormous meal. Then I went to bed and slept for twelve hours.

I worked hard for my Finals but always at the back of my mind was a question which had to be answered. The Mary Ward had by this time become oddly interlinked with our family. Apart from myself three cousins had been residents. Michael was the next to live there. After leaving the army he had gone back to Cambridge and was now studying in London. In due course he married one of the girls who had lived at the Mary Ward for a long time so I can include Alison, who was to become my sister-in-law, in the list of residents from our family. Because he knew Lene and also must have known what the family thought, I put to him casually the possibility of Lene and I

189

getting married. He was obviously horrified at the idea. However, I sensed some of the others felt we were morally engaged, if not in fact, and because Lene was unhappy they were sorry for her. I avoided going to the Mary Ward as much as possible but at weekends Lene often came up to Canonbury House where everyone was friendly. We played foursomes on the nearby tennis courts and sometimes went out to the country, either as a group, or just the two of us. Life drifted on and the Finals came ever closer.

Then Destiny stepped in again. Lene and I had been out for the evening and caught a late tube train back. We had had a good time and as the carriage doors slid open we jumped on the train cheerfully and sat down on the nearest seats opposite a girl who was sitting alone. It was Alice. Lene was saying something but I was not listening.

'Alice.'

'Christopher.'

She was older than I remembered and I thought she looked tired. She had a pile of cardboard folders on her knee. Neither of us knew what to say. After a while I remembered Lene was sitting next to me.

'Alice,' I said, 'this is Lene.'

They shook hands. I think there must have been a look of appeal in my eyes. Alice turned her face towards the window where the hoardings flashed by as the train gained momentum.

'Are you still at college?' I said.

'No, I left a long time ago. I'm doing social work now.'

Our eyes met again and, to keep the conversation going, I asked, 'What sort of social work?'

'It's to do with the church,' she said, but she did not elaborate.

Looking at her I had a feeling 'belief' had taken over her life. That, maybe, was her solution. I wanted to know but it was not the sort of thing one could ask.

'Do you still sing?'

'No. I've more or less given that up.'

I asked after her mother and she asked after my family. It was all very polite.

'How's Eidy?' she said, and I could see the faint familiar smile playing round her lips.

'Getting older.'

Alice had to leave the train fairly soon so the meeting was brief. She stood up, tucked the folders under her arm, smiled at Lene and in a moment was gone. I tried to speak casually to Lene but we soon lapsed into silence.

We went back to the Mary Ward. It was after midnight and everyone had gone to bed. The corridor lights had been turned off. Lene sat on the stairs and started to cry.

'What's wrong?' I kept saying but she shook her head and would not answer. I knew what was wrong. After a time she dried her eyes and spoke.

'When we met that girl in the train you said "Alice, this is Lene." You should have said, "Lene, this is Alice." '

'It doesn't matter. It's the way people say things.'

'It does matter.'

'I knew Alice a long time ago. It's all in the past.'

'I don't think it is in the past. You should have said "Lene, this is Alice." '

'I'm sorry I've upset you. There's nothing to it.' But I knew there was. She sobbed again.

'We aren't ever going to be married, are we, Christopher?'

'If it's what you want we'll get married as soon as you like.'

'No, it is not possible I think.'

'I'm asking you to marry me, Lene.'

'No,' she said, 'no, we will not be married.' I tried to comfort her. I told her I loved her. But all the time I was thinking of Alice.

'Lene, I want you to marry me.'

'We should never have met.' She gave me a quick kiss on the forehead and ran up the stairs.

I suppose it was lucky for me that the Finals were so close. I had to work hard. There was no option. I continued to go out with Lene once a week or so. Neither of us wanted a dramatic end to our friendship and now that the question of marriage had come and gone we were happy in the brief time left to us.

In June I went up to Cambridge for the exams I had dreaded for so long. Here I met friends I had not seen for years, including Tom, who had done his clinical training in a northern hospital. In spite of the excitement and worry of the exams we sat up late talking. His affair with Janet had dwindled and come to nothing.

'And what about the beautiful Alice?' he asked.

'We met again in London but that came to nothing too.' I told him about Lene and asked his advice.

'Avoid bicycles,' he said, 'that's my advice. You always seem to get tied up with girls because of bicycles. You are a bicycle pervert.'

'Be serious.'

'Serious? I think you're stupid. Fancy going on a bicycle tour with a girl half the way round the country.'

'It meant nothing.'

'It might have meant nothing to you. It probably meant a hell of a lot to her. You're a fool. You always were a fool with women. Don't you remember that girl on the fruit-picking camp? Then there was Alice.'

'I don't see why it's foolish to have love affairs. I bet you have plenty.'

'But mine end quickly. You hang on to yours. You're a melancholy bastard. It's about time you stopped feeling so sorry for yourself. I think you really enjoy being miserable.' This was very true, in part at least.

'I won't feel miserable if I pass the Finals.'

'No doubt you'll find something to cry about . . . or someone else to upset.'

I saw a lot of Tom in the next two weeks. The exams seemed to be going well for him and I was, on the whole, satisfied with my progress. There were no nightmare examiners dropping questions on me from a great height. In the practicals, which were the most worrying, I seemed to find the right answers. The patients, many of whom were experienced examination subjects, were well disposed and my 'long case', the most important of all, gave me a helping hand.

'I've got a large liver,' he whispered to me, 'three inches they usually say. It's due to me drinking half a bottle of whisky a day. And don't forget my rupture. That's here,' and he pointed it out to me. This was really cheating but I accepted what the gods offered.

Immediately opposite the hospital was the Fitzwilliam Museum and I mooched round there in between my oral exams looking at Egyptian mummies and other things. It made my Finals insignificant in relation to the whole extent of human history, which would be a good excuse if I failed. For old time's sake I bought a cherry cake from Fitzbillies – no queueing now – and shared it with Tom and some of my other friends. We had a much better time than I had expected and fitted in some games of tennis. Once we took a punt up the river. It was nice to be back at Cambridge.

Then my last oral exam was over. The results would not be posted on the board outside the Senate House until next day, so I decided not to wait and went back to London. One of my friends promised to phone me as soon as he knew the results.

I was not expecting the call until evening so I spent the day with

Lene. We went to Madame Tussaud's. We had been there before but Lene was so fascinated by each waxwork figure that it would have taken her a week to see everything.

'Look, is that really King Henry the Eighth? Where are all his wives?'

'There they are. All six of them.'

'He was a very unhappy man, I think.'

'I expect he was a lot happier than his wives. Most of them had their heads chopped off.'

'I'm glad I'm not going to marry you. I do not want my head chopped off.' She said this lightheartedly but I had a terrible feeling of regret. I remembered her as she was the first day we met, kneeling among the flowers in Kew Gardens.

'No one will chop your head off, Lene.'

She turned away and stared at the waxwork figure of Anne Boleyn. Poor Anne Boleyn. Her head had been chopped off and she had been a frightened child. Poor Lene, too. She was frightened, for all her gaiety and charm. She longed for safety and she had chosen me. It was a bad choice.

After tea I went back to Canonbury House because I was expecting the phone call to come through there. We played endless games of poker round the kitchen table and waited and waited. At six o' clock the call came through. My friend had failed the exam and was so disheartened he had forgotten to phone me earlier. I was lucky. I had passed. I was now a doctor.

We had a party that evening to celebrate, but in the middle I felt strangely sad. All these years I had worked for this particular moment. Now it had come. I went to the window and looked out at the lights of the London traffic. Lene came and stood by me. Tom had been right. I was a melancholy bastard.

Two days later I left London and went home to Cornwall. There was no chance of getting a job of the kind I wanted at the Middlesex and I had no immediate plans. I decided to have a short break then look for something suitable.

Lene came to see me off at Paddington station. She stood smiling on the platform and waved goodbye. She was so pleased for me that I was now a doctor. I closed the carriage window and sat down, choked with tears. There was an aching void inside me. Never, never again must I fall in love. It was always the same. The heartbreak of parting was ten times more than the joy of loving someone. No doubt I would have girlfriends but I decided, as I sat in the Cornish Riviera Express while it steamed through the countryside, that I would not commit myself to anyone, not until I was sure she was the girl I was going to marry. It had taken me too long to learn the bitter truth that reality can never be based on dreams with any hope of success. It is only when dreams are based on reality that one has the slightest chance of being happy.

XIV

Crossing the Tamar
1948–51

When the Cornish Riviera Express crossed the River Tamar into Cornwall I left behind more than one illusion. I could no longer play the part of a medical student, looking at life from its fringes. I was going to be in the thick of it and the sooner the better. The black void within me was more than the sadness of leaving Lene. It was leaving the unreal life I had led from childhood onwards.

Mother and father welcomed me in their fashion and although I was fond of mother and at least understood father, they could contribute nothing of value to fill the void. Lene was not mentioned. They must have guessed the affair was over and done with but I did not want their sympathy, although I expect mother was desperate to show me sympathy, in spite of her obvious relief. Joan was a good friend but was away most of the time so there was no one of my own age to talk to. The new house was on Kenwyn Hill overlooking the city of Truro on one side and on the other sloping down towards woods of oak and birch, a place of great beauty, but I did not wish to fall into the trap of becoming addicted to solitary walks. This would lead only one way and that would be backwards. I had to wait for Destiny to come to my aid and I did not have to wait long, because it was a few days later that I went reluctantly to a cocktail party with my parents and met a surgeon from the nearby hospital. He was looking for a houseman and I accepted the job he offered on the spot. The following Monday I was at work at the Royal Cornwall Infirmary.

The hospital, as it then was, could justifiably be described as a 'dump', everything being small and cramped and designed, it appeared, with the express purpose of making it difficult to look after patients. None the less the Cornish people had a great affection for it and in the pubs they used to sing a little song which started

> Come and die,
> In the RCI.

As the Greeks said, 'It is men who make a city, not walls or ships without crews.' So with hospitals. It is the staff and patients who are important and what they *feel* about the hospital is more significant than what the buildings are like. Under the circumstances the place and the job were just right for me. Although I was nominally the house surgeon, the hospital was small and understaffed and the residents had to share the work between them and cover for each other. So I turned my hand to anything that had to be done and, looking back, I am amazed at the responsibilities I undertook with virtually no experience.

I was extremely nervous that first Monday and, to raise my morale, wore a blue pin-stripe suit for my first Outpatients as a doctor. I looked ridiculous because Mr Hood, the consultant, was a country type who always looked as if he had just returned from a fishing trip or a day with the hounds, which indeed he often had. He was nicknamed Lord John. He obviously thought me peculiar and made a rude remark which I did not quite catch. I did not make that mistake again.

That night I was on duty and delivered a baby in casualty, still in my dressing-gown. Next morning I was giving anaesthetics, a procedure about which I knew little. Fortunately the patients I practised on survived without blemish. All this was terrifying and during the first week, when I was operating, sometimes on my own, my hand shook so much that I had to steady it by pressing my wrist against the patient's body.

The fact of being a qualified doctor, I soon found out, gave hidden resources and, because people expected of you more than you were capable of giving, there was no choice but to grow up quickly. I soon learnt to accept anxiety as a way of life, in fact a necessary stimulus to keep going.

There were eight of us on the resident staff and we were all desperately overworked and dependent on each other. I found friendship of a new kind and the black void within me shrivelled away because I ignored it. Illusions, when I had time to think of them, were luxuries I could well do without. There were patients waiting to be seen and problems waiting to be solved.

My chief absorption was with the patients and in time I formed enormous respect for the Cornish people. They came, of course, in all shapes and sizes, but there was an imaginativeness about them which attracted me. They lacked the Anglo-Saxon solidity I was used to but they knew all about being afraid of pain and illness and overcame them by experiencing them to the full.

In particular I remember an old fisherman from Mevagissey who was twice in the ward before he at last succumbed to cancer. Shortly before his final illness he took me fishing in his small boat and we hauled in mackerel as fast as we could throw out the lines. The silver fish danced in the sunlight as we pulled them in. 'Poor buggers,' he said, 'but it's my turn next.' He seemed reluctant to set sail for the shore and we sat for a long time watching the orange sun settling down on the horizon while the boat rocked gently. When we finally came to land and tied the boat up again on the jetty, tears were running down his face. He knew it was his last trip and he was not afraid to show me his fear. It was brave of him, much braver than hiding his feelings.

Another patient I remember was a wizened old lady paralysed after a stroke. She loved talking because it was about the only thing she could do and I sat by the bed and listened to her stories of piskies and other strange creatures that lived in the woods near her farm, or came into the bay on the evening tide. She really believed in these beings and, as many Cornish people then did, she put a saucer of milk on her doorstep each night before going to bed to show the piskies she was a friend.

These were special patients and another I remember was a middle-aged woman from the Channel Isles who came into hospital to die from an infection of her heart valves. Perhaps she was an echo from the past because her eyes were dark and her smile was soft. I sat holding her hand as she was dying and I wondered if this was love as it really should be, a sharing of fear and peacefulness. It made nonsense of the things I usually associated with the word 'love' − the dancing and kissing, the dreaming and heartbreak. Petty affairs compared with the practical matter of helping someone to die.

Those were rich days for me. As I learnt my trade as a doctor I learnt respect for myself. Tom had once called me a 'melancholy bastard' and being melancholy was another luxury I could not afford.

We had little time off duty but we made the most of what we had. We were not far from the sea and one of our great pleasures was to hire horses from a stable near Perranporth and ride along the sands. For half a crown we could gallop through the spray with the waves breaking over the horses' hooves. The horses loved it as much as we did.

I did not seek company outside the hospital and rather neglected mother and father, who lived so close. This was partly because they could not understand the life I led and partly because whenever I went home I promptly fell asleep and woke up when it was time to leave. I was stretching myself to the limit and needed constant stimulus even to keep me awake.

Mother made one disastrous visit to the hospital over Christmas. She wanted to see where I worked and when I introduced her to the ward sister she thanked her profusely for 'looking after her boy'. She then did a kind of vicar's wife's tour of the ward. Fortunately I was pretty drunk at the time, it being Christmas, and this dulled the embarrassment but I was careful not to invite her again. Poor mother! She wanted so much to share in the lives of all her children but it was not possible. She did not realise I had been drunk and confided in Joan, 'Christopher's got a very high colour. I wonder if it's blood pressure.' Joan was very amused but did not tell mother the awful truth.

After I had been at the hospital for a month or so I became friendly with a nurse called Sarah, who became my walking companion. Because she knew Cornwall by heart she showed me obscure inlets where the sea crept in between rocks and paths across the fields which were not marked on any map. I was not in love with her but found her calm and kind-hearted. She was an ideal friend for me at that time because she did not talk much so with her I found solitude on long walks without the dread of being alone. Selfishly I did not pause to consider if she loved me.

Sarah was a great provider of food and would carry a small haversack over her shoulder full of all sorts of delicacies, such as ham sandwiches, chocolate and oranges. Rationing was still strict although the war was over and I never found out where she got her supplies of food. Probably she 'borrowed' them from the hospital store cupboards.

After walking miles we would have our meals on the seashore, or sitting on the grass of the cliff tops, with the gulls circling round us waiting to be thrown scraps. With Sarah I found relaxation without the immediate desire to go off to sleep and because there was little 'love interest' the relationship was easy-going. Sarah had fair curly hair and an upturned nose and did not challenge me with great beauty.

The intensity of our lives in the hospital did not leave much room for idle emotions, as I liked to think of them, but emotion was there nonetheless and without it the work would have become drudgery once the novelty had worn off. A particular incident was important to me and made me wonder about this strange job of being a doctor. It happened like this.

One morning I found a letter under my bedroom door which puzzled me. It was from one of the theatre nurses whom I will refer to as Nurse Smith. She was in great trouble, she wrote, and needed my help. Could we meet and talk somewhere away from the hospital? It sounded very secretive and aroused my latent feelings of knight errantry. I managed to slip a note to her in the scrubbing-up room in between operations and we met the following night at the end of the lane leading down to the estuary.

Here, sitting on a gate in the moonlight, Nurse Smith told me, with tears running down her face, that she was expecting a baby and had to get rid of it. I should, of course, have been prepared for this but I was not and, fool that I was, I promised to help her. In those days, especially in Cornwall, to have an illegitimate baby was a disgrace and for a doctor to carry out an abortion meant being struck off the register without much chance of appeal. I was, therefore, jeopardising my career at the very outset, trapped by the moonlight and the sight of a weeping girl.

I was so naive I did not even ask her when the baby was due. Her figure was slim and I assumed she was in early pregnancy, so it would be no great problem for me to carry out an abortion, provided I had the necessary facilities. I did not dare take anyone into my confidence but I could not think how I would keep my promise. From what the girl had told me I felt it was the right thing to do in spite of my Hippocratic Oath and all the risks involved. Once more Destiny came to my aid.

I was worrying about it a lot but a few nights later I was woken by someone shaking me by the shoulder. It was the night sister. She asked me to come at once because one of the nurses, she said, was in great pain and she thought it might be appendicitis. I found it difficult to shake off sleep but when I saw the face of the patient on the pillow, I became alert very quickly. Nurse Smith's eyes looked at me appealingly and I did not know what to do.

When I pulled back the bedclothes it was obvious to me and the night sister that the patient was in labour. Somehow she had kept her pregnancy secret until near the full time, and the apparent slimness of her figure had deceived me and everyone else. She had been working in the theatre the day before.

The night sister was a friend of mine and between us we arranged an ambulance to take Nurse Smith to a private nursing home. The financial side would have to be sorted out later. We managed to do this with no one else in the hospital knowing, apart from matron whom we took into our confidence next morning. The word was put round that Nurse Smith had been called away suddenly to a sick relative.

A few weeks later I received one of the nicest letters I have ever had.

Nurse Smith wrote to say the baby had been born later that night and she had arranged its adoption. She was now working in a hospital in another county. 'Thank you for keeping the secret,' she wrote, 'and thank you for keeping your promise. I know I really have nothing to be ashamed of but other people would have made me feel ashamed. That is why I came to you. I am happy now. If ever you feel a patient is ungrateful think of me because my gratitude will make amends for the ingratitude of a thousand other patients.'

I was quick to realise she would have written in a similar way if I had carried out an abortion, and been condemned by the medical profession. I was lucky because I had helped her to 'get rid of the baby' without breaking the law as it was at that time. I treasured her words and they were a great help to me in a time of disaster which came all too soon. It struck me that this was yet another form of this odd thing 'love', helping someone who was desperate.

This disaster was an episode in my life that I would prefer to forget and it was the only time I seriously considered giving up medicine. It happened a fortnight before I left the hospital. I had already finished my tour of duty as a house surgeon and was waiting to go into the RAF to do my national service. To fill in time I did a locum job as house physician, which included looking after the childrens' ward.

There were six babies when I started work there and one in the side ward was seriously ill with gastroenteritis. He was three months old but was so shrivelled that he looked as if he had just been born. There was no effective treatment at that time and all we could do was inject saline under the skin with large syringes, which probably did not help at all. The parents took it in turns to sit by his cot day and night and I was too inexperienced to tell them what I knew to be the truth, that their baby was going to die. Instead I tried to encourage them by saying, 'Tomorrow we should see some improvement.' And they believed me because it was what they wanted to believe.

After three days the baby gave a gasp and died. I was called from the main ward and found the mother holding the dead baby in her arms. She gave me a look I will never forget.

'You said he would get better,' she said, with terrible bitterness, 'you lied to us all along.'

'We did our best,' I mumbled.

'Well, it wasn't good enough. It's my baby you've killed,' and she walked out of the ward and, I believe, into the street carrying her dead baby, his head lolling over the fold of her arms.

It was a dreadful moment. The woman's eyes were wild and I could see she hated me. I did not understand hatred like this. I deluded myself into thinking it was my fault and inexperience was no excuse. I was inconsolable and although everyone told me how unjust the remark had been, and how it was really the mother's grief transformed into anger towards me, none the less I could not put it out of my mind.

Next morning two of the other babies were ill with gastroenteritis and there started a nightmare which continued until all six babies had died. I remember the hopeless expression in the eyes of the parents sitting by the cots and I wanted to give them hope but knew I had no right to. By now I was given the support I needed, supervision from a more senior doctor and extra nurses but I still felt the weight of responsibility on my own shoulders.

The grief of a mother over a dead child is beyond words. I was not faced with anger again. If anything it was sympathy on the part of the parents but I could not express my sympathy to them in return because I was as shrivelled up inside as were the poor dying babies. Words would not come. The thin veneer of professionalism was stripped from me and I could not protect myself from the anguish of the mothers in particular nor from the consciousness of my own ineptitude.

I did not sleep and would get up in the middle of the night to go down to the ward, hoping to see some improvement in just one of my small patients. There never was.

I suppose it must have been one of the last outbreaks of fatal gastroenteritis in any hospital in the country and I was unfortunate to be involved. I had not yet come to terms with work by knowing how to control my feelings of compassion, a most difficult lesson for any young doctor to learn. In fact my obvious concern was probably of more comfort to the parents than a more detached professionalism but I did not see it that way at the time.

When I finally left the hospital I went home and slept for twenty-four hours in my bedroom overlooking the valley. I woke with the sun shining through a gap in the curtains. It was then that I heard a bird calling from the garden and suddenly everything seemed all right. This, as I have mentioned before, was a moment of transcendental beauty, and from then on I ceased to think of any anonymous Destiny as the controlling force of my life or anyone else's.

The next two years were an interlude, an escape from medicine and from thinking about anything with great seriousness. In the RAF I was able to indulge myself in various ways. The silver monoplane of my childhood had altered shape to become the Wellington bomber, an aircraft which had seen service right through the war but its use was now limited to training. I was lucky to be posted to a unit in Flying Training Command in Wiltshire so had unlimited opportunity for flying and, because one of my duties was to give instruction in aviation medicine, this was encouraged. My eyesight did not allow me to be trained as aircrew but I sometimes took over the controls with the connivance of friendly pilots. However my favourite position in the Wellington was up front in the gun turret where there was nothing but perspex between the ground and me.

The war was a thing of the past so in a way I was cheating by having the thrills without the danger. This was not completely true because there is always some danger in flying and on a few occasions I experienced fear which, in a paradoxical way, I enjoyed. It absolved me from not having taken part in the war. Night flying I especially loved and I remember many flights over the North Sea when I looked down and watched the lights of fishing fleets on the invisible sea far below. Then we would turn back and cross the coastline, flying on until the runway came rushing towards us. After that I would sit and eat fried eggs and listen to the air crew chat before going off to bed and deep untroubled sleep.

There were frequent training flights overseas, usually to Malta, an island I came to love. My fellow officers found me naive and used to play tricks on me. Once they staged a pretend ditching in the sea and, perversely, I was quite disappointed when the Wellington skimmed the surface of the waves then lifted its nose and flew on towards the island.

Malta in 1950 was still a military island and the harbour at Valetta was crowded with warships. The town had notorious facilities for rampant sailors, soldiers and airmen. One of our amusements was to go to a famous street called The Gut, although the small group I went with treated this strictly as a sightseeing tour. Here again my fellow officers were amused at my naivety.

In one dance hall, as it was euphemistically called, I met a very nice girl from Manchester who had the strange habit of asking me to stand her a drink, tipping the contents down her throat, then plonking the glass on the bar and asking for another. When I mentioned this odd behaviour to one of my friends he almost killed himself laughing. It became known as 'Christopher's first meeting with a prostitute'. It turned out that I bore a resemblance to Mr Mintoff who was then a labour politician and later became prime minister. When we went into the more sleazy joints I was often met with the cry, 'Meester Meentof, I lova you de horseshit,' and this also became a proverbial expression amongst the aircrew. It was all fun to me. It was a great thrill too to be mixing freely with men who had flown many bombing missions over Germany and a few who had flown Spitfires and Hurricanes in the Battle of Britain.

On the flight back from Malta we always stopped to refuel at Marseilles. Here, on one occasion, there was considerable discussion amongst the senior officers as to whether we should delay our return because the Met report showed unexpected storms over central France. I didn't understand the technicalities but it was decided that our flight of five Wellingtons should proceed and 'fly over the weather'. This was the one occasion I really was in danger because the Wellington I was in developed engine trouble and lost the power to climb. I sensed the anxiety of the aircrew over the intercom as we headed towards a mass of black clouds towering above us. We flew straight into an electric storm and lightning rippled along the wings and round us before we became enveloped in impenetrable gloom. The Wellington staggered through the sky and I could hear one engine repeatedly cutting out so I wedged myself against the framework near the diamond shaped hatch through which I knew I would have to squeeze if the worst happened. This time I really was afraid but I was more frightened of making a fool of myself through my ignorance of parachuting, than the possibility of flying into a mountain side. Quite suddenly the faulty engine picked up and we were soon through the storm and flying over the Channel in sunlight. The aircrew later behaved as if it had been a routine matter but I knew it had not been.

The trips to Malta were great fun and it was a delight to swim in the blue Mediterranean a few hours after taking off from a foggy airfield in Wiltshire. We were also able to buy rare commodities such as tinned food and nylons, the latter especially being in great demand and, as one pilot put it to me, 'a useful bargaining point'. It was rumoured that these were dropped in a sack from the bomb bay of one of the Wellingtons on its approach to the airfield to avoid the customs inspectors who would be waiting for us. I never saw this happening.

My other indulgence in the RAF was sport. I had always been keen on games, especially rugger, but I had never before had the chance to treat it as almost a full time activity. In the peacetime services of those days sport was considered to be of great importance, almost a substitute for fighting a war, and it was a way of occupying the time of crowds of rather bored national service men. I was lucky in that our

RAF unit had a very good rugger team. I played at scrum-half with, outside me, a Welsh fly-half who could, I am sure, have become an international if he had not been rather lazy. The other station medical officer was a county wing-forward and we formed a trio of which I was the link man. To someone who is not a games player it is difficult to portray the sheer beauty of playing in a team with complete under-standing. Our trio, of which I was very much the junior member, became quite well known. We had a strong pack and fast three-quarters, of whom one was a New Zealander, and we won every cup we could. I can remember losing only one game the whole season. This was when, due to a mix-up in the fixture list, we were challenged by Bridgwater, at that time one of the leading West Country clubs. Unfortunately we could field only a half-strength side because of the short notice and I was acting captain that day. In spite of this we lost by the narrowest of margins. It was a memorable match and I think, for once in my life, I went almost berserk and tackled everything in sight. It was a strange experience, rather like the occasion at my preparatory school when I turned on my tormentors using the top of the desk as a weapon. It was frightening too because the quality I had in me that day was brutal rather than heroic, yet I enjoyed it. I regret that we did not win that match. It would have been an extra bonus in my life, like winning the Shakespeare medal when I was a mere scientist.

With flying and sport there was not much time for anything else and my work as a doctor seldom occupied more than a couple of hours a day, much of which was signing forms in triplicate. There was little of the anxiety I had felt in the hospital in Cornwall and my work became lazy and haphazard. The only upsetting experiences were dealing with infrequent aircraft crashes. Once I had to inspect the bodies of the crew of a burnt out Wellington, all unrecognisably shrunk and charred. Two had been friends of mine and I felt sick at heart. I was reminded of the candlestick I had carried to bed as a child in Springwell with its blackened, twisted match ends. The smell of those incinerated bodies lingered for days and led to the only nightmares I have smelled rather than seen. The incident pulled me up with a start and made me question the self-indulgent enjoyment which had become my life.

At this time I was also shaken by the death of Eidy, our old nanny. She had a stroke and I visited her in hospital a few days before she died. I went in full uniform because I thought it would please her, but to her I was still a little boy. She was very ill so we did not talk much and before I kissed her goodbye I showed her my handkerchief so that she would not worry about me having a 'clean hankie'. I was heartbroken when I heard of her death. I did not believe that someone so dear to me could cease to exist.

During this period of my life I often went out with girls, each delightful in her own way, but I was careful not to fall in love. These affairs suited my mood of the time and I am sure none of them loved me any more than I loved them. There was a general desire for pleasure and a return to peacetime luxury. In the services we had plenty of food and frequent dances or other entertainment laid on for us, while the rest of the population were weighed down by restrictions and rationing. An RAF officer was therefore considered a good catch and this is why I had no lack of girlfriends but a considerable lack of real affection. For a long time my chief companion was a charming lady doctor from a nearby hospital, but our minds were never at one and the physical attraction pointed towards a physical solution for which I was still not prepared. There were opportunities galore and I expect she found me the most boring and unpredictable partner imaginable. But the angels were not singing for me and this I could not explain to her. When we finally parted she probably had some regrets for my uniform but, if she had any sense, none for me.

I met Lene once again when I went to the Mary Ward for Michael's wedding and she was one of the guests. She was engaged to a Swedish boy and I felt a mixture of jealousy and relief. We spent an evening together and she seemed an older and more serious person than the Lene I had known, with her Scandinavian charm. When we said goodbye we wished each other luck and her last words to me were, 'I will be very happy I think.'

I met Alice, too, out of curiosity. One day when I was on forty-eight hours leave in London, I phoned her. She recognised my voice at once and said, 'Hullo, Christopher,' as I expected she would. That was her way. So we arranged to meet for dinner and I had the fascination of talking to someone I was no longer in love with about our past love affair. I think I must have been apologetic about myself as I had been, because she became quite angry and leapt to my defence. She told me frankly that she preferred me shy and tongue-tied. 'That's why I couldn't give you up,' she said. This remark made me realise that life in the RAF had made me brash. I was now a squadron leader but Alice was not the person to be impressed by that sort of thing and after this brief passage of arms we got on well together. As I had suspected her life had become more and more bound up with her ideas of religion and I envied her this and was not at all proud of what I had become. I can remember saying to her, 'By the way I've given up believing in Destiny.' She smiled. 'Don't start on that again,' she said. We had a very happy evening together. I was no longer impeded by dreams that were unattainable and at last understood what a wonderful companion she had been to me in spite of my attempts to spoil everything with my obtusity. The mould of perfection into which I had tried to squeeze her could, in the long run, be nothing but uncomfortable for her, but she had coped with the role of an unwilling goddess extraordinarily well.

'It wasn't really me you were in love with,' said Alice, following my train of thought. 'I'm an ordinary sort of person. I think it was someone from long ago. Or something.'

'It's all rather confusing . . . no, it was you I loved, Alice. I loved you very much.'

We decided to make this meeting an annual event, but it was not to be. Alice married and went to live in New Zealand, so passed out of my life forever.

I left the RAF with many regrets and was tempted to take a permanent commission, but I knew that if I did I would finish up behind a desk, which meant I would be a doctor in name only. On the last evening I had a farewell drink with my commanding officer and he said to me, 'When you came to us you were a boy. Now you are a man.' This sounded so corny that I almost choked on my beer and I half expected him to play the headmaster and add, 'If ever you are in trouble don't hesitate to get in touch with me, day or night.'

When I returned to civilian life I was reluctant to go back to hospital work straightaway because I knew I would lose my freedom. Instead I went on a tour of Europe, a Europe still desolate and stricken with bomb damage, travelling in a battered old car with a musician and two girls. The mix did not work very well because the musician and one of the girls quarrelled round France and half Spain. But we saw many beautiful places and did many interesting things. It expanded my personality, as Tom would have said.

When we got home I picked up a copy of the British Medical Journal and applied for the first suitable job I could find.

XV

Nurse Thompson
1952–3

The first suitable job turned out to be at the Northampton General Hospital, where I took a post as house physician. This was to be my home for two and a half years and I did a cycle of jobs to prepare for general practice which I was convinced was to be my lot in life. If I had happened to pick up a different copy of the British Medical Journal I would now be living in some other part of England with a different wife and different children.

Father and mother moved back to Essex, their final move as it turned out, and settled in Saffron Walden within a few miles of Springwell, and in a house which had a remarkably similar name, Freshwell, the last in a long line of family homes. They were both getting old and I felt I should be within striking distance but not too close, as I had been in Cornwall. I did not like the idea of mother descending on the ward where I was working. Northampton was a convenient distance. Edward still lived in Edinburgh and was in the Civil Service while Michael was a lawyer and had settled in Surrey. Joan remained at Freshwell House until mother's death when the property was sold, and father spent his last two years in hospital.

My new job was very different from the one in Cornwall where my fuel had been excitement and romance with little experience to back it up. I now got down to the serious study of medicine with experienced colleagues to show me what to do. I rarely had to attempt anything beyond my capabilities, which was greatly to the benefit of the patients, but I do not regret the flair and self-reliance I had picked up the hard way in Cornwall. Nor did I regret my two-year holiday in the RAF. But now I longed to get down to hard work.

The physician I worked for was a charming but eccentric old gentleman on the point of retirement. I did not see much of him but he liked to do a ward round once a week and for this he sometimes wore a black cloak and carried a silver headed cane. He would not let go of this which meant it was almost impossible for him to use a stethoscope which was to everyone's advantage because his skills lay very much in the past. The patients adored him and I felt deep respect for him and was careful not to catch him out, a thing which would have been very easy to do. We all made sure to tell him what was wrong with the patient before asking his opinion.

One of the obstacles to work in those days was the ward sisters, powerful, matriarchal figures, who could be divided into two categories – those who liked you and those who did not. Those who liked you were resolute companions and advisers and, because they ran the ward with an efficiency almost unmatched nowadays, they made life less complicated. The only authority over them was matron who did a daily round with her cairn terrier, which used to pee against the side of the beds and ladder the nurses' stockings. We were all a little frightened of her, which is what matrons are for.

The ward sisters who did not like you could make life very difficult indeed. In my next job, which was on the children's ward, my first duty of the day was to inject antibiotics into the spinal canals of children with tuberculous meningitis, a dreadful disease which is now very rare. The injections required quite a lot of skill and patience on the part of the doctors and nurses and when the sister was in a bad mood she would refuse to let me have a nurse to help because 'they were too busy'. This became quite a problem because the work had to be done. The matter was solved by the paediatric registrar, my immediate superior. Sister's great pleasure in life, apart from baiting house physicians, was to do the *Daily Telegraph* crossword over her cup of coffee in the morning. If ever she was intransigent he would fill up the crossword with stupid words like 'knickers' and this annoyed her so much that we finally came to a sensible compromise. She was, needless to say, an excellent sister and very kind to the children. It was just junior doctors she was not very partial to.

The paediatric registrar was an interesting character, a South African Jew called Abe. He was imperturbable and on the ward rounds, which tended to be rather long, he would sometimes sit in a chair by the door and go to sleep, waking up in time to join the procession on its way to the next ward. The consultant got very cross but never did anything about it. Abe was a keen amateur flier and when he was meant to be on duty for me he was often to be seen circling above the town in a Tiger Moth. I could do little but shake my fist at the sky. His argument was that he was in sight of the hospital.

He was a wonderful doctor and, in spite of his peculiar habits, he somehow managed to be present and awake when he was really needed.

Hospitals in those days always had a few extravagant personalities around, who made life interesting because the work was hard and the hours long. It was not at all unusual to be up all night and have to work the following day, and I sometimes managed seventy-two hours on duty without sleep, especially when I was involved with midwifery. Babies do not work to a timetable and we would never have dreamed of trying to arrange for them to be born at a time convenient to the staff, which is the present day practice. I enjoyed midwifery. My boss, Mr Gordon Sturtridge, had once played fly-half for Australia, so when we were not talking about mothers and babies we were discussing the state of British rugby and in particular our own local team, the Saints, at that time about the best in England. I still played undistinguished rugger but was usually so short of sleep that I staggered round the field like a zombie, praying for the final whistle to come. Soon I was to hang up my boots after twenty consecutive seasons, and I still miss it.

The food in the doctors' mess was awful because rationing was only just coming to an end and the meals had a dreadful sameness. For this reason we relied heavily on the nursing staff to provide us with extras and we considered one of the chief qualities of an efficient nurse was to be able to make good scrambled eggs without Sister finding out.

The doctors' mess was a closed community and, because young doctors could not afford to marry on the nominal salary they were paid, the relationships were more intense than they are today. We all worked hard but when we had parties or decided to get drunk, we really kicked over the traces. This was usually all in good spirit but at one time we had two rival factions, one Irish and the other Australian. After a few pints of beer they would fight it out on a grand scale. Once I remember finding the dining room ankle deep in broken crockery. This was vandalism but the pressures were so great that it was understandable. The consultants were very angry about it and came to have a look at the mess, shaking their heads solemnly, while at the same time remembering their own days as young doctors.

Another form of extravagant behaviour was the wheelchair races round the corridors, based on the general idea of chariot races in a Roman arena. These were exciting and dangerous for the person in the wheelchair. They were also noisy and disturbed the patients and once a policeman threatened to arrest us until the night sister explained that we were doctors, not hoodlums. The distinction was slight on these occasions.

I was once nearly responsible for burning the hospital down during a party. One of the house surgeons had gone to the toilet to be sick and came back in some distress because he had lost a tooth-cap. Feeling good-natured I promised I would find it for him. The light bulb was not very powerful so I decided to improve the illumination by setting fire to a pile of toilet paper in the corner. It seemed entirely reasonable at the time and I did, in fact, find the tooth but the flames spread and the smoke in the corridors caused a great deal of alarm. I was quite rightly in trouble over this and decided to control my drinking more carefully in the future.

At that period of my life I still did not really want to fall in love with anyone and was thought to be a studious type who was not very interested in the opposite sex. Soon after my arrival at the hospital I was shown, in great secrecy, a rather tatty notebook in which was recorded the names of the small cadre of nurses who, I was told in a hushed whisper, would 'leap into bed with anyone'. Most of the girls mentioned seemed ordinary pleasant people and I had a feeling that the book was something of a myth. The idea of permissiveness had not yet arrived on the scene but I was, even for those days, old-fashioned in my outlook and did not understand that people could be nice and leap into bed at the same time. There was a set of Jane Austen's novels on my bookshelf and, although I had little time for reading, they still exerted an influence on me.

I got on well with the nurses but treated them with formality and avoided the intrigues which are part of hospital life. I had formed a brief friendship with one nurse but when I found she was engaged to someone else I let the matter drop. It was unfair on her, me and the fiancé. My colleagues thought I was overscrupulous.

Although I was against the general idea of falling in love I felt a need to belong to someone and for someone to belong to me. One could form deep but obviously limited relationships with patients and we had a lot of fun in the doctors' mess but all this was not enough. The voice of the angels could not be silent and soon my protective fence was to be blown over by a gust of wind.

It started in the most unpropitious manner imaginable, at a party of the kind which often springs up spontaneously in hospitals. We were all feeling rather jaded and decided to retire to the doctors' quarters with a bottle of whisky and an adequate supply of beer. At about midnight one of the house physicians decided that what we really needed to cheer us up was additional female company and he managed to pass a message round the wards that any of the night nurses would be welcome during their 'lunch break'. This was forbidden because nurses were not allowed in the doctors' quarters but half a dozen dodged the prowling night sister and put in a brief appearance. Amongst them was a girl with dark hair and deep brown eyes. I had not met her before.

I was pretty drunk at the time and she realised this and didn't like it. She was very shy. I spent the time I was with her trying to find out her name but she would not tell me and I tried to kiss her but she skilfully avoided this too. Then she must have quietly gone back to her ward because I can remember sitting alone, feeling rather desolate, with an empty chair in front of me. I also remember saying to myself, 'This is the girl I am going to marry and I don't even know her name.'

Next morning I woke with a slight hangover. The image of the girl's face was blurred and I thought, 'I not only don't know her name but I can't remember what she looks like,' which was really very strange because I was still pretty sure we were going to be married.

All that day I thought about her and in the evening my old friend Destiny came to my aid. As I was walking back from the wards I glanced up the staircase which led to the nurses' dining room and there she was. She looked over her shoulder, saw me, and with the slightest toss of her head went on up the stairs and was gone.

I had at least to find out her name so I approached the house physician who had organised the party and said, 'You know that dark-haired nurse I was talking to. . . .'

He laughed and told me her name was Thompson. 'I don't know her first name but everyone calls her Tommy,' he added. So Tommy she was and has remained ever since, to the initial consternation of my family and to the confusion of strangers who usually get the names 'Tommy' and 'Chris' the wrong way round. It often creates situations like the Elliott-bloody-Binns mix-up in the Home Guard. This, of course, was all in the future.

The house physician told me Nurse Thompson was on night duty on Compton Ward. There was no possible reason for me to visit that particular ward and, remembering that slight toss of the head, I thought it would be embarrassing and confusing for both of us if I did. The only way round the problem was to use a go-between and the house physician, obviously amused, agreed to do this for me. Through him I invited Nurse Thompson to tea, not expecting for a moment that she would accept — but she did.

We went to a small café, owned by two elderly ladies, in a village called Wootton. There was a chequered cloth on each table with a posy of flowers exactly in the middle. We looked at each other over the flowers and did not know what to say. One of the old ladies fussed round with teacakes and a pot of tea and, when she finally left us to ourselves, we talked about the hospital and the people we knew there, which was the most obvious common topic.

Then we talked about ourselves. Tommy's family were working-class people, of whom she was proud, and by winning a scholarship and taking up nursing she had 'bettered herself' as she put it, with faint irony in her voice and a shrug of the shoulders. I loved her for her frankness. There was nothing special about our conversation and neither of us overcame our shyness but by the time we had got up from the table and thanked the two old ladies for the tea and cakes we were deeply in love. What is more we both knew it. There was no special reason why this should have been so but that is how love works.

'It was eye language,' Tommy said many years later, 'we looked at each other's eyes and that told us everything.'

'And what did you think of me that day?'

'I was too nervous to think much but I was pleasantly surprised.'

'Surprised?'

'Yes. I came prepared to dislike you. I thought you were after the usual thing.'

'What, at afternoon tea?'

'I suppose that made it a bit safer. Mind you, if you had asked me out for the evening I wouldn't have come.'

'Wouldn't you?'

'You were terribly drunk the first time we met, remember, but . . . yes, I probably would have come.'

'And what did you really think of me?'

'I liked your politeness. I thought it quite funny at first, then I decided it wasn't. I liked your shyness too and, as I said before, I was surprised we could look into each other's eyes although we were both so shy.'

'You seem to have sized me up.'

'Not really. I was mystified by you. It seemed – but I only understood this later – that sometimes when you were laughing happily you were really crying deep inside. Does that make sense?'

'In other words I was a melancholy bastard.'

'No, just a bit on the solemn side sometimes. My turn now, what did you think of me?'

'Oh, I was head over heels in love. I didn't think at all.'

And that was the truth. For the first and only time in my life I was *completely* in love. It was not a dream and there was no need for me to think. Dear Tommy!

Although the outcome was beyond doubt we had to have a courtship of some sort. This was a little difficult because Tommy was on night duty and it was awkward to arrange meetings. Notes passed between us and we still keep these in a special 'memory box'. Our favourite rendezvous was in the matron's garden at midnight. This was forbidden territory but it had privacy and there was a hut by the tennis court where we could sit. I would usually arrive first and wait for the gleam of the white nurse's cap as Tommy came hurrying down the path. It was a 'Come into the garden Maud' situation but Maud always came.

The nights were starlit and over the hospital buildings we could see the constellation Cassiopeia, the lady reclining on her couch. I will not say the stars were tipped with steel – an expression I have used more than once in this book – because such expressions seem strangely irrelevant. This was love of the kind that leads to marriage, which is of a different quality from a 'love affair'. Of course the angels sang but their voices were harmonious and joyful rather than exuberant and this meant they could go on singing forever, which they have done. Sometimes the voices have been muted, sometimes discordant, but the important thing is that the angels have kept on working at it and those voices are always in the background.

We kept our love to ourselves at first because we were shy of it but after a fortnight we became engaged and then we lost our privacy. Tommy's mother came hurtling down from Birmingham to interview me and later, when the engagement became official, Tommy had to survive the ordeal of a family inspection at Saffron Walden. All brides-to-be have to suffer this sort of thing.

Just over a year later we were married and after four years we had three children. This meant toys scattered all over the nursery floor and a lot of love and laughter.

To write more about Tommy would be to write another book. Besides it is virtually impossible to write about a love affair which still exists as mine does with Tommy.

Has there been any point in all this looking back? It is one of the oddities of middle age that a person feels less secure and needs to find some kind of meaning in things and in himself, or herself. Life has somehow to be pieced together and childhood and youth are the blocks that form the foundations. They are a resource on which one depends more and more. That is why I have explored the past, the intent being 'to arrive where we started and know the place for the first time'. A vain hope.

Mostly I have thought of love, that strange crystalline object with so many surfaces reflecting in so many different ways. Sex is one of the brighter facets but the deeper glow of affection and just being there are equally important. Rarely the entire crystal blazes with light quite unexpectedly but this happens only a few times in a person's life.

Before I met Tommy I was groping for love and the exposure of all the imperfections and insincerities of these earlier love affairs makes them even more precious and makes my life with Tommy more precious too.

Love is a tyrant from which I, like anyone else cannot escape. I suppose escape would bring peace of a kind, but the peace would be a form of desertion, like the Munich postponement of war, or the failure of a doctor to feel for his patient. That is the kind of peace I do not want.

If there is a solution to the enigma it is to expand this word love until it means one's feelings for people and things in general. Curiously this is why my learning to love and learning to be a doctor have been entwined and it was a happy chance that my marriage to Tommy coincided with my entering general practice. A doctor sees the whole spectrum of humanity with its folly and courage and either learns to love it or falls under the dark shadow. And learning to love starts as love of one's home and family, continues as the love between a boy and a girl grows and grows until it becomes a more important idea altogether. By this I mean such things as the music of Bach and the suffering of King Lear and so on and so on, until you think of Time and Destiny and God. This is the 'intolerable shirt of flame which human power cannot remove'. Nor would I wish to remove it.